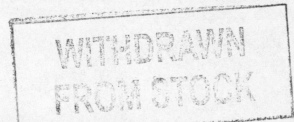
The Professional Engineer in Society

A Textbook for Engineering Students

of related interest

The Engineers: A History of the Engineering Profession in Britain 1750-1914
R A Buchanan

The Professional Engineer in Society

Stephen Collins, John Ghey and Graham Mills

with a foreword by J. C. Levy,
Director - Engineering Profession, The Engineering Council

Jessica Kingsley Publishers
London

First published in 1989 by
Jessica Kingsley Publishers Ltd
118 Pentonville Road
London N1 9JN

British Library Cataloguing in Publication Data

Collins, Stephen
  The professional engineer in society.
  1. Great Britain. Engineers. Professional
  education
  I. Title II. Ghey, John III. Mills,
  Graham
  620'.007'1141

ISBN 1-85302-501-1

Printed and bound in Great Britain by
Biddles Ltd, Guildford and King's Lynn

Contents

PART III: COMMUNICATION

Figures

Foreword

Like life, engineering changes but does not change. From time immemorial there have been people whom we would describe as engineers, who have led developments to improve the quality of everyday life, all the way from the wheel to the microchip. But within that slow and hard-won progress there have been profound changes of kind, character and responsibility in engineering activity. These changes have gradually accelerated throughout the ages, but spectacularly so in recent years.

Of all the professions engineering is, almost by definition, the first to feel the impact of new technology and the new problems which it generates. Nowadays it is not just manufacturing industry which has to accommodate rapid technological change. Transport and service industries too such as banking, retailing and medicine are all underpinned by the need for high precision measurement and information storage and retrieval.

It used to be said that an engineer was someone who could make for £1 what anyone else could make for £2. Not so any longer. It is more likely that in today's world the engineer can make, and make function, for a million pounds, what nobody else can make at all.

But the point of the old definition remains. Engineering activities must be economic or in the long run they will be abortive.

Another change lies in the old saying 'If it looks right, it is right'. Can that be true of the moon buggy or a North Sea oil rig? But again, who can deny the continuing importance of aesthetics to engineering designers who are in the consumer durable market place?

The social and managerial domain is where the role of the engineer is now changing most rapidly and that makes the publication of this book particularly timely. In the past the engineer has usually been under a professional obligation to a patron, client or employer and these responsibilities are undiminished. Gradually, however, a wider responsibility to the community at large has had to be acknowledged in the face of life-endangering failures and accidents on the one hand, and natural catastrophes and the poisoning of the biosphere on the other with, as yet, unpredictable consequences.

Some may hold engineers at least partly responsible for environmental damage caused by industrialisation. The paradox is that the world must rely on engineers to provide the remedies, yet not allow an unacceptable drop in the standard of living. Where safety to people or danger to the environment are concerned, the engineer has both technical and ethical problems to face.

In the United Kingdom the establishment of the Chartered Engineering Institutions in the nineteenth century coincided with the growing awareness of the need for public accountability. In acknowledgement of this duty one of their innovations was a code of conduct for professional engineers to which was later added a qualifications function, now carried out under the auspices of The Engineering Council.

All engineers, whatever their discipline - civil, mechanical, electrical, aeronautical, chemical, marine, mining etc. - and whatever their activity in research, development, design, manufacture, marketing, management or maintenance, need to be made well aware of these matters during their education and training, which should extend throughout working life and not terminate with graduation. At every stage of their development, engineers face new problems and new challenges, an almost unique feature among the professions and one which makes it so satisfying as a career. Moreover, communication, verbal and written, and management responsibility form continuous threads through the lives of many engineers.

This book examines in a commendably informed and enlightened manner the organisation of the profession and the interlinked technical, social and economic dimensions of engineering in the modern world. It constitutes a most excellent commentary, and not just for its primary audience who are entering the profession via a degree course or The Engineering Council examination. For practising engineers, too, it provides shrewd insights into the activities and obligations of professional engineers into the year 2000 and beyond.

J.C. Levy
Director - Engineering Profession, The Engineering Council

October 1989

Acknowledgements

We would like to pay special thanks to Professor Maurice Kogan and Professor John Brown of Brunel University for their helpful comments during the formation of the book. We also acknowledge the help given to us by the Engineering Council in allowing us to reprint bibliographical material and for much useful advice: in particular, we would like to thank Professor Jack Levy, Director - Engineering Profession, Dr Kenneth Miller, past Director General, and Mr Ron Kirby, Director of Public Affairs.

Thanks are also due to the library staff and colleagues of Southampton Institute of Higher Education and UKAEA (especially Mr John Collier, Chairman) for supplying much useful information.

Finally we would like to thank our families for their help and continual support over many long months during the preparation of the book.

Introduction

The 1980s have been a time of change for the British Engineering Profession. The need for change was highlighted early in the decade by a Government report which exposed the lack of recognition accorded to professional engineers, despite their importance to the wellbeing and wealth of society. The report, entitled *Engineering Our Future* (Finniston, 1980) uncovered crucial weaknesses in the education and training of engineers which devalued their professional standing.

One important finding was that British engineers were being produced hastily and superficially compared to engineers in France and West Germany. At the top of the British profession, Chartered Engineers took only a three-year degree course (requiring a maximum attendance of 90 weeks), followed by little more than token 'on the job' training. The syllabuses of these courses also failed to reflect the practical needs of engineering, and to acknowledge the fact that the majority of engineers would end up in management positions where they would require skills in organisation and management, report writing and face-to-face communication.

The report concluded that: 'the British system does not give students sufficient grounding in the synthesis of technical ... (and) human ... considerations nor does it adequately encourage the development of the wider skills and outlook required by engineers within the engineering dimension. In consequence employers have often taken the attitude that few engineers are properly equipped to take on broader management responsibilities and have employed them instead as providers of technical services, thereby closing the vicious circle' (Finniston, 1980).

Following the publication of *Engineering Our Future*, the Engineering Council was granted a Royal Charter in November 1981 to maintain the momentum for change and to improve co-ordination in what was a fragmented profession. One of the Council's top priorities was to 'raise the standard' of British engineering by improving the quality of the education and training of engineers, and it has worked hard to achieve this throughout the 1980s. The groundwork laid by the Engineering Council in this decade will radically change the shape of the profession in the 1990s.

After 1992, only enhanced courses accredited by the Engineering Council and designated as Bachelor of Engineering (BEng) or Master of Engineering (MEng) will lead, after a period of accredited training and responsible experience, directly to Chartered Engineer status. The engineering institutions will also require all those who aspire to Chartered status to prove their suitability through a formal interview (known as the 'professional review') after finishing their periods of responsible experience.

Similar changes have been introduced for those completing BTEC Higher Certificates and Diplomas who wish eventually to register as Incorporated Engineers. In addition, ladders and bridges have been provided for Incorporated Engineers, and others who have prepared themselves for the profession by non-degree routes, to transfer to the Chartered Engineer path.

These improvements, in both the quality of courses and the routes to registration, will place additional demands on the personal qualities and skills of engineers. If the calls for improvement made in many recent publications are achieved, engineers in the twenty-first century will have to be of an extremely high calibre. For example, in an Engineering Council paper, *Raising the Standard*, we are told that: 'qualified engineers of tomorrow must be technically competent, market conscious, commercially adept, environmentally sensitive and responsive to human needs' (Engineering Council 1985a).

In a similar vein, an initiative entitled *Opening Windows on Engineering* called for young engineers who are 'personable, articulate, enthusiastic, sincere and skilful' (these 'missionaries' will be sent into schools to tell children about the joys of engineering. (Engineering Council, 1986a)). And the Women Into Science and Engineering (WISE - 1984) campaign has sought to encourage women of a similarly high calibre to join the profession in much greater numbers - partly to help break down the outmoded 'boiler suits and spanners' image of engineering. Finally, in the United States, engineers have been ordered to 'get human' in recognition of the fact that: 'a professional engineer can no longer be narrowly focused. He or she lives and operates in a social system and needs to understand cultural and human values'.

In conclusion, the engineering profession is looking for young men and women who are more than technically competent. The new engineers must be humanist and environmentally sensitive as well as market conscious; and they must be good managers and communicators; in other words, men and women who will be well able to raise the profile of the professional engineer in society.

We hope that this book will make a contribution to this process of raising the standard and status of British engineering. We have been concerned that few books have dealt systematically with the changes going on in the profession itself or have offered linked advice on key areas such as the relationship between technology and society, energy and the environment, engineering safety, management principles, leadership and communication skills. The book is aimed at ambitious engineers currently undergoing the formation process of approved education, integrated training and work experience leading to Incorporated or Chartered Engineer status. This includes the 40,000 students studying for first degrees in engineering and technology at universities, polytechnics or other institutes of higher education and the 40,000 students studying for BTEC Higher Diplomas and Certificates in the same subjects.

It will be especially relevant for those 1,000 or so students intending to gain Chartered status by sitting the Engineering Council's Part 2 examinations. All these students will take the compulsory *Engineer in Society* paper (Part 2B) which is common to all engineering disciplines. Similarly, it is pertinent to those sitting examinations such as the Institution of Civil Engineers' paper - *The Place of the Engineer in the Community and Management Topics*. It will also be useful to those students embarking upon the pilot *Integrated Engineering Degree Programmes* (IEDP) in selected polytechnics and universities. These inter-disciplinary courses, encouraged by the Engineering Council, are intended to integrate engineering disciplines with management training and project and design work and are likely to include a new subject called 'Enterprise, Organisation and People.'

The book is also intended for those who have already gained their degrees, diplomas and certificates and who are embarking upon their training and experience programmes before applying for registration with the Engineering Council.

Finally, we hope it will appeal to all registered engineers who wish to widen their knowledge about their profession and enhance skills in management and communication as part of a continuing education and training programme. In 1988 some 260,000 persons were registered in the Engineering Council's Chartered or Incorporated Engineer Sections.

The structure of the book is based on the three main aims of the Engineering Council's own Part 2B examination, *The Engineer in Society*.

Part I - Technology and Society

This relates to aim one of the examination: 'Awareness of the impact of technology on society, and of the responsibilities of professional engineers to the community that they serve.'

Chapter 1, 'The Professional Engineer in Society', begins by examining the proposition that the lack of status accorded to professional engineers is partly attributable to the fact that Britain is an industrial country with an 'anti-industrial culture'. This proposition is examined with special reference to the relationship between engineering and education. The second part of this chapter looks at some of the criteria of a 'true profession' and examines the engineering profession against these. We conclude that engineering does not fulfil all the criteria for a true profession. This, however, is not necessarily a disadvantage, as a softer model of professionalism encourages flexible working relationships and allows engineers to accept the positive, altruistic aspects of professionalism, while rejecting the inflexibility and restrictive practices sometimes associated with traditional models of professionalism.

Chapter 2, 'The Work of the Engineering Council', describes the efforts of the Council to 'raise the standard' of the engineering profession. It is vital that all engineers understand the routes to registration and the standards expected of them as professional engineers, and in Chapter 2 we examine the changes in these areas which have been overseen by the Engineering Council. We describe the series of public awareness campaigns run by the Council, on an almost continuous basis, in order to reverse the effects of the anti-industrial culture discussed in Chapter 1, and to secure the future supply of well qualified and able engineers of both sexes.

Chapter 3, 'Technology and Society', explores the hypothesis that technological changes act as 'creative gales of destruction', which travel round the globe and create and destroy whole economies and societies. We critically examine the proposition that the Western industrial nations are currently undergoing a technological revolution, based on information technology, which is taking them out of the industrial age and into a new 'post industrial society'. Next we analyse the problems associated with the transfer of advanced technology from the developed nations to the 'Third World'. Finally, we put forward a framework for analysing the effect of technology and society and apply this to the Channel Tunnel as an illustrative case study.

Chapter 4, 'Energy Sources and the Environment', highlights some of the most intractable and controversial environmental issues of the past decade. The widespread use of fossil fuels for the creation of energy is implicated in two major environmental problems: the creation of acid rain and the global warming associated with the 'greenhouse effect'. These two problems, together with their possible technical solutions are discussed.

Many people see the expansion of nuclear energy as one way of avoiding the environmental problems associated with fossil fuels. In the second half of *Chapter 4* we examine the proposition that this would merely exchange one set of environmental hazards for another. Two environmental problems associated with the generation of nuclear power are the danger of reactor accidents (in this context we describe the Three Mile Island and Chernobyl disasters) and the problems associated with the disposal of radioactive nuclear waste. Finally, we examine the exciting possibility that research currently being conducted into nuclear *fusion* (as opposed to nuclear *fission*) may lead to an abundant, and environmentally safe, source of energy for the next century.

One of the public relations problems affecting the position of the engineering profession in society is that engineers are often in the news for the wrong reason: when they are blamed for a spectacular technological disaster which hits the headlines. *Chapter 5*, 'Issues in Engineering Safety', examines six of these disasters and poses the question: what lessons can engineers learn from technological accidents? The case studies are: the Flixborough explosion, the release of dioxin at Seveso, the release of methyl isocyanate at Bhopal, the explosion of the space shuttle *Challenger*, the capsize of the *Herald of Free Enterprise* at Zeebrugge, and the King's Cross Underground fire.

Part II - The Organisation of Engineering Activities

This is relevant to aim two of the *Engineer in Society* examination: 'knowledge of the basic principles involved in the organisation of engineering activities that provide goods and services - from design to marketing and from manager to workforce.'

Although the practice of management has been around for thousands of years, three engineers working in the late nineteenth and early twentieth century can claim to have invented management as we know it today: Frederick Taylor, Henri Fayol and Alfred Sloan. The ideas of these three are examined in *Chapter 6*, 'The Pioneers of Management Thought'.

However, the ideas of these pioneers of 'classical management' have been criticised by more modern theorists who argue that the classical managers mistakenly believed that human organisations could be run as if they were machines. We examine these criticisms with particular reference to some of the historical problems of British manufacturing industry - including the de-humanisation of work and poor industrial relations.

Chapter 7, 'Modern Approaches to Organisational Design', analyses three modern approaches. First, aspects of the internationally admired Japanese style of management are described - with special reference to techniques adopted by the Matsushita organisation. Next we examine the management principles espoused by America's best-run companies as described in the world-wide best seller, *In Search of Excellence*, and set these principles in a European context by describing case studies based on the successful turn-around of Jaguar Cars in the UK, and the introduction of 'computer integrated manufacturing' (CIM) to the Ford plant in Cologne. Finally, we draw attention to a new type of organisation - described by Charles Handy as the 'federal organisation' - which has grown in response to the turbulent environment for manufacturing in the 1980s and the decentralising influence of information technology.

A hard, autocratic management style is often inappropriate to the modern organisation of engineering activities. The emphasis today is more often on flexibility, adaptiveness and co-operation in multi-disciplinary teams. *Chapter 8*, 'Team Leadership', outlines the more imaginative approach to leadership that this implies. It focuses on the key characteristics and skills of leadership in an attempt to answer the question: what is leadership? First, we examine various theoretical and practical approaches to individual motivation and team-building before exploring the 'power of the group' to motivate individuals. Next we analyse the advantages of a participative style of management and compare this with a 'contingency' style of leadership which emphasises that different styles are appropriate to different situations. Finally, no discussion of leadership would be complete without an examination of the network of power and authority relationships which underpin all organisations, and we focus on 'leadership and organisational structure' in the concluding section of the chapter.

Part III - Communication

This is pertinent to aim three of the *Engineer in Society* examination: 'skill in the verbal communication of subjects within the purview of engineering.'

If engineers are to play a more prominent role in society, they will need high level communication skills. *Chapter 9*, 'Face-to-Face Communication', examines the key oral communication skills needed for effective leadership. A recurring theme of this chapter is the importance of inter-personal skills and of preparation.

The chapter is divided into three areas of activity which all engineers will encounter within their own organisations or when they are playing a wider role in the community - for example when giving a careers talk or acting as a school governor. These three areas are: making a formal presentation, chairing a meeting, and conducting a selection interview.

Finally, *Chapter 10*, 'Written Communications', examines an area of work in which engineers are often criticised. We discuss some of the problems associated with written communications, before setting down some guidelines for the production of reports, written instructions and technical manuals. These guidelines are set down under three main headings: style; structure and logical order; and presentation. The chapter ends with a discussion of the particular techniques associated with the production of letters and memoranda.

Suggestions for Further Study

Each chapter ends with a section entitled 'Suggestions for Further Study'. These sections give practical advice to students on how to follow up key learning points contained in the relevant chapters. They also provide a guide to the extensive bibliography which can be found at the end of the book.

Study Questions and Assignments

These can be found at the back of the book. Most are taken from the Engineering Council Part 2B examination - *The Engineer in Society* - and are ideal for student engineers who wish to prepare themselves for this, and other similar examinations.

Part I

Technology and Society

Chapter 1

The Professional Engineer in Society

On 11th March 1988 the House of Commons held its first full-scale debate on the state of the engineering profession since 1980. In the opening speech, Patrick Thompson MP praised the economic performance of the engineering industry in the 1980s:

> 'Although the overall size of the workforce fell by almost one third between 1978 and 1985, output was higher at the end of that period than in 1980 and has continued to rise since then. Productivity per head rose by 31 per cent between 1980 and 1985. The most spectacular gains were in electronics and office equipment where the volume of production rose by over 80 per cent in the years between 1978. Significantly, the percentage of professional engineers, scientists and technologists employed in the engineering sector more than doubled over that same period.'

However, the careful use of percentages in the figures presented to Parliament cannot alter the fact that the engineering industry has failed to keep up with the increasing demand for manufactured goods in an apparently booming national economy. The reality is that during the 1980s Britain - once the 'workshop of the world' - became a net importer of finished manufactured goods (see *Figure 1.1*).

Fortuitously, a combination of North Sea Oil, tourism, the financial and insurance institutions of the City of London, and the traded services generally, have helped to balance the nation's books in the 1980s (although the gross figures for 1988 showed the worst balance of payments deficit since records began). It has been calculated that a 2.5 per cent rise in earnings from services is needed to offset a 1 per cent fall in export earnings from manufacturing and maintain the balance of payments (Finniston, 1980). Moreover, the oil will run out eventually and the stock market crash of October 1987 exposed the dangers of relying too heavily on the financial sector for economic

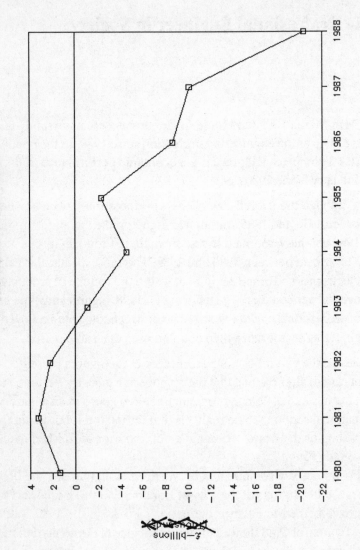

Figure 1.1
The UK Balance of Payments 1980-1988 (CSO, 1989)
The Visible Trade Balance

survival. As for the contribution of tourism, Sir John Harvey-Jones, ex-chairman of ICI, expressed his opinion bluntly in a speech during 'Industry Year', 1986: 'If we think we can get by with a bunch of people in smocks showing people around medieval castles, we are quite frankly out of our tiny minds.'

A further indication of the relative weakness of the manufacturing sector is illustrated by a comparison of the numbers of annual entrants to the engineering profession in the United Kingdom and Japan. A recent survey indicated that the Japanese higher education system produces roughly *three times* as many graduates with a qualification in engineering or an allied subject (at the Higher National, degree, and post-graduate levels) as the UK. And, at first degree level, the Japanese produce over *four times* as many engineering graduates (see *Figure 1.2*). (However, it must be noted that the total population of Japan is over twice that of the UK).

Moreover, the survey suggested that the figures do not account for the fact that:

> '... in Japan, the cream of school leavers can be selected for university engineering places. This is not the case in the UK, where many relatively low level A level achievers are admitted, particularly, but not exclusively, to polytechnics' (Engineering Council, 1988a).

The survey also found that the pool of Japanese school leavers with mathematics qualifications suitable for a career in engineering was around *ten times* higher than that in the UK.

Many reasons have been advanced for the poor performance of UK manufacturing industry. One popular explanation is that an autocratic and unimaginative management style has led to poor relations between management and trade unions. Another view is that excessive Government interference and successive cycles of nationalisation and privatisation have undermined industry's self-confidence and ability to plan ahead. However, a fashionable view in the 1980s has been that the roots of the problem lie in the nature of British society itself. Sir Geoffrey Chandler expressed this view succinctly during Industry Year, 1986: 'Britain, uniquely, is an industrial nation with an anti-industrial culture.'

Supporters of this viewpoint, who include many influential voices within the engineering profession, argue that a deep-seated bias against industry is largely to blame for the lack of societal recognition and prestige accorded to the engineering profession, when compared to other professions such as me-

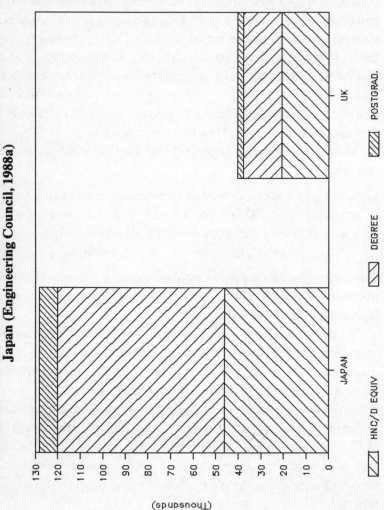

Figure 1.2

A Comparison of Home Students Successfully Completing Higher Education Programmes in Engineering and Allied Topics in 1983 in the UK and Japan (Engineering Council, 1988a)

dicine and law; and that this has led to the failure of the profession to attract enough suitably qualified young people to a career in engineering.

We shall now analyse the proposition that the weakness of UK manufacturing industry today is at least partly due to the lack of status accorded to the professional engineer in society, by examining aspects of the relationship between *Education and Engineering* and by posing the question: 'Is Engineering a True Profession?' Finally, as a postscript, we will explore the work of the organisation which stands at the pinnacle of the engineering profession - The Fellowship of Engineering.

Education and engineering

The economic background to an earlier major Parliamentary debate on the engineering profession in 1980 was particularly gloomy. Various Government reports (Feilden, 1963; Dainton, 1968; Swann, 1968) had charted the relative decline of British manufacturing industry since the Second World War and expressed concern about the dangers of de-industrialisation. In addition, pressure on the balance of payments was particularly severe in the period before Britain enjoyed the benefit of North Sea oil. And, in the early 1970s, a world-wide economic crisis had been precipitated by the decision of countries belonging to OPEC (the Organisation of Petroleum Exporting Countries) to quadruple the price of oil.

The Finniston Report

The Labour Government which came to power in 1974 was faced with recurring balance of payments crises and expressed its dissatisfaction with manufacturing industry's export performance.

At the same time the leading professional institutions were engaged in the so-called 'Great Engineering Debate' on the future of the profession (Stanstell and Valery, 1977). In 1977 the Government responded by appointing Sir Montague Finniston, a Fellow of the Royal Society and lately Chairman of British Steel and Sears Engineering, to chair a committee to investigate the state of the engineering profession. The committee's terms of reference were, 'to review (and make recommendations) for manufacturing industry and in the light of national economic needs':

1. the requirements of British industry for professional and technician engineers, the extent to which these needs are being met, and the use made of engineers by industry

2. the role of the engineering institutions in relation to the education and qualification of engineers at professional and technician level

3. the advantages and disadvantages of statutory registration and licensing of engineers in the UK

4. the arrangements in other major industrial countries, particularly in the EEC, for handling these problems having regard to relevant comparative studies (Finniston, 1980).

The report of the working party, entitled *Engineering Our Future* (but more commonly known as the *Finniston Report*), was published in 1980 and formed the focus of the debate in the House of Commons in the same year. The report remains the most recent and most comprehensive inquiry into the engineering profession in Britain.

The Finniston Report lamented the fact that Britain's accepted creativity and inventiveness had not been harnessed effectively because not enough people with those talents had been attracted into engineering. Finniston also contrasted the poor status of engineering with the great prestige associated with science, medicine and the creative arts. The report also regretted the fact that there was no basis for according esteem to British engineers equivalent to that conveyed by the European concept of *Technic* - the synthesis of knowledge from many disciplines to devise technical and economic solutions to practical problems. The report argued that this third culture (alongside science and art) was well understood in Continental Europe, in Japan and to a lesser extent in the USA. In Britain, by contrast, engineering was often regarded as a subordinate branch of science - symbolised by national institutions such as the *Science* Research Council and the *Science* Museum: institutions whose titles belied the fact that they were more frequently concerned with engineering and technology than with science. The report argued that the award of Bachelor of *Science* and even Bachelor of *Arts* degrees to engineering graduates further devalued the separate standing of engineering.

The Wiener Thesis

Wiener (1981) pinned the blame for the engineering profession's failure to attract sufficient numbers of the brightest national talents firmly on an anti-industrial bias in the British education system which has existed since Victorian times. He argued that an ethos of gentility and service was cultivated in the Victorian public school and replicated in the universities.

This ethos served a useful purpose, at the time, in meeting the need for an army of administrators to run the Empire efficiently and with a measure of humanity. The first choice of many young people in those days was a career in the Indian or the Sudan Civil Services, the Army or the Navy. Industry provided careers only for those who could find nothing better and thus education paid little attention to its needs. Later, the public school ethos was transferred to the state grammar schools, which appeared in the twentieth century, and the study of practical subjects such as engineering was left to the sons of the skilled working classes who attended secondary modern schools and the technical colleges.

Academic drift

The low status of engineering was reflected in the development of higher education in the twentieth century. In recognition of a national need to train more highly qualified technologists and in an attempt to raise the status of engineering and technology, some of the larger technical colleges were upgraded into colleges of advanced technology (CATs) in the 1950s. In the 1960s, the same institutions were upgraded into universities and, at the same time, a completely new type of institution was created - the polytechnic. Many of these new universities and polytechnics introduced innovative and relevant approaches to engineering education, especially full-time sandwich courses and project work. However, most soon began to compete for status by trying to emulate the traditional universities in developing more 'pure' (as opposed to 'applied') science courses and running a full range of arts and social science courses. In an interview, Wiener described this process:

'New institutions have been created - universities, polytechnics and so on - which have been meant to educate people into a more technological and competitive ethos. But they have gradually turned into copies of the old ones with the same anti-materialist values' (Allison, 1983).This process is commonly known as 'academic drift.'

The Robbins expansion

Ironically, expansion of full-time higher education in the 1960s in the aftermath of the Robbins Report, which should have improved the flow of high quality entrants to the engineering profession, caused new recruitment difficulties. Previously the vast majority of engineers had qualified through part-time study for Higher National Certificate qualifications while working in industry; but since the mid 1960s most engineers have come via full-time degree courses at universities and polytechnics. The effect of this change was that the engineering industry lost touch with many able young men who previously would have joined it straight from school. Engineering had become only one of many career options awaiting the 21 or 22 year old graduate.

Take-up rates in higher education

Engineering's recruitment problem has been compounded by a national failure to increase the percentage of young people in full-time higher education since the 1960s. In the early years of that decade, approximately seven per cent of 18- and 19-year-olds went on to full time higher education. By the end of the decade, the 'take-up rate' had been boosted to 13 per cent. However, since 1971, the figure has stayed at around 14 per cent. Meanwhile other advanced industrial countries have persuaded much higher proportions of young people to stay on in higher education. For example in Japan 22 per cent of 18-year-olds go on to universities, a further 10 per cent go on to two year colleges, and another 14 per cent go to 'Special Training Schools' (Engineering Council, 1988a). So in Britain engineering is competing with other industries to catch the best young people from a pool of higher education students which is smaller than in countries such as West Germany, Japan and the USA.

Career choice

Another hindrance to engineering recruitment are the many critical-decision 'gateways' affecting young peoples' choice of career. For example, entry to an engineering degree course normally requires passes in mathematics and physics at 'A' level. This means that potential engineering students must have made a positive decision at the age of 13 or 14 to include mathematics and physics among their 'O' level or GCSE subjects. According to Finniston this was much too early to expect young people to commit themselves to a particular career. The report lamented the fact that too many students, particularly girls, dropped mathematics or physics in favour of other subjects when choosing their 'O' or 'A' level specialisms - thus effectively, and perhaps inadvertently, ruling out the choice of a career in engineering. Finniston attributed this problem to the uniquely restrictive nature of English and Welsh sixth-form study. The report compared the system in England and Wales unfavourably with that of Scotland, where pupils can combine mathematics and physics with three or four 'Highers', and continental Europe where school pupils study for a broadly based *Abitur* or *Baccalauréat*.

Women and engineering

Finniston had one more telling point to make: the profession has consistently failed to attract half of the available population - women. Only half a per cent of all engineers were women at the time of the Finniston report.

Finniston argued that there was 'no intrinsic reason why women should not become engineers' and suggested three main reasons why women had not entered the profession. Firstly, the conventional school curriculum, reinforced by attitudes of parents and teachers, tended to steer girls away from educational choices which might lead to engineering careers. Secondly, there was a lack of suitable 'role models' for girls. Girls may know women who are doctors or solicitors and will certainly know women teachers, but they are less likely to know, or even know of, women engineers. Thirdly, conventional working patterns discriminated against women. Employers were often reluctant to provide expensive training for women who might leave work soon after they qualified. Women engineers with dependent children faced the problem and expense of employing childminders if they wished to return to work - a problem exacerbated by the lack of tax relief upon such expenses. Another aspect of the problem was that women in engineering were being lost to the profession when they left to have children and failed to return. One of the main reasons cited here was a loss of confidence: women engineers felt that they had been unable to keep up with technological changes since they had left employment and worried that this would be exposed if they returned to work.

Much discussion has taken place within the profession on the special benefits that women could bring to engineering. Some research suggested that women would make good engineers because of their mathematical aptitudes; others pointed to the traditional role of women in Western society which would make them more conscious of safety, design and the peaceful uses to which technology could be applied. Also, as Finniston remarked, the recruitment of more women into the industry might 'demolish the myth of the "boiler suits and spanners" image which engineers have long been trying, with limited success, to shake off.'

Is engineering a true profession?

British engineers do not feel that they are members of a true profession like barristers, solicitors or doctors. Many have compared their situation unfavourably with other European countries where the word 'Engineer' is used as a prestigious title and form of address in the same way that 'Doctor' is used in Britain.

In order to establish the reasons why engineering does not appear to receive the same recognition as the medical and legal professions, we need to define the characteristics of a 'true' profession. These are generally agreed to include:

1. custody of a clearly definable and valuable body of knowledge and understanding associated with a long period of training

2. a strong unitary organisation which ensures that the profession generally speaks with 'one voice'

3. clearly defined and rigorous entry standards, backed up by a *requirement* to register with the professional association

4. an overriding responsibility to maintain the standards of the profession for the public's benefit.

The engineering profession clearly meets the first of these conditions, but serious question marks must be placed against the remaining three, which we will now consider in turn.

A strong unitary organisation which ensures that the profession generally speaks with 'one voice'.

In Britain, the British Medical Association and the Law Society are vociferous in their protection of the interests of doctors and solicitors respectively. The accountancy profession is represented by four main bodies, although the Chartered Institute of Accountants is more powerful and prestigious than the other three. In the United States the vast majority of engineers belong to four main professional institutions. Yet, the main co-ordinating body for the engineering profession - the Engineering Council - is committed by its Charter to working through nearly 50 existing professional institutions covering the whole range of established engineering, industrial and technological activities (see *Appendix 1*).

The reason for the large number of engineering institutions can be traced back to the nineteenth century. The first to be formed was the Institution of Civil Engineers in 1818. In 1847 a group of engineers broke away (after Robert Stephenson was refused entry) and formed the Institution of Mechanical Engineers; and in 1860 the Royal Institution of Naval Architects was created. This process of division and creation was to be repeated many times. Amalgamations were much rarer and hence, over the years, the number of institutions multiplied.

The Engineering Council has been well aware of the problem of proliferation and has tried to rationalise the number of institutions (or 'nominated bodies') through which it has to work. An Executive Group Committee system has been adopted which divides the institutions into five clusters based broadly upon disciplines:

1. Mechanical and Production

2. Civil and Structural

3. Electrical and Electronic

4. Chemical and Materials

5. Transport and Marine.

This decision was taken to encourage the constituent institutions to work more closely together and to foster the possibilities of amalgamation.

Some mergers have occurred and these have been welcomed by Sir William Barlow (1988), Chairman of the Engineering Council, who went on to say that:

'Further mergers are desirable but not necessarily essential ... So much, anyway, can be achieved by agreement within the five institution groupings which are now working well. The committee structure is such that all institutions have an opportunity to influence policies. We now have a Council that can speak for all engineers and that is extremely important.'

The Council has made further progress towards creating 'one voice' for the profession with the formation of 19 Engineering Council Regional Organisations (ECROs). Their main roles are to publicise the profession, arrange meetings and conferences, and deal with careers and education issues - all at the regional level. Their activities are co-ordinated by the Engineering Council Regional Organisation Co-ordinating Committee (ECROC).

The ECROs each elect four Chartered Engineers plus two others (drawn from the Incorporated and Technician sections of the profession) to serve on the National Engineering Assembly which provides a forum for grass-roots opinion among professional engineers. Although the Assembly has no direct executive power, it is able to put the Engineering Council's policy under the microscope and to pass resolutions reflecting the profession's views, to which the Council has to respond.

The first national conference of the Assembly was held in Birmingham on 3rd September 1985 and was graced by the presence of the Prime Minister, Margaret Thatcher. Subsequent assemblies have been held successfully at Swansea (1986), Edinburgh (1987), Belfast (1988) and Huddersfield (1989).

Clearly defined and rigorous entry standards are backed up by a requirement to register with the professional authority.

Medical practitioners cannot describe themselves as doctors unless they are on the official register of the General Medical Council. Furthermore doctors who are 'struck off' or 'erased' from the register immediately lose their right to practise.

In contrast anyone in Britain can call themselves an engineer if they want to. In the 1981 Census there were 365,000 economically active people who described themselves as engineers. Yet in the same year, there were only approximately 200,000 names on the Title and Register of the Engineering Council.

This issue can be traced back to the 1920s, when the engineering institutions turned their attention to the protection of their titles. They could have chosen to protect the title *Engineer*; instead they chose the term *Chartered Engineer*. Subsequently there has been a marked reluctance within the profession to erect a rigid barrier around the work of the Chartered Engineer for fear of driving wedges into the profession and disrupting close working relationships between Chartered and Incorporated engineers and Engineering Technicians. Thus the profession itself is at least partly to blame for any confusion which exists in the public mind about the different levels in the profession. Sir Barney Hayhoe MP (one of the tiny number of Chartered Engineers in the House of Commons) drew attention to this problem in the 1988 Parliamentary debate: 'There is never any confusion between surgeons and hospital porters but there is great confusion between highly qualified and highly skilled professional engineers and skilled or semi-skilled people who work in the industry.'

This situation is exacerbated by engineers' lack of face-to-face contact with the public (compared, for example, with doctors). Moreover, while the work of doctors and lawyers is often highlighted in soap operas and dramas based in hospitals or the courts, the engineering profession receives little positive media reinforcement. More commonly the engineering profession is the focus of media attention only when it is implicated in a spectacular technological accident which has hit the front pages (see *Chapter 5*).

Another source of the confusion over who are entitled to call themselves engineers is that there is no requirement for qualified engineers to register with their professional institutions. Indeed many engineers see no practical advantages in registering and do not bother to do so. This particularly applies to the two lower levels of the profession: Incorporated Engineers and Engineering Technicians. A glance at the numbers on the register at the end of 1987 shows an inverted pyramid:

- Chartered Engineers: 196,920
- Incorporated Engineers: 59,205
- Engineering Technicians: 17,034

The Council has admitted that it is in 'dire need' of more engineers at the two lower levels, but this places it in a dilemma. On one hand, it wants to seek more widespread recognition of the title 'Chartered Engineer' and promote this as the true professional level. On the other, it does not want to be seen to be too overtly elitist and alienate the engineers at the lower levels whom it desperately wants to attract on to the register.

Finniston considered engineers' reluctance to register and suggested that there were three main advantages in introducing a statutory requirement for them to do so. These were:

1. Many employers manifestly did not accord engineering or engineers the importance and priority required and in the absence of compulsion would not insist that the engineers they employed were properly qualified

2. Unless failure to register implied a serious loss of employment opportunities for engineers, the incentive for them to seek registration would be weakened and the power of the new machinery to influence engineering formation attenuated

3. Unless registration was necessary for significant areas of engineering employment, and was withdrawable, no effective sanction would exist against professional misconduct or incompetence.

But in the end Finniston rejected the principle of statutory registration. The main reason given was that registration would inhibit the breaking down of departmental barriers needed for the effective organisation of modern engineering companies:

'attempts to draw lines around functions within the engineering dimension and to prescribe who should be allowed responsibility within them would ossify and departmentalise even further the working relationships which we have argued should be opened up and made as flexible as possible' (Finniston, 1980).

For similar reasons Finniston rejected adoption of the Canadian model of a more rigorous system for *licensing* engineers. In Canada, an engineering degree is regarded as a good general foundation for a variety of careers in industry or commerce. Thereafter those entering engineering careers (as defined in law) are obliged to register their qualifications under the relevant Provincial Act. Registration is controlled by the engineering profession under delegated authority from the Provincial Governments. A single register is maintained for each Province, membership of which is required before an engineer can practise. The register also defines the individual's area of competence and places an onus on him or her not to work outside this area.

In Britain licensing does exist in the nuclear, aeronautical and marine industries, where public safety issues are particularly prominent. A good example is the 'ticket' needed by marine engineers which licenses them to practise at sea.

While it is still not the Engineering Council's policy to press for widespread licensing of engineers, in 1987 it expressed the intention of examining this issue and considering whether any extensions should be sought:

'work is commencing to examine the practicability of defining the type and level of responsibility which, it may be recommended, should be reserved for registered engineers. This would fall short of a full licensing arrangement but would indicate to employers and Government the views of the Engineering Council on this important matter' (Levy, 1987).

An over-riding responsibility to maintain the standards of the profession for the public's benefit

One view of the 'real' professions such as law and medicine is as benevolent associations which establish professional standards and ethics. These standards and ethics emphasise altruism and service to the public rather than narrow self interests. Thus the lawyer is seen as the guardian of the law in the interest of society as a whole; and medical practitioners, directed by their Hippocratic oath, are primarily concerned with the health of their patients and that of the community at large. The reward for this altruism is the high degree of trust accorded to such professional groups by the public. One reflection of this trust is the way that professionals are allowed to police their own profession. For example, doctors are judged and disciplined by a panel of their peers, nominated by the professional body, rather than by their employer.

This is a model to which many would like the engineering profession to aspire. Indeed, Professor Meredith Tring (1988) has suggested that Engineers, Scientists and Technicians should have their own Hippocratic Oath:

'I vow to practise my profession with conscience and dignity; I will strive to apply my skills only with the utmost respect for the well being of humanity; the earth and its species; I will not permit considerations of nationality, politics, prejudice or material advancement to intervene between my work and this duty to present and future generations. I make this oath freely and upon my honour' *Chemical Engineer*, 1988.

However, in contrast to many professional groups, most engineers are employed on a full-time basis in organisations and thus it is likely that *their first loyalty will be to their company rather than to the public*. This also means that, more often than not, it is the employer who has to accept legal responsibility for any fault in an engineer's work. In other words if a mistake by an engineer causes injury or loss of life, the employer, rather than the engineer, is likely to be sued. Consequently, it is more likely that the employer, rather than the professional institution, will initiate disciplinary action against the engineer. Although the professional engineering institutions have well-defined disciplinary procedures, these are rarely applied. Even if they are applied and an engineer is expelled, there is nothing to stop him or her continuing in employment as an engineer (see our earlier debate on registration).

Incidentally, the situation is rather different if the engineer is working as a consultant. All consultants take on 'professional liability', for their work and should take out insurance in case they unwittingly or negligently give wrong advice to a client (doctors have to take out similar insurance). There is a case for saying that only engineers who are working as consultants are working as 'true professionals'. Finniston indeed argued that the work of consultants was one area which should be covered by a strict licensing system.

However, the perception of professional bodies as benevolent associations has been challenged by those who take a more negative view of professionalism. George Bernard Shaw once described all professions as 'conspiracies against the laity'. And there is a view that professionalism is simply a self-interested strategy for improving the market share of an occupational class. Seen from this perspective, self-policing allows a profession better to guard the monopoly of whatever service it provides. Professional ethics and the emphasis on altruism, care and community service are then seen as a smoke-screen which serves to disguise professional self-interest.

A certain ambivalence towards professionalism is understandable in today's society when the professions in general are on the defensive. Critics of self-policing by the medical profession argue that the system is too lenient and punishes moral misbehaviour more harshly than negligence or incompetence. Architects have been denounced for designing houses and flats which they themselves would never live in, and planners have been condemned for spoiling the urban environment and creating urban chaos. Teachers continue to be blamed for an alleged decline in educational standards and for not responding to the wishes of parents. And the Conservative Government, fresh from its victories over the trade unions in the 1980s, has decided to challenge some of the restrictive working practices which it claims are to be found within the professions.

Any move to impose the full model of professionalism on engineers would therefore probably be counter-productive and out of tune with the times. But one major advantage of an ambivalent approach towards professionalism is that engineers themselves can choose the *positive* aspects of professionalism while rejecting the *negative* ones. So in this book we assume that a *professional approach* is synonymous with the positive, altruistic values of professionalism identified earlier. And a professional approach implies a mastery of not only the technical knowledge and skills owned by the profession, but the overriding responsibility to maintain the standards of the profession for the public's benefit.

Conclusion

We can state that the engineering profession does not receive the recognition it deserves for its contribution to the economic and material well-being of society, and that this lack of status has contributed to the relative decline of UK manufacturing industry in recent times.

The root cause of the problem may be the deep-seated cultural bias against industry identified in the Finniston and Wiener theses discussed at the beginning of this chapter. This, in turn, may have had a negative effect on the supply of high-quality entrants to the engineering profession.

However, the lack of status accorded to the profession is also due to the fact that it does not fully meet three of the criteria of a 'true' profession we have identified. Firstly, although the creation of the Engineering Council has made a significant difference, the profession still does not possess a strong unitary organisation which ensures that engineers generally speak with 'one voice'. Secondly, although entry standards have been more clearly defined and made more rigorous, these have not been backed up by a *requirement* to register with the professional association. And, finally, the engineering profession's overriding responsibility to maintain its standards for the public's benefit is diluted by the fact that engineers' first loyalty is normally to their employers. Consequently, the profession's responsibility to the public is *implicit* rather than *explicit*, and not immediately self-evident to the public.

However, as we have argued, young engineers should seize the positive aspects of professionalism and strive to bring a professional approach to everything they do. Implicit in this approach is a sensitivity to the way in which engineering interrelates with those affected by its activities - the effect that engineering has on society. Hence the title of this book - *The Professional Engineer in Society*.

Postscript - The Fellowship of Engineering

The final achievement for any Chartered Engineer who aspires to reach the pinnacle of the profession is to join the elite ranks of the Fellowship of Engineering.

During the mid-1970s the Duke of Edinburgh and a group of distinguished engineers set about the creation of this powerful body which, it was hoped, would perform the same function for engineering as the Royal Society had successfully performed for science over the last 300 years. This body would work for, and reflect, excellence in engineering.

The Fellowship of Engineering was set up by the Council of Engineering Institutions in 1976, with an initial membership of 126. Membership comprised those engineers who were already members of the Royal Society and an equal number of the most eminent Chartered Engineers from all branches of the profession. It was intended that this number would grow at a rate of not more than 60 per annum and should not exceed 1000. (By 1987 membership had reached 707.) Members are allowed to use the prestigious title 'FEng'.

Finniston, having explored the successful role of similar bodies in the USA and Sweden, was in favour of an enhanced role for the Fellowship. He saw it as being undecided on its role and objectives and suggested that it should concentrate on the identification and promotion of new directions for engineering research, development and innovation which had not yet been exploited. He saw future functions as advising Government, undertaking studies of important issues in engineering and identifying the need for new academic Chairs of Engineering.

The Fellowship was granted a Royal Charter in 1983 and is committed to 'the pursuit, encouragement and maintenance of excellence in the whole field of engineering to useful purpose in order to promote the advancement of the science, art and practice of engineering for the benefit of the public'. It has now begun to fulfil the role that Finniston wished for it and has carried out a major study of the engineering aspects of acid rain, and has organised discussions on key topics such as 'science parks', 'finance for innovation' and the 'relationship of standards of education and training to industrial performance'. It also organises a major competition (the MacRobert Award) for an outstanding contribution by way of innovation in engineering or in the application of the physical sciences, which is designed to enhance British prestige and prosperity.

Suggestions for further study

The Engineering Council produces regular newsletters which give the latest news from the regions and the activities of the national assembly: these should be required reading for all student engineers. Student engineers should also apply for student membership of their own professional institutions and attend local meetings and conferences wherever possible.

We also suggest that student engineers carefully read and memorise the code of conduct contained in their professional institution's handbook, and consider the full implication of this code for their present and future working lives.

The Finniston Report remains the most up-to-date and comprehensive inquiry into the state of the engineering profession, and we recommend that all student engineers should consult a copy of it in their library. Martin Wiener's influential but controversial book, *English Culture and the Decline of the English Industrial Spirit 1850-1980*, provides an outsider's perspective of the anti-industrial culture which is said to exist in Britain - Wiener is an American Professor of History at Rice University, Texas.

Chapter 2

The Work of the Engineering Council

The central recommendation of the Finniston Report (1980) was the establishment of a powerful new statutory body to take overall responsibility for the running and development of the engineering profession. Finniston hoped that this new body, to be known as the *Engineering Authority*, would act as an 'engine of change' to overcome the inertia and negativism of prevailing attitudes, arrest the decline in Britain's manufacturing industry and create a market-orientated 'engineering dimension' - a new pillar in British society distinct from the arts and sciences - to help the nation towards economic recovery.

There had been earlier attempts to introduce greater co-ordination to the profession. The *Engineering Joint Council* was formed in 1924 and in 1962 the 13 largest institutions (who each held a Royal Charter) formed the *Engineering Institutions Joint Council*. When this organisation was itself awarded a Royal Charter in 1965, it changed its name to the *Council of Engineering Institutions* (CEI). However, Finniston considered that the CEI did not have sufficient credibility to provide the leadership needed.

Although the Finniston Report was never fully implemented, the Government did accept its recommendation for a new national co-ordinating body and the *Engineering Council* was duly awarded a Royal Charter on 27th November, 1981. However, the Government did not give the Engineering *Council* the statutory powers that Finniston had wanted the Engineering *Authority* to have. The reason for this was that the established professional institutions (such as the Institution of Civil Engineers, the Institution of Mechanical Engineers, and the Institution of Electrical Engineers) were justly proud of their long history and traditions; and, in the aftermath of the publication of the Finniston Report, they fought a hard and ultimately successful battle for continued autonomy and independence.

Consequently, the emergence of the Engineering Council was the outcome of a process of bargaining and compromise which preserved the power of the professional institutions and not the dramatic change in policy intended by Finniston (Jordan and Richardson, 1984). Many people inside and outside the profession thought that the Council would fail because of the lack of statutory 'teeth' given to it by the Government. Others saw the resultant need for the Council to work by persuasion rather than by edict as an advantage, as it meant independence and freedom of operation unimpeded by the Government of the day.

Today the Engineering Council works through the 47 professional institutions (Engineering Council, 1988b) and itself employs fewer than 60 people. Of these employees, about a dozen are exclusively engaged in maintaining a Register of qualified engineers and in running the Engineering Council examinations. The other staff are concerned with the qualifications and training functions of the Council. They also maintain contact with the engineering institutions and industrial affiliate organisations (currently numbering 210) and promote and service an annual Engineering Assembly. In addition, they look after the 19 regional committees and maintain contact with a large number of national organisations (Levy, 1987).

The Engineering Council was initially helped by a three-year Government grant but it is now financially independent. Some 50 per cent of its annual income of £3 million is derived from Registration fees, 20 per cent from examination fees, and 10 per cent from specifically supported projects. The last 20 per cent is attracted, significantly, from the growing number of Industrial Affiliates who pay a subscription relative to their number of employees (from £250 to £10,000 at the time of writing). Support from this area is one indication of the Council's success.

The work of the Engineering Council has been based on the premise that Britain is an industrial nation with an 'anti-industrial culture'; and that these negative attitudes towards industry and engineering must be countered, if Britain is to achieve long term economic recovery. Its three aims are:

1. to improve standards and routes to registration for the engineering profession

2. to create awareness of engineering and technology in society and thus secure the next generation of engineers and technicians

3. to improve the supply of qualified engineers and technologists of all grades and disciplines.

In this chapter we shall examine the work of the Engineering Council in relation to the first of these aims by describing its plans to improve the *Standards and Routes to Registration* of engineers. We will then evaluate the various *Campaigns and Initiatives* run by the Engineering Council in pursuance of aims two and three.

Standards and routes to registration

One of the Council's earliest tasks was to take over the 'Title and Register of Engineers' from the Council of Engineering Institutions (CEI) and to set up a new Board for Engineers' Registration (BER). The new Register maintained the three sections of the old Council of Engineering Institutions Engineering Registration Board (ERB), namely: *Chartered Engineer* (CEng), *Technician Engineer* (TEng), and *Engineering Technician* (Eng Tech). The Technician Engineer section has since been renamed as the *Incorporated Engineer* (IEng) section.

But the Finniston report had called for a set of reforms in the registration process and introduced a new concept: that of engineering *formation*. This concept was intended to cover a 'cradle to grave' approach to the *integrated* education, training, and continuing education and training of high quality engineers. Finniston found that these activities were generally treated as unconnected functions by education and industry. In order to integrate these functions, the Engineering Council defined three stages in the formation of an engineer. These stages are:

Stage 1: *Accredited education* - denotes that the person has acquired an appropriate academic standard.

Stage 2: *Approved training* - denotes that sufficient training of the right type has been undertaken.

Stage 3: *Responsible experience* - denotes that sufficient experience at an appropriate level of responsibility has been obtained.

The important step of linking the three stages of formation to the three sections of the Register occurred with the publication of the 'Standards and Routes to Registration' or SARTOR (Engineering Council, 1984a). SARTOR set out clear paths leading to the three sections of the register. Thus the routes by which the majority of engineers will be expected to register in future are to consist of accredited courses and approved training programmes, followed by monitored responsible experience. Ladders and bridges are to be provided to enable progression from stage to stage and from section to section of the Register (see *Figure 2.1*). The Engineering Council expects these regulations to be effective from 1992. However, the Engineering Council will still not be able to compel anyone who wishes to practise as an engineer to join the Register (see *Chapter 1*).

Stage 1 - Accredited education

The Council has delegated authority to the major engineering institutions to accredit new Bachelor and Master of *Engineering* (BEng and MEng) degrees to replace the old Bachelor and Master of *Science* degrees and to give a symbolic boost to the profession. Yet these new qualifications are more than just a change of name. The new courses aim to give a fuller educational experience to the young engineer and integrate the theoretical and practical elements of the study of engineering more successfully than in the past. There is also a requirement that material is included which is related to the environment and to the social and professional role of the engineer. Such provisions apply no less to National Certificate and Higher National Certificate courses than to BEng courses.

The MEng degree is one year longer than the BEng. This lengthening allows the whole of the undergraduate course to be further broadened and deepened: primarily in engineering content, but also by the inclusion of topics such as business studies, management and marketing.

The Engineering Council expects that the majority of those who aspire to Chartered status will obtain an honours degree in engineering awarded by a British university or the Council for National Academic Awards (CNAA). However, the Engineering Council conducts its own Part 1 and 2 examinations for prospective registrants who have prepared themselves for the profession in other ways. The Part 2 examination is equivalent to a British university honours degree in Engineering and is itself divided into three parts. Part A consists of technical subjects relevant to the candidate's specialisation; Part B is common to all disciplines and concerns 'The Engineer in Society'; Part C is a design project (note that some professional institutions substitute their own examinations for this part).

Finally, the Council has agreed that courses in fields adjacent to engineering may now be 'part-accredited'. This is intended to act as a signal to students taking physics degrees, for example, that a career in engineering is open

Figure 2.1
Definitions of the Three Sections on the Register and the Stages in their formation (Engineering Council, 1987).

Chartered Engineers ... are concerned with the progress of technology through innovation, creativity and change and should be able to develop and apply new technologies, promote advanced designs, introduce new and more efficient production techniques, marketing and construction concepts and pioneer new engineering services and management methods. They need the ability to supervise others and in due time the maturity to assume responsibility for the direction of important tasks.

Incorporated Engineers ... perform technical duties of an established or novel nature in posts demanding a detailed understanding of a particular technology. They are concerned with maintaining and managing existing technology efficiently. They need communication skills and an awareness beyond the limits of their specific responsibility.

Engineering Technicians ... are competent to apply proven techniques and procedures with an element of personal responsibility. They should have an understanding of general engineering principles applicable to their role, rather than by relying solely on established practices or accumulated skills.

Only after the three stages in formation have been completed can the designatory letters be used after an engineer's name. The intention is to place emphasis on the role of training and responsible experience.

Chartered Engineer Section
Stage 1 Academic standard exemplified by an accredited degree in engineering or a pass in the Engineering Council Part 2 Examination
Stage 2 a period of approved training
Stage 3 a period of acceptable experience and professional responsibility; the aggregate of training and experience shall not be less than four years; minimum age 25.

Those entering the Register at Stage 3 are authorised to use the style or title of Chartered Engineer and the designatory letters CEng providing they are members of a nominated Chartered Engineering Institution or Institution-affiliated body.

Incorporated Engineer Section
Stage 1 Academic standard exemplified by the BTEC Higher National Certificate in approved programme areas
Stage 2 a minimum of two years approved training
Stage 3 five years engineering experience including the period of training shown above; minimum age 23.

Those entering the Register at Stage 3 are entitled to use the style or title of Incorporated Engineer and the designatory letters IEng.

Engineering Technician Section
Stage 1 Academic standard exemplified by the BTEC National Certificate in approved programme areas
Stage 2 a minimum of two years' approved training
Stage 3 three years' engineering experience including the period of training shown above; minimum age 21.

Those entering the Register at Stage 3 are entitled to use the style or title of Engineering Technician and the designatory letters Eng Tech.

to them and could lead to early interest and involvement in using the practical applications of their knowledge. After graduation such students would need to make good the difference between their degree and the design and project work of fully-accredited BEng courses by participating in open-learning schemes (Engineering Council, 1985a).

Stage 2 - Approved training

All three grades of engineer now have to satisfy training programmes which are seen as no less important than accredited academic courses. The Council was determined that Stage 2 training should be properly planned and structured (not an extension of discredited 'time serving' or 'sitting next to Nellie' methods of training) and decided to accredit training schemes in the same way as academic courses. Thus organisations authorised by the Engineering Council to supervise Stage 2 training for the Register are required to liaise closely with employers, maintain registers of the trainees and record their progress in log books. Trainees must be supervised by qualified engineers at the place of training and supported, where appropriate, by academic staff responsible for sandwich and block release courses.

Stage 3 - Responsible experience

After the first and second stages have been completed, each candidate for Registration must satisfy the third stage - 'Responsible Experience'. Candidates have to produce solid evidence of their experience including proof of employment in a post carrying some professional responsibility. This means exposure to the reality of making decisions (and taking personal responsibility for the outcome) in manufacture, construction, health and safety or in business negotiations.

For those applying for Stage 3 Registration at the Chartered or Incorporated Engineer levels this evidence must be presented at a 'Professional Review':

'Professional Reviews are occasions when candidates are assessed by senior representatives of the Nominated Body on the whole of their formation. The Review normally includes an interview and a written report which contains a description of the types of work on which the candidate has been engaged and indicates his or her responsibility. The occasion acts as a final check on competence and, if successful, the candidate is eligible to become a Chartered or Incorporated Engineer. This is not, however, the end of the story, for, as in previous generations, the new registrant then carries a personal charge to maintain his or her knowledge in a field which may be expected to alter as rapidly in the next generation as in the last' (Engineering Council, 1985a).

For example, a candidate wishing to seek election or transfer to Corporate or Associate Membership of the Institution of Production Engineers, and subsequent admission to Stage 3 of the Chartered Engineer or Incorporated Engineer registers of the Engineering Council's Board for Engineers' Registration, has to write a 2000 word 'Professional Review Report'. This document is subsequently used as the basis for questioning by an interview panel of leading engineers. The first part of the report is intended to highlight aspects of the applicant's career after completion of the academic and training requirements, 'which demonstrates (their) ability to practise as a professional production engineer'. The second part must state, '[the candidate's] commitment in the future to the Production Engineering profession, its Code of Conduct and to ... continuing education and training' (Institution of Production Engineers, 1987).

The Institution of Production Engineers' Code of Conduct states that the candidate must:

1. order, at all times, their conduct so as to uphold the dignity and reputation of the Institution and of the Profession of Engineering and to safeguard the public interest in matters of safety and health and otherwise

2. exercise their professional or technical skill and judgement to the best of their ability and to discharge their professional or technical responsibilities with integrity

3. not abuse their connections with the Institution to further their personal or business interests.

Once the interview has been successfully completed, the candidate becomes eligible for a certificate, issued by the Engineering Council, which bears the Council's Coat of Arms and the candidate's Registered title.

Continuing education and training

As implied by the preceding description of the professional review, an important post registration stage in the formation of an engineer is 'Continuing

Education and Training' (CET): the continuous up-dating and extending of knowledge and skills.

All the main professions recognise the need for some form of Continuing Education and Training (known variously as 'Continuing Professional Education or Development' or just 'Continuing Education'). The Engineering Council suggested that CET should become a part of a professional code of practice for engineers:

> 'it should be the responsibility of every Chartered and Technician (Incorporated) Engineer to maintain professional standards by keeping up-to-date with the latest technology and anticipating future needs as they may arise. CET implies the need for an individual to undertake life long learning in order to keep in the forefront of the thinking and skills required in their profession' (Engineering Council, 1986b).

CET is particularly important to engineering as new technological developments take place so quickly. In order to remain competitive, it is vital that employers have engineers and technicians who are up-to-date and able to help their organisations improve their cutting edge in the world market.

The Engineering Council found evidence of industry's neglect of CET in a survey of 31 organisations commissioned in 1985. This survey provided information about the attitudes towards up-dating displayed by senior and middle managers and by the engineers themselves. It found that CET was seldom treated as a subject in its own right and that most CET was haphazard, reactive to current problems and rarely part of long-term planning. Moreover, CET was rarely exploited as a method of introducing the technologies needed to give future products a competitive edge. Performance reviews and career development procedures were widely available but their application was patchy and many engineers and technicians expressed little ambition to reach the top. Finally, the survey concluded that, as suppliers of CET, academic and professional institutions needed to market their products better to stimulate demand.

In order to generate interest in CET, the Council has constructed a model of a typical pattern of education and training activities around the three stages of a professional engineer's career.

In the *early stage*, the Council recommends that young engineers should be participating in full-time education at university or college or in short specialist courses in computer applications and other specific topics. They should attend and contribute to meetings of their professional institutions and receive 'mentor guidance' from experienced colleagues. In addition, they should be receiving in-house training in design methods, attending management meetings, and writing reports.

At the *mid-career stage*, they should be participating in full-time postgraduate courses or in research and development activities in industry, lecturing, producing articles and papers, and contributing to conferences and seminars. They should also be undergoing advanced training in communication, legal, financial, and management skills and have acquired fluency in at least one foreign language. Finally, they should be involved in the affairs of their professional institution and acting as mentors to junior engineers.

At the *later stage*, engineers at the top of their profession should be directing research activities and be involved in arbitration, consultancy or corporate management roles. They should be providing management instruction for others, running in-house seminars and playing a leading role in institutional affairs and in the community (as, for example, a school or college governor). They might also be involved in writing, giving careers advice and part-time teaching (Engineering Council, 1985b).

In order to put its ideas into practice, the Engineering Council has started a number of pilot CET schemes, sponsored by the Department of Education and Science's PICKUP updating programme (Engineering Council, 1988c). In this context, the Engineering Council believes that engineering education, training and experience provide an excellent base from which engineers with the right commitment and leadership qualities can be developed into effective managers. Consequently, the Council has issued a firm policy statement which calls for employers to provide more generous opportunities for CET in management and business skills at all stages of an engineer's career (Engineering Council, 1988d).

The European engineer

Chartered Engineers can now achieve the status of 'European Engineer'. The British National Committee for International Engineering Affairs is a member (with all other relevant organisations from other EEC countries) of the *Fédération Européenne d'Associations Nationales d'Ingénieurs* (European Federation of National Engineering Associations or FEANI) which was founded in 1951. This is a non-governmental organisation to which the national engineering associations of 20 European nations are federated. Its main aims are to co-ordinate the requirements, qualifications and recognition of engineers; and to assert the status, role and responsibility of engineers in the European community.

FEANI has had the difficult task of equating the qualifications of European engineers. Until recently British Chartered Engineers were classified in section Ab of the FEANI Register rather than Aa because of the limited length of their initial engineering degree course (three years as against Continental courses lasting four, five or six years). Deadlock resulted, and Britain was under pressure to increase the length of engineering degree courses to four years. However, these attempts to harmonise apparently irreconcilable systems were eventually abandoned in favour of accepting the co-existence of differing schemes of education provided that they were effectively monitored to produce a competent engineer at the end. The deadlock was broken in May 1986, as a result of an initiative by the British National Committee of FEANI. Since this date all 20 National Committees have agreed to recognise a new basis for the European Register, namely a seven-year package of education, training and experience which strongly resembles the requirement for British Chartered Engineers. This places British Chartered Engineers in the new FEANI Group I and makes them eligible as European Engineers alongside their previously better-placed European counterparts.

In 1987 this agreement was used to launch the new title *Euro-Engineer* which could be used as a pan-European title of address - 'EurIng Smith'. The Engineering Council hopes that British Chartered Engineers will now be able to obtain a FEANI 'passport' on application enabling them to get international recognition more readily. This is all the more important given the move to a single European Market by 1992 which will create a genuine multi-national employment market within the European Community.

However, at the 1988 Engineering Assembly, the Chairman of the Engineering Council, Sir William Barlow, attacked European bureaucrats for ignoring the FEANI agreement and pressing ahead with a General Directive on professional qualifications (including engineering) issued by the European Commission as part of harmonisation arrangements. Sir William reported that some countries, particularly Germany and Denmark, had refused to accept the EuroIng qualification because they wanted to protect their technical colleges and he stated that: 'Our intention now is to follow up on the General Directive with increased pressure to win an Engineering Directive, and I think that this is feasible within a time scale of two or three years.'

Campaigns and initiatives

The Engineering Council has been involved in many campaigns and initiatives since its creation in 1981.

Public awareness campaigns

The Engineering Council's first major publicity campaign was launched in 1984 with a series of advertisements in the quality press. These carried some striking slogans such as:

'Once more the world is beating us at our own game. And it's not cricket.'

'Last year we imported more manufactured goods than we exported. It was the first time. And it was the last straw.'

'Why isn't there an Engineers' Corner in Westminster Abbey? In Britain, we've always made more fuss of a ballad than a blueprint' (see *Figure 2.2*).

The Engineering Council's finances at the time dictated that the campaign had to be run on a 'shoestring' budget of £140,000. Subsequently the Council has run an almost continuous series of public awareness campaigns - the latest of which is the 1987 'Industry Matters' campaign.

A *Financial Times* journalist summed up the effectiveness of these campaigns: 'If engineers have been negligent in beating their own drum, the emergence ... of the Council ... shows they are at last learning how' (Engineering Council, 1985c). Although it is still too early to judge the Engineering Council on its ambitious aim of contributing to a national change of culture, a start has been made on the long-term task of changing attitudes and alerting the nation to the importance of engineering (Engineering Council 1985c).

Women into science and engineering

Another Engineering Council campaign was launched in 1984 in collaboration with the Equal Opportunities Commission (EOC). This initiative was known as Women Into Science and Engineering, or WISE '84. One of the joint chairpersons of this campaign, Baroness (Beryl) Platt of Writtle, has the ideal credentials for the job: she is an aeronautical engineer and the first woman to serve on the governing body of the Engineering Council (Ferry, 1984).

The campaign was aimed largely at schoolgirls. Schools and universities held open days; there were parents' evenings, 'WISE weeks' and careers con-

Figure 2.2
Why isn't there an Engineers' Corner in Westminster Abbey?

Why isn't there an Engineers' Corner in Westminster Abbey?

In Britain we've always made more fuss of a ballad than a blueprint.

Heaped more honours on our poets, statesmen and military heroes than our inventive geniuses.

But why?

It was our engineers 200 years ago who transformed this country into a mighty power.

It is our engineers we have relied on ever since for so much of our prestige and prosperity.

It is our engineers we turned to in the crisis of the war.

And it is our engineers we need just as desperately, today, if we are to survive as an industrial power.

To make the cars, the computers, the turbines and the telecommunications the world markets are crying out for.

But who would guess?

How many schoolchildren daydream of becoming great engineers?

How many parents encourage them to do so?

Why don't we put more emphasis on engineering in our universities and polytechnics?

Japan produces 10 times as many engineering graduates.

Why are our engineers paid less well than other professions?

They aren't in Germany, Sweden or the States.

Why do they so seldom rise to the top of industry or Government, as they do in France?

Is it any wonder that we are short of professional engineers,

and that our economy is feeling the effect?

Last year was the first time since before the Industrial Revolution that we imported more manufactured goods than we exported.

It is a crisis – and The Engineering Council has been formed to tackle it.

To impress upon the City, the Government, educationalists and industry alike the importance of the profession, and to put more engineers where they belong.

In the schools, universities, polytechnics, factories, boardrooms, Parliament and Government.

Even in Westminster Abbey.

THE ENGINEERING COUNCIL

THE ENGINEERING COUNCIL CANBERRA HOUSE, MALTRAVERS STREET, LONDON WC2R 3ER 01 240 7891 ventions. The EOC acted as a clearing house for information on WISE events and ran two advertising campaigns, (one on information technology and the other on engineering). These aimed to reach schoolgirls through information packs and advertisements in teenage magazines and elsewhere. A colourful poster with the slogan 'Engineering - A Woman's Touch', was printed and distributed to every school in Britain. Special 'WISE Buses' were adapted to hold electronically controlled equipment for girls to operate and these embarked upon a national tour of schools. The buses also provided careers literature and videos showing working conditions in engineering. A publication by the Women's Engineering Society (an organisation which has been dedicated to promoting the cause for more women in engineering since 1920) illustrated over 20 case studies of successful women engineers to act as role-models for those thinking about a career in engineering (West, 1984).

A later Engineering Council publication, *Career Breaks for Women*, drew attention to the commercial sense of encouraging women engineers to return to industry after having their children (Engineering Council, 1985e).

The WISE campaign demonstrated the ignorance of girls over career choice and highlighted the propensity of girls to drop the study of mathematics and science subjects at an early stage in their secondary education. It also demonstrated the need for work experience for schoolgirls in science and engineering based areas and the crucial need to break down stereotypes that discouraged girls from a career in engineering and science.

In 1986 the Engineering Council conducted a survey to examine the impact of WISE and found that the number of women studying on full-time engineering and technology courses in universities had risen, modestly, from 8.7 per cent to 10.9 per cent, (between 1982-3 and 1985-6) (see *Figure 2.3*). Analysis of these statistics showed that this increase was not achieved at the expense of science places, which had similarly grown. However, the number of women studying engineering and technology in higher education as a whole (universities, polytechnics, and colleges - full time and part time) was less encouraging. As *Figure 2.3* also shows, in the academic year 1984-5, there were only 10,200 females (or 6.5 per cent) on all such courses.

Industry Year

Although Industry Year 1986 was run under the leadership of the *Royal Society for the Encouragement of Arts, Commerce, and Manufactures* (better known as the Royal Society of Arts or RSA), the Engineering Council played

Figure 2.3
**(a) Percentage of Women on Full Time University Courses in Engineering
and Technology (CSO, Annual Abstract of Statistics, 1987)**

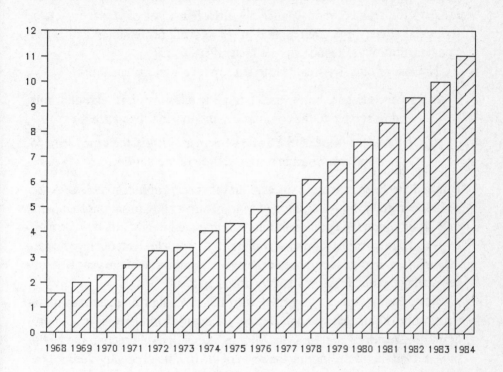

(b) All Students Studying Engineering and Technology in Higher Education in 1984-85 (CSO, Annual Abstract of Statistics, 1987)
(in thousands)

	POST GRAD		UNDERGRAD		OTHER H.E.		TOTALS
	FT	PT	FT	PT	FT	PT	
MALE:	7.7	4.1	54.9	3.9	19.6	57.1	147.3 (93.5%)
FEMALE:	0.8	0.4	5.4	0.2	1.8	1.6	10.2 (6.5%)

FT = full time
PT = part time

a major supporting role. Some 135 years earlier the RSA had conceived and summoned support for the Great Exhibition of 1851: an event widely regarded by historians as the zenith of Britain's industrial world leadership. In addition to the support from the Engineering Council, the RSA's 1986 campaign enjoyed the full backing of Government, the Confederation of British Industry, the Trades Union Council, the British Institute of Management, the Industrial Society, the Church, and other relevant professional and educational institutions (Engineering Council, 1986e).

The aim of Industry Year was to act as a lever for change and:

1. to encourage a better understanding of industry, its essential role, and its service to the community, and to win acceptance for it

2. to foster the pride of those who work in industry in their own achievements and contribution to the welfare of the nation.

Doubts have been expressed since about the success of Industry Year. A survey conducted by the Association of Market Survey Organisations found that only 1 per cent of the population had participated in any Industry Year activity and one sceptical journalist commented: 'don't feel left out if you sailed through 1986 in total ignorance of the event ... at the end of the year Britain's resounding apathy remains virtually untouched.'

Nevertheless, those concerned with the campaign thought that it was worthwhile. Diana McMahon (Deputy Director of Industry Year and programme director of the 'Industry Matters' campaign) claimed at the beginning of 1987 that: 'considering the scale of the task that Industry Year set out to tackle the response has been remarkable' (McMahon, 1987). She saw most progress in the area of the relationships between education and industry, especially in linking secondary schools with local industries, and pointed to the benefits of giving schools a better understanding of the changes occurring in industry and *vice versa*.

The campaign for quality in industry

The foundations of a National Quality Campaign were laid down in a 1982 Government White Paper entitled 'Standards Quality and International Competitiveness.' And, having spent so much effort in raising the quality of the engineering profession, it was natural for the Engineering Council to become involved with efforts to raise the quality of British manufactured goods (see *Figure 2.4*).

Figure 2.4
What is quality in manufacturing? (Source DTI, 1986)

Quality is the sum of:
1. knowing the customer's needs and expectations
2. designing to meet them
3. faultless construction
4. reliable bought-in components and sub-assemblies
5. certified performance and safety
6. clear instruction manuals
7. suitable packaging
8. punctual delivery
9. efficient back-up service
10. feed-back of field experience.

These elements add up to fitness for purpose and value for money - into ownership satisfaction that brings customers back to buy a company's products again and again. This is summed up in the slogan:

'If you want your customers to come back you need to ensure that your products don't.'

As a contribution to the National Quality Campaign, the Engineering Council published two concise pamphlets entitled *Appraising the Technical and Commercial Aspects of a Manufacturing Company* and *Technical Reviews for Manufacturing, Process and Construction Companies* (Engineering Council, 1983a, and 1983b). These, together with a third pamphlet, entitled *Managing Design for Competitive Advantage* (Engineering Council, 1986d) - a joint initiative between the Engineering Council and the Design Council - were aimed at raising international competitiveness. The first of these pamphlets reminded the reader what the engineers had to achieve at company level if British manufacturing industries were to be successful:

1. assessing and/or anticipating market needs and opportunities

2. assessing the company's potential to meet or create these opportunities

3. conceiving, designing and continually developing products and systems to meet market requirements

4. developing, operating and improving processes for manufacturing such products profitably, making optimum use of materials, energy, capital and human resources

5. ensuring that engineering support for products is efficiently sustained throughout product life

6. responding quickly to changes in market requirements.

Managing Design for Competitive Advantage pointed out that 'the engineering of a product, process or system is a complex activity comprising many complementary and interrelated factors. The importance and interdisciplinary nature of design and its management are frequently misunderstood.' It outlined the management and role of design and the four recognised phases of design, namely:

1. Definition of Objectives

2. Conceptual Design

3. Embodiment Design

4. Detail Design.

The 'Design and Build' courses now being included in MEng and other engineering degree schemes should help engineering students to anticipate some of the problems inherent in producing good design and quality while remaining economically competitive.

Education and industry links

The Engineering Council can take credit for many new initiatives designed to make school syllabuses more practical and relevant to the needs of industry. The Council encouraged engineers to become school governors (either as parents or as co-opted members) (Engineering Council, 1986f), and it has published teaching materials in collaboration with the Standing Conference on Schools Science and Technology (SCSST). These materials offer a framework within which teachers in primary schools can give young children experience in practical problem-solving, help them to work in groups and begin to appreciate the principles of 'design and make' (Engineering Council, 1985d). In this way, a sound foundation is laid for more advanced work in Craft, Design and Technology in Secondary schools.

The Council places great importance on participation in school careers functions and has taken over responsibility for the Engineering Careers Co-ordinating Organisation (ECCO). Through ECCO, the Council has developed and financed an engineering database, linked to an electronic mail system on the Times Network.

'Opening Windows on Engineering' is a scheme run by the Council to encourage and train successful young engineers to visit schools and spread knowledge about industry, engineering careers and the role of engineering in wealth creation for Britain. The main target group is boys and girls aged between 12 and 15 years and their teachers (Engineering Council, 1986a). More recently, the Council has established, in partnership with the Department of Trade and Industry, a 'neighbourhood engineer' scheme to link engineers with local secondary schools. The scheme will help schools with curriculum development, careers advice, and community involvement. Finally, the Council's annual 'Young Engineers for Britain' competition has generated positive publicity for engineering (Engineering Council, 1986c).

Other achievements

The Engineering Council can now point to a number of changes which have been achieved, at least in part, as a result of its publicity and lobbying activities. It was one of the bodies which lobbied the Government to introduce a core curriculum to ensure that all children study science and mathematics at least until the age of 16. This argument was won, and with the passing of the 1988 Education Reform Act, thousands of children, especially girls, are less likely to forfeit the chance of becoming engineers by an ill-judged choice of subject options. The Government has also introduced an 'Advanced Supplementary' ('AS Level') qualification which will enable pupils to increase the range of subjects they are able to study after the age of sixteen years. The Engineering Council supported this move as it wants potential engineers to receive a broad and balanced education.

When the Government announced an increase in the number of places for engineering students in higher education in March 1985 as part of a new 'Engineering and Technology Programme' (popularly known as the 'Switch') it acknowledged that this action had been taken on the Engineering Council's advice. The Council can also claim credit for the 'Manufacturing Systems Engineering Initiative', which was launched in the Spring of 1988 and created an additional 1,500 places on relevant degree courses in universities and polytechnics after the Council, following discussion with its affiliates, had identified a serious shortage of production engineers.

Finally, the Engineering Council organises the prestigious *Prince of Wales Award for Industrial Innovation and Production*. This award highlights the necessity of bringing inventions through to production, a matter of the greatest importance for national industrial revival (Engineering Council, 1988e).

Suggestions for further study

The Engineering Council has published many excellent pamphlets on all aspects of its work. Most are freely available on request to the Engineering Council (see the *Appendix III: 'Useful Addresses'*). The Engineering Council's *Opening Windows on Engineering* gives young engineers an excellent opportunity to show their commitment to their profession. And most schools and colleges are pleased to welcome back their ex-students to give brief talks on engineering in the classroom situation and at careers conventions.

Chapter 3

Technology and Society

The pace of technological change is increasing at an exponential rate. Only 66 years separate man's first powered flight at Kitty Hawk, USA (by Wilbur and Orville Wright on 17th December 1903) from Neil Armstrong's message from the Moon on 21st July 1969: '... that's one small step for a man, but a giant leap for mankind.' And when the first electronic computer ENIAC (Electronic Numerical Integrator and Computer) was built in the United States in 1946, it weighed 30 tons, filled the space of a double garage, had 18,000 vacuum tubes (one of which failed every few minutes) and cost half a million dollars at *1946 prices*. Today a cheap games computer costing less than $100 could out-perform ENIAC.

Although humanity has existed for nearly three million years, the most dramatic technological advances have occurred in the last two hundred:

2,600,000 BC   Stone Age (first man)
3,000 BC   Bronze Age
1,200 BC   Iron Age
1760   Industrial Age
1945   Nuclear Age (Hiroshima)
1957   Space Age (launch of 'Sputnik')
1971   Information Age (based on the micro-chip)

But, while the material benefits of technological progress are self-evident to those living in the advanced Western nations, the uneven rate of economic and technological progress in the world as a whole has left us with a major dilemma. How do we reconcile the fact that advanced industrial countries are enjoying an ever-increasing standard of living, while millions of human beings in the under-developed countries are struggling to cope with squalid living conditions and are exposed to nature's excesses, such as famine, flood and plague?

Koestler (1978) paints a pessimistic picture of our future.

Acknowledging that 'history is accelerating along dizzy exponential curves,' he argues that 'since the day when the first atomic bomb outshone the sun at Hiroshima, mankind as a whole has had to live with the prospect of its own extinction as a species.' He contrasts the growth curves of mankind's technological and moral achievement. While technological growth has been dramatic, it is almost impossible to demonstrate evidence of any significant moral and intellectual growth. There has been little progress in controlling the arms race or in reaching international agreement on how to tackle mass starvation. Half the Earth's five billion inhabitants starve while surplus food is destroyed elsewhere. Thus, like Janus, the ancient Roman god who faced two ways, technology has two faces.

One example is the motor car. One face shows increased freedom, convenience and comfortable travel, but the other face shows thousands of deaths and injuries; lead and carbon monoxide pollution; fertile and attractive countryside buried under concrete to provide motorways; the hearts of cities destroyed for car parks; historic buildings crumbling from the vibration of heavy lorries; and frustration caused by traffic jams, car thefts, and parking problems (see *Figure 3.1*).

In recognition of the importance of the relationship between technological change and social change, nearly all syllabuses for advanced engineering courses now provide an opportunity to study the impact of *technology on society*. These syllabuses should cover three principal themes:

1. the concept of a technological revolution

2. technology transfers to the Third World

3. the impact of new technology on society.

These themes also form the focus of this chapter.

The concept of a technological revolution

Today, many centres of past technological change and innovation can only be found with the aid of an archaeologist's trowel. This demonstrates that the ability to produce dramatic technological breakthroughs and gain regional supremacy gives no guarantee of the survival of any particular society. Look at the ancient civilisations of China, Egypt, Greece, Rome, Peru, Babylon, and Persia.

Figure 3.1
The Unacceptable Face of Motoring

1. Deaths and Injuries (CSO, *Annual Abstract of Statistics*, 1988)
In the UK in 1987, there were:
    5,125 deaths on the road
    64,300 serious injuries
    242,000 slight injuries

2. Environmental Pollution
The internal combustion engine belches out five main chemical elements which put our health and the environment at risk :
    Carbon Dioxide - the main 'greenhouse' gas
    Nitrogen Oxides - which contribute to the formation of acid rain and to the green-
        house effect
    Carbon Monoxide - a human toxin which adds to the greenhouse effect
    Hydrocarbons - which cause respiratory problems by irritating the lung
    Lead - which is known to damage the brain.
(see *Chapter 4* for explanations of *acid rain* and the *greenhouse effect*)

3. The Statistics of Chaos (*The Times*, 1989)
In the year of the city 'super-jam' in the UK:
    £2.5 billion is spent each year on roadworks
    3 million holes are dug in our roads every year
    £220 million is spent each year on re-doing substandard work
    £225 million costs are caused each year by delays due to roadworks
    One hole a year on average is made in every 80 yards of road in London.
And in 1987 there were 17,000,000 licensed cars and 2,500,000 motoring offences were committed (CSO, 1988).

Waves of technological innovation

In fact, technological leadership seems to travel from one part of the globe to another. Joseph Schumpeter, an economist working in the 1920s and 1930s, described major technological changes as 'creative gales of destruction' which create or destroy entire economies. His contemporary, the Russian economist, Nicholai Kondratiev speculated that 'long waves' of economic development associated with periods of successful technological innovation occurred every 50 years or so. He argued that while inventions occur all the time, they are transformed into successful innovations only in very specific historical periods. These waves of innovation are related to long-term economic cycles from slump to boom and back to slump. The first long wave in the modern world economy was from 1789 to 1849 (going up until 1814, then down) the second from 1849 to 1896 (with a peak in 1873) and the third upswing from 1896 to 1920.

Handy (1982) has drawn on Kondratiev's theory to speculate that the first wave had its focus in England during the Industrial Revolution and was based on the technology of the steam engine. The wave then moved on to Germany and Northern Europe with the development of chemicals, steel-making and oil-refining. The third wave occurred in the USA with the birth of the automobile industry and the development of the telephone. A fourth wave, after the Second World War, was centred on the Pacific basin (primarily California and Japan) and was based on the development of electronics.

Technological determinism

The concept of a technological revolution is associated with a belief in 'technological determinism'. This is a theory of social change in which technology is viewed as part of an inescapable economic force which affects the future of entire economies and societies and over which people have little control.

Merrifield (*The Times*, 1987) presents a typical technological determinist perspective. He argues that 'technology is now the engine driving the World economy', and that 'the innovation process has become more important than anything else'. In manufacturing, he predicts continuous change, with no product life-cycle being greater than a few years. This perpetual revolution means that industrial management has become synonymous with the management of change. Therefore, industrial competitiveness requires the mastery of the management of change in three areas:

1. the realisation of the urgent need to accelerate the innovation process

2. the requirement for lifelong, continuous re-skilling of the workforce - any set of skills can now be obsolete in five to ten years

3. the move to computer-integrated manufacturing (CIM) - automated plants that can produce different products at the flick of a switch (the 'make anything factory').

In further support of the technological determinist argument, Freeman (1987) quotes the example of communist countries which attempted initially to opt out of a pattern of technology characteristic of capitalist states. He argues that, sooner or later, these states have to conform to worldwide trends in technological innovation. This was the case in the USSR as long ago as the 1920s, where, after considerable controversy, 'Fordist' assembly line technology and scientific management or 'Taylorist' techniques (see *Chapter 6*) had to be adopted in an effort to catch up with the capitalist countries. It could be argued that the recent reforms introduced by President Gorbachev, with the aim of modernising the USSR economy, are a manifestation of the same inexorable process.

Technological determinists tend to be visionaries and write in Utopian terms about the impact of technological innovation. This was true of those who announced the onset of a new age after the Second World War. Two candidates for the title of a new era were the 'nuclear age' and the 'space age'. But popular confidence in these two technologies has been shaken in recent years by a combination of spiralling costs, disasters, and concern about the environment. With the benefit of hindsight we can classify these technologies as major changes of technology system - but not as technological revolutions.

The Information Age

Today many observers argue that we are living at a time when parts of Earth's society are undergoing a technological revolution based on the use of information. Sola Pool (Freeman, 1987) describes the process leading up to the information revolution:

> 'For untold millennia humans, unlike any other animal, could talk. Then for four thousand years or so their uniqueness was not only that they could move air to express themselves to those immediately around them, but also that they could embody speech in writing, to be preserved in time and transported over space. With Gutenberg [1400-68] (the inventor of the printing press) a third era began, in which written texts could be disseminated in multiple copies. In the last stage of that era phonographs and photographs made it possible to circulate sound and pictures, as well as text, in multiple copies. Now a fourth era has been ushered in by an innovation of at least as much historical significance as the mass production of print and other media. Pulses of electromagnetic energy embody and convey messages that up to now have been sent by sound, pictures, and text. All media are becoming electronic.'

This fourth era has taken workers out of the factory (where they are being replaced by robots) and put them into the office or even back to working from home (in an 'electronic cottage') to provide services for others. In these new workplaces, information is the resource and communication is the main activity.

Similarly, Stonier (1982) argues that an 'information revolution', based on silicon chips, microprocessors and robotics has led Britain into a 'post-industrial society' in which most of the new jobs will be in the information sector. He predicts that, early in the next century, only about 10 per cent of the working population will be actively engaged in the production of material things. Toffler (1981), describes the move from industrial to service economies as the 'third wave' (the first wave was into agriculture; the second wave from agriculture to industry). While Naisbitt (1984) describes the change from manufacturing to service industry as one of history's 'megatrends' (see *Figure 3.2*).

The information sector of the economy is the area where information is collected, absorbed, transcribed, analysed, transmitted and communicated. Millions of jobs have been created in this sector: systems analysts and computer programmers, stock exchange jobbers, consultants of all types, engineering researchers and designers (rather than craftsmen and technicians), educators and trainers, journalists and broadcasters, public relations officers and marketing officers and so on. Eyeions (1988) suggests that the categories of work used in the official employment figures, such as industry and manufacturing, tend to disguise the fact that they contain a high percentage of information workers and concludes that over half of Britain's working population are already in the information sector.

Believers in the information revolution show little concern for the relative decline in the importance of manufacturing industry and argue that it is old-fashioned to think that wealth can only be created by making things. They state simply that wealth is created by giving value to something that had no value before. Traditional wealth-creation is associated with such activities as growing crops from barren land or producing finely machined parts from crude steel. Today we can use human ingenuity to produce new computer programs or new ways of educating people, new systems for passing information or new procedures for insurance or investment. And 'information' itself is a commodity which can be sold and bought in the same way as more tangible and visible 'things'.

But the optimistic scenario of a post-industrial society described by such technological determinists as Toffler, Naisbitt and Stonier has been challenged by other writers. Notable among those who take a more sceptical view of the effect of the 'information revolution' is Theodore Roszak.

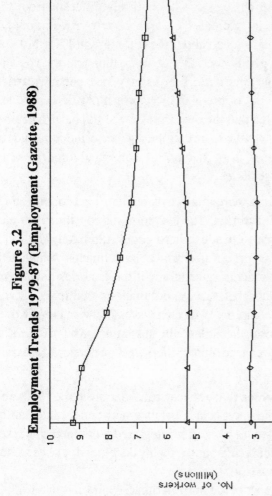

Figure 3.2

Employment Trends 1979-87 (Employment Gazette, 1988)

1. Production
2. Agriculture, Forestry and Fishing
3. Services - Hotels, Catering and Retailing
4. The Information Sector - Banking, Finance, Insurance, Public Administration, Education

No. of workers
(Millions)

He argues (1986) that historians have always attempted to attach dramatic labels to different periods in history. Every age has its 'godword', such as 'the Age of Faith' the 'Age of Reason', and the 'Age of Discovery'. So it is understandable that modern historians have attempted to pin godwords like 'the Age of Information' to our own age. Roszak does not deny that information technology has caused important changes in society and economic activity. But he does deny that these changes are dramatically different from the changes caused by earlier technologies or are, indeed, 'revolutionary'. Rather, he argues that no one worried about these trends until Naisbitt and Toffler's best-selling books popularised and made fashionable the concept of the information revolution. Such writers, he asserts, have become carried away by the seductive potential of the glamorous world of microchips and floppy disks and have forgotten that the necessities of life still have to be provided for. Fields still have to be tilled, ores mined and heavy industrial goods manufactured. Roszak stresses, in particular, the continued importance of manufacturing in advanced societies:

> 'An industrial economy is fundamentally a manufacturing economy: high tech itself requires manufacturing. The technology is constituted of machines; the machines exist to produce hard goods, ultimately the food, clothing, shelter, and transport our flesh and blood demands. A high tech economy remains a manufacturing economy if the factories have been automated and the number of service occupations multiplies....Even when industrial capital is exported to foreign places (Taiwan, Hong Kong, South Korea), manufacturing has still not been eliminated from the economy, but only internationalised under the same ownership' (Roszak, 1986).

Whoever is right, we can now see that a successful economy in the 1990s and early twenty-first century will consist of a balance between a highly automated industrial sector (based on computer integrated manufacturing) creating a large proportion of the *wealth*, and a highly developed service sector providing most of the *employment*.

At present the global impact of the information revolution is patchy. It is known to have originated in the cluster of high-tech companies in *silicon valley*, California, and to have spread rapidly to Japan and parts of Western Europe. In Britain the revolution is popularly associated with *silicon alley* (following the route of the M4 and including Reading, Swindon, and Bristol) *silicon glen* (Glenrothes, Scotland) and *silicon fen* (Cambridgeshire). It may eventually spread to cover the whole of the country and provide service sector employment for the workers who find that automation has deprived them of their jobs in the industrial sector. But this is not guaranteed to happen if industry continues to use so few robots (in 1987 there were only 3,200 robots in 740 firms in the UK); and if the nation continues to spend less than 3 per cent of gross domestic product on research and development into new technology.

Even if overall employment levels are maintained, inequalities and social tensions are likely to increase. Roszak argues that high tech pays off handsomely for some, 'especially if those who are collecting the profits are excused from paying the social costs that result from running down old industrial centres and disemploying their work force.' He goes on to argue that: 'some two thirds of the "new jobs" created in the late 1970s and 1980s and so loudly trumpeted by the Carter and Reagan administrations are low skilled, part-time service employment. When once highly skilled factory workers are squeezed into work of this kind ... they have taken an economic drubbing.'

Much the same could be said of the jobs created in Britain during the Thatcher era (see *Figure 3.3*). Inequalities between a prosperous south of England and the rest of the country (the so-called 'north-south divide') continue to cause concern. It seems that technological revolutions always have winners and losers - another illustration of the two faces of technology. However, historians are still fine-tuning our understanding of the origins of the eighteenth/nineteenth century British Industrial Revolution; it may be that future historians will argue about the origins of the twentieth-century information revolution, or even debate whether one occurred at all.

Technology transfers to the third world

Rostow (1960) identified five stages of economic growth based on the historical experience of the Western industrial nations:

1. traditional society

2. pre-conditions for 'take-off'

3. take-off

4. drive to technological maturity

5. age of high mass consumption.

Figure 3.3

Growth of Part-Time Employment (*Employment Gazette*, 1987)

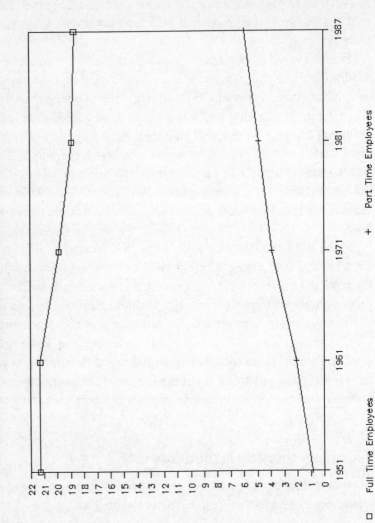

Millions

□ Full Time Employees   +   Part Time Employees

His pre-conditions for take-off stress the systematic translation of the insights of modern science into both agriculture and industry. Other requisite human and resource factors include:

1. health, education, and employment programmes for the population

2. the discovery and utilisation of natural resources

3. the need to produce economic growth by quantitatively and qualitatively improving investment

4. investment in social overhead capital - for example, the building of bridges, ports, roads, dams and air strips.

It is often difficult to convince a population clamouring for basic material goods that, if technological progress is to be achieved and sustained in the long term, the state must first spend massive sums on social overhead capital. It is all too easy to create conditions where the population expands so rapidly that no development policy can sustain itself, because the size and structure of the population now exceeds the supply of resources, and any attempt to counter these conditions by introducing birth control measures raises long-term political and social issues, as experience in India and China shows.

However, it is in the area of technological transfer from First World to the Third World that most problems have occurred. In the 1960s, developing nations were first presented with the possibility of a solution to their problems by accepting offers of advanced technology from the West. These offers were hard to resist when Western materialistic values and mass advertising techniques began to influence even the poorest societies. But this 'quick fix' solution often led to political exploitation and economic disaster.

Since that time, Western technology has been transferred to Third World countries on a large scale. This technology was characterised by high capital investment costs, and developing countries borrowed massive sums in order to finance its transfer. Subsequently many of them have threatened to default on their repayments. This poses a danger both to imprudent Western banks and their governments, and, in turn, creates a negative attitude towards future lending. Only major economic structural adjustment programmes can hope to avert a total breakdown in relations between donor and client nations.

Moreover, advanced Western technology is designed to save labour and its transfer often created unemployment and worsened the recipient's economic position. For example, some countries imported huge, automated, textile machines only to witness the plight of local weavers who gave up the struggle to improve their meagre output and joined the masses of the unemployed.

High technology is generally unsuitable for developing countries. Instead, these countries need low technology with low capital investment costs to avoid the need to borrow large sums of money from the West. They also need technology which is highly labour intensive, in order to employ some of the vast reservoir of unskilled labour. Today, much of the costly, labour-saving technology exported by the West lies in 'graveyards' which are to be found throughout the Third World. These graveyards contain the rusting hulks of caterpillar tractors, trucks, diggers, and bulldozers. The developed nations were guilty of gross insensitivity to the political, social, economic, cultural and environmental conditions pertaining in the recipient nations. Schumacher (1973) was instrumental in highlighting the fact that 'the ruling philosophy of development over the last twenty years has been: What is best for the rich must be best for the poor.'

Schumacher showed how this belief had been carried to extreme lengths with the export of nuclear reactors to such countries as Taiwan, South Korea, Philippines, Vietnam, Thailand, Iran, and Venezuela. What these countries really needed was simple, labour intensive, agricultural technology to help feed their populations and rejuvenate rural life, which had virtually collapsed due to the mass exodus to the urban sprawl and squalid shanty towns.

Schumacher recognised that high technology needs a social infrastructure of education, organisation and discipline that exists only in the Western donor countries. The developing countries need to acquire such an infrastructure before high technology transplants from the West would be appropriate. Until then they need some form of *intermediate technology*, or '$100 technology', to close the gap between what Schumacher symbolically termed the $1 indigenous technology and the $1,000 imported technology from the developed nations.

Intermediate technology fits smoothly into the relatively unsophisticated environment in which it is to be used. It offers small working units, communal ownership, and regional working places utilising local labour and resources. The equipment is simple (and therefore easily understandable) and suitable for maintenance and repair on the spot. Such equipment is less dependent on raw materials of great purity or exact specifications and is much more adaptable to market fluctuations than more sophisticated equipment.

In addition, workers are more easily trained; supervision, control, and organisation are simpler; and there is far less vulnerability to unforeseen difficulties.

However, aid workers have found that you can take nothing for granted, even in the transfer of quite simple equipment, when it comes to the recipient nation's ability to install, operate, repair, up-date, and replace it. They have found that even low-tech pumps installed to provide unpolluted drinking water for a village might be abandoned once repairs were needed. Is it any wonder that sophisticated, labour saving, energy consumptive, high technology lies all over the Third World in need of repair?

Schumacher (1973) started a revolution in thinking about technology transfer based on his philosophy of 'Small is Beautiful'. The formation of the Intermediate Technology Development Group (ITDG) and the production of periodicals such as *Intermediate Technology* are tributes to his ideas. His theories brought a sense of reality to some Third World politicians who had been beguiled by the prospect of rapid change and material advancement offered by advanced technology. And some countries who have continued to espouse Western material values and import Western 'quick fix' technology, have faced social upheaval and even revolution. The return of whole nations to fundamentalist religions is one result of a reaction against Western materialism. And Schumacher's focus on the gross economic inefficiency, environmental pollution and inhumane working conditions, caused by the pursuit of profit and progress have also had a major impact on discussions about our own dilemmas in the developed nations.

Most developing countries are now aware of the nature and meaning of an industrial revolution and the need to tackle all the prerequisite areas systematically in order to achieve it. They also recognise that they have no need to rely solely on their own devices to produce the preconditions for take-off, while being aware of the danger of economic and political exploitation.

Some developing nations now attempt to create realistic five-year plans, often against a background of unstable political conditions. These plans must be based on aggregates of the social and economic costs of activities related to change, from population control to savings and investment. Planners must also attempt to match their plans to *realistic* projections of bilateral and multilateral aid, in the realisation that these are now only a fraction of the total economic interchange between First and Third Worlds.

It is now possible for the developed nations to offer high-tech aid in a more subtle way to help the recipients. For example, satellites can be launched into space which can improve communications across the most impenetrable jungle, locate oil and mineral deposits, provide weather forecasts and warn of locust swarms using remote sensing techniques (DTI, 1983). On the ground, it is now possible to provide a wide range of practical help with computer software such as models of irrigation schemes and expert systems ready for the easy input of local data.

But the greatest sensitivity must be still shown in these latest high-tech transfers from First World to Third if we are not to repeat earlier mistakes. Delicate and complicated computer systems have every chance of breaking down in the developing world and we must be sure that cultural relationships and indigenous expertise, borne of years of observation of natural phenomena, are harmonised rather than alienated in the process of change.

Finally, opening up the Western education system to students from the developing countries is another way of closing the technology gap. But even these programmes have potential dangers if insensitively handled. Is the education tailored to the needs of the students from the developing nation? Will they be corrupted by exposure to high-tech solutions? Will they form an unfavourable impression of the donor nation and become politically alienated? Or, in the opposite case, will they fail to return to the country of origin? If all goes well, they should be able to handle the high-tech possibilities that the micro-chip holds out while adhering to the proven principles of the school of intermediate technology.

The impact of technology on society

Not all technological innovations have dramatic effects. We need a model to help us distinguish between changes which are small and localised and changes which are truly 'revolutionary' in scope. Freeman (1987) has put forward a model which defines four categories of innovation:

1. incremental
2. radical
3. change of technology system
4. technological revolution.

Incremental innovations occur continuously and account for most new patents. They are often the outcome of inventions and improvements suggested by engineers and others working in the production process. Examples include new ways of improving production generated by company 'suggestion schemes' or groups of workers meeting in 'quality circles' (see *Chapter 9*). Many such innovations pass unnoticed and unrecorded and rarely have one single dramatic effect; but their cumulative effect may be very important. Incremental innovations often occur as a series of improvements after a *radical innovation*.

Radical innovations are exceptional and unusual events which are usually the result of deliberate research and development programmes. Over a period of decades a radical innovation, such as the development of nylon or the birth control pill may have some dramatic effects on society. But its economic impact is limited unless a whole cluster of radical innovations are linked together to form a major *change of technology system*.

A system change is a far-reaching change in technology, affecting several branches of the economy and generating entirely new activities. As an example, Freeman quotes the cluster of innovations in plastic materials, injection moulding and extrusion machinery in the period 1930-50 and the many new uses found for plastics. Although these changes were important, we do not normally talk of the 'plastics revolution' or the 'age of plastic'. Finally, as we have seen, some changes in technology are so far-reaching in their economic effects that they can be described as true *technological revolutions*.

However, Freeman's model does not offer us a framework for judging the effect of technological change on society. If we are to judge the impact of new technology on society before it happens and before mistakes are made, we need a mental or conceptual framework for judging the value of technology to that society.

We now offer such a model here. The framework draws on nine disciplines from the social sciences, humanities and human sciences to form a collection of mental or conceptual 'boxes': *history, philosophy, sociology, psychology, politics, law, economics, ecology* and *physiology*. Into each box we can put questions which ought to be asked about any piece of new technology (see *Figure 3.4* applied to television).

We may not be able to generate answers in every box: the important point is that the questions are asked in the first place. In this way, areas can be identified in which more investigation is needed. Also, we can expect to find contradictory evidence within the same headings. It would be surprising if all evidence for the introduction of new technology pointed in the same direction and we are hampered by the fact that technology can have unpredictable

Figure 3.4
A Framework for Analysing the Effect of Technology on Society

How will the increase in the number of TV channels, stimulated by satellite and cable technology, affect society?
The supplementary questions that we might ask are:

History
How and when was television invented? What lessons can be learned from its interaction with society in the past?

Philosophy
Does television improve the quality of life? Are ethical considerations involved? Is television a 'good thing'?

Sociology
How will the increase in new channels affect family life and relationships? How will it affect different groups in society - the old, the young, the infirm? Will it change social attitudes? Will it create or destroy jobs in the TV, video and film industries?

Psychology
Will more television change individual behaviour? Do children become more violent, lazy, less creative? How much do we learn from television?

Politics
Who will decide what we watch, what channels are available, what it costs to watch? What should people be allowed to watch - pornography, violence? What is the right balance between a government's desire to control information and individual freedom?

Law
What new laws will be required to ensure that political decisions can be enforced?

Economics
How much will the new technology cost? Should new channels be financed by advertising, licence fee or subscription? Who will take the profits?

Ecology
Will satellite dishes and 'squariels' spoil the neighbourhood environment?

Physiology?
What effect does television have on our health? Does it make us idle and fat?

long-term effects. Furthermore, we start from a point of no reference, i.e. we have no agreed position on mankind's ultimate purpose on Earth. The advantage of this method of analysing technology, however, is that it may help us to separate our subjective values and ideologies from what appears to be objective reality when we are involved in technological change. Thus our answers will help us to make an impressionistic, but systematic, evaluation of possible implications before reaching a tentative judgement on the value of that technology to society.

As an illustration, we will now use the framework to analyse some aspects of the effect of a pending piece of new technology: the *Channel Tunnel*. When drilling of the 38 km tunnel began in 1987 it heralded the start of the biggest privately funded engineering scheme in Europe.

History and philosophy

The philosophical value of international travel as a means of broadening the mind and improving links between peoples of different nations has long been accepted in Western society. History shows that the reasons why we have had to wait nearly 200 years for a fixed link across the Channel are political and economic rather than philosophical.

Ten years after the end of the Second World War, the British Government finally conceded that the prospect of an invading army marching through the tunnel was becoming remote and removed its objection to the tunnel on political grounds. Since 1955 the main obstacle to the tunnel has been cost. In 1980 an impoverished British Government announced that it had no objection to the building of a cross-Channel link as long as it did not have to commit any public funds to the project (see *Figure 3.5*).

Sociology and psychology

With the threat of European war diminishing, with full membership of the European Economic Community and regular holidays abroad, the 'psychological' barrier of the English Channel is less obvious than it used to be. It remains to be seen whether the removal of the last physical barrier between Britain and mainland Europe will contribute to the further erosion of the British feeling of being a separate 'island race'.

Social attitudes towards travel and leisure seem certain to change. Some London commuters are already buying cheaper properties in northern France whence they plan to travel via the tunnel to work. Other projected

Figure 3.5
The Channel Tunnel - key dates

1802 Plans for a Channel Tunnel, for horse-drawn vehicles, proposed by French engineer Albert Mathieu-Favier. These were approved by Napoleon but later abandoned.

1867 Queen Victoria and Napoleon III favour a modified scheme at Paris Exhibition.

1872/1875 Channel Tunnel Companies formed in Britain and France respectively.

1881 Companies begin drilling near Calais and Dover.

1882 Channel Tunnel Bill is rejected at Westminster on defence grounds. (These Government objections were lifted only in 1955.)

1930 New Tunnel initiative defeated in House of Commons.

1957 Channel Tunnel Study Group formed - suggests twin rail link.

1964 Joint Government declaration in favour of two railway tunnels and service tunnel scheme.

1975 After trial bore, scheme rejected on financial grounds.

1980 British Government announces that it has no objection to a privately financed cross-Channel fixed link.

1981 Prime Minister Thatcher and President Mitterand commission a Joint Study

1985 April: Invitation for private tenders for development, financing, construction and operation of Tunnel, produces four major bids with varying schemes.

1986 January: Channel Tunnel Group/Franche Manche (Eurotunnel) design chosen.

1986 February: Channel Tunnel White Paper (Cmnd. 9735). Channel Tunnel Treaty (Cmnd. 9745).

1987 July: Channel Tunnel Act 1987; drilling starts in December

1993 Planned opening date: 15th May.

uses of the tunnel include day-trips to the new Disneyland being built just north of Paris, and short skiing breaks in the Alps (Eurotunnel, 1987a).

The success of the whole project now rests on the attitudes of people towards using the tunnel. Forecasts of tunnel use must rely on questionnaires and interviews in which the public's perception of their future needs for travel are assessed. We are likely to see major shifts of attitude towards the tunnel and European travel over the next few years as various construction hurdles are crossed or obstacles encountered - for example, the rate of drilling progress, the meeting of financial and time targets, and the final joining of the British and French ends of the tunnel. A favourable response from the media is vital in shaping the general public's perception of the scheme, and the builders and operators will need to cultivate good public relations.

An independent study of the employment impact of the tunnel on the county of Kent calculated that 3,200 new jobs directly related to tunnel operation activities will be created. On the other hand the same study calculated that between 4,300 and 6,600 jobs will be lost in the ferries, container terminals and other port facilities in East Kent, giving a net loss of 1,100 to 3,400 jobs (DoT, 1987). However, the secondary employment effects of the tunnel in Kent were calculated to be some 13,000 to 14,000 new jobs in the service industries (1,800), manufacturing (5,200), distribution (4,000), and tourism (2,000-3,000).

Some experienced seamen from Dover have already lost their jobs. In 1988 the shipping company, P&O European Ferries, imposed new working conditions and efficient working practices in anticipation of competition from the tunnel. The result was a strike which was defeated when the company sacked hundreds of seamen for allegedly breaking their contracts and hired new crews.

The old-established community based on the port of Dover will face more disruption and stress in the future. Those dockers and seamen who find that their skills do not transfer easily to the service sector where most of the new jobs will be created will have to face a hard choice between a long period of unemployment or an unskilled job on low pay. Some may never work again.

Politics and law

The Conservative Government of the early 1980s was ideologically opposed to the commitment of large sums of taxpayer's money to major public projects. It argued that such projects are best handled by the private sector. Hence the decision to seek private funding for the tunnel was a political one.

The City of London has often been criticised for its failure to invest in risk-taking projects which do not produce short-term profits but are essential to the long-term economic health of the country. At one time it looked as though the City would fail to produce the goods and the Government had to put considerable pressure on the City behind the scenes to make sure that the finance was forthcoming.

The decision to issue shares to the general public, with the incentive of free travel for life for those who invested enough, was another political decision based on the Government's ideological commitment to a 'share-owning democracy'.

Before the final go-ahead, the project had to undergo the normal Parliamentary process, including scrutiny by the Select Committees from the House of Commons and the House of Lords. The Government consulted relevant local authorities and interest groups such as the Nature Conservancy Council and the Countryside Commission. The general public were also given a chance to voice their views. Controversially, the Government rejected a full-scale public inquiry into the project - arguing that such an inquiry would be too bureaucratic and time-consuming.

The claim of the Conservative administration to have created a new 'enterprise culture' is partly dependent on the completion of the tunnel on time. Consequently legislation has been passed which imposes strict targets on the tunnel builders. Huge fines of £333,000 per day, rising to £500,000 per day (up to a maximum penalty of £163 million), will follow if there is delay in opening the tunnel. At the same time Eurotunnel has to pay close attention to all laws governing the safe building of the tunnel and the employment of staff. Already the Health and Safety Executive has prosecuted five companies for failure to comply with safety regulations (Bailey, 1988).

Economics

We have yet to find out whether the cost of construction will exceed the funding so far raised. Once the tunnel is finished in 1993 and the amount of use (currently estimated at 100 train movements per day in each direction) is established, the cost of each trip for private and commercial users can be decided. This figure will have a further effect on the flow of users through the tunnel and will determine whether the service will reach economic viability in the late 1990s as planned (*The Economist*, 1987).

We have already seen that parts of Kent will benefit economically from the generation of new jobs. Undoubtedly, that benefit will spread to other parts of the London and South East region. The economic benefits that the rest of the country will achieve depend very much on the quality of connections with the tunnel. Without good, fast road and rail connections the rest of the country will gain little.

Finally, we might consider just one other cost - that of policing the tunnel. This has been projected to be £5 million a year, involving a special unit of 154 officers, about 40 of whom will be armed, when the tunnel opens in 1993.

Ecology

The economic growth which will be generated by the tunnel is a threat to the Kent countryside and its beautiful towns and villages. So the planners and designers have had to be sensitive to the environmental impact of the tunnel at all stages of the project. Eurotunnel commissioned 18 specialist studies on the potential environmental impact. These were reviewed by independent assessors and published in November 1985. The Government stated later that Eurotunnel's careful consideration of the environmental impact was one of the main reasons why their bid was selected (Cmnd. 9735).

The Government did call for a reassessment of Eurotunnel's proposals to dump 4.75 million cubic metres of spoil which will be produced by the tunnel excavations (Eurotunnel, 1987c). A 'Surplus Spoil Working Group' was set up for this purpose and drew up a short-list of seven potential off-site disposal locations. The Government and Eurotunnel then each commissioned independent consultants to advise on the final choice of a disposal site.

The consultants concluded that all the short-listed disposal sites had significant technical or environmental problems and would adversely affect local residents. In the end the Government decided to accept Eurotunnel's original plan to dispose of the remaining 3.75 million cubic metres of spoil at the foot of Shakespeare Cliff - directly above the route of the tunnel (see *Figure 3.6*). The remaining one million cubic metres are required for chalk fill at the Folkestone terminal.

The environment at the foot of the cliff had already been affected by the blasting of the cliffs in the 1840s to accommodate a railway line. It was also

Figure 3.6
A Map of Channel Tunnel Route (Eurotunnel)

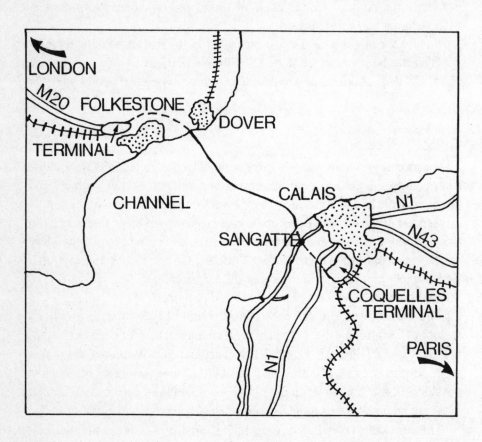

used for coal mining and was the site of the workings for a tunnel which were abandoned in 1974 (Eurotunnel, 1987b). The dumping of the spoil here will have the effect of extending an existing platform of reclaimed land further into the sea. After completion of the tunnel, this platform will be landscaped and adapted for informal recreation use.

Unfortunately, the waste dumped at Shakespeare Cliff will cover a natural chalk inter-tidal zone supporting flora and fauna of considerable scientific interest, and will also spoil the cliff top views of part of the Folkestone to Dover Heritage Coast. The Nature Conservancy Council remains concerned that dumping will stop natural cliff erosion processes.

Methods and timing of soil disposal, landscaping and other treatment of the land are subject to the approval of Kent County Council, the waste disposal authority, after consultation with the Nature Conservancy Council and the Countryside Commission (Eurotunnel, 1987b).

Noise, vibration and air pollution have also been the subject of intensive investigation by Eurotunnel, with a view to mitigating their likely impacts (Eurotunnel, 1987d).

Physiology

Physiological factors influenced the decision to build a rail rather than a road tunnel. It was considered that driving through the tunnel would be monotonous, tiring and dangerous. The effect of poisonous car and lorry exhausts was also of concern. In contrast, a rail tunnel poses no serious physiological problems; although there was speculation at one point that people's ears would pop due to the piston effect of the trains in the narrow tunnel.

However, one physiological danger which has had to be taken very seriously by the tunnel designers is that rabies-infected animals might find their way through the tunnel from France to Britain (House of Lords, 1987). Rabies, a deadly viral disease of the central nervous system, can be carried by most warm-blooded animals and is particularly prevalent among carnivores. Humans are at risk from the bite of an infected animal, especially a cat or a dog. Britain eradicated the disease in 1922 and has kept it out ever since through strict controls at sea and airports on the importation of animals. However, West Germany reported 6,862 rabies cases in animals in 1985 and, although it has yet to be reported within 100 km of the Calais terminal, the disease is also widespread in France.

Proposals to protect the tunnel against the entry and passage of wild or stray rabies-susceptible animals include the building of a small-mesh boundary fence to prevent animals as small as mice and rats from getting through. The fence will be sunk to present a barrier to burrowing animals, and where the fence line is broken, an alternative barrier such as a cattle grid with a sunken pit will be used. Strict measures to prevent the build-up of rubbish and for the collection of discarded food will be introduced, along with security measures such as dog patrols and video cameras. Additional measures such as electrified mesh, and slow-scan movement triggers have been discussed.

These measures, together with the continued enforcement of strict customs controls to prevent the smuggling of pets, should ensure that control over the illegal importation of rabies-susceptible animals through the tunnel will be as good, if not better, as the current arrangements for sea and airports (Eurotunnel, 1987e).

The threat of rabies reaching Britain via the tunnel appears to have receded. However, one nightmare still remains: the prospect of a fire on a train in the middle of the tunnel. If the fire is minor, the plan is to evacuate passengers into neighbouring carriages and put fire curtains in place to prevent the fire spreading. The train will then exit from the tunnel as quickly as possible.

If the fire is more serious, passengers would again be evacuated into adjacent carriages, the problem carriage would be uncoupled and the locomotives at each end would then pull the two halves of the train in opposite directions. Meanwhile a fire crew would be travelling to the scene via the service tunnel - a journey which could take up to 25 minutes (Jones, 1987).

However, an American consultant to Eurotunnel has described the problems experienced in a real fire on a train in a tunnel under San Francisco harbour in 1979. This tunnel was of the concrete tube variety similar in construction to the Channel Tunnel (but only one tenth of its length). An efficient safety system had been designed for the tunnel, but when the fire broke out the operators in the central control room became confused and, instead of extracting smoke and letting air in, they diverted fresh air and concentrated the smoke. The evacuation of the passengers was not smooth and, to make matters worse, instead of sending in a train full of fire fighters, the operators sent another train filled with passengers into the tunnel (Jones, 1987). A major fire in the Channel Tunnel leading to loss of life would cause a serious loss of public confidence and could even result in its closure.

Postscript

If British Rail is to fulfil its contract with Eurotunnel, it has to provide a new high speed rail link with London. This will spread the environmental, economic and political impact of the Channel Tunnel even farther afield.

At the time of writing a major political controversy is still raging over British Rail's choice of a rail route from the Channel Tunnel to the King's Cross terminal in London. This controversy has focused on the likely environmental disturbance to the suburbs of South London and the Kent countryside - with particular concern about the noise levels of the new 180 mph trains, which will be similar to the French TGV. *The Times* reported that 'affluent, articulate and indignant committees are preparing for what promises to be the biggest planning battle since the campaigns about the third London airport twenty years ago' (Hill, 1989).

An early indication of the scale of the protest was illustrated by a political rally which attracted 15,000 people to central London on 26th February 1989. This rally called for more consultation and more consideration of the environmental impact of the rail route.

The strength of feeling against the scheme was such that British Rail has agreed to tunnel stretches of the line under South London and Kent as a means of reducing the environmental impact of the rail link in these areas.

Suggestions for further study

There are a number of books which extol the virtues of the Information Revolution. We recommend that student engineers read one of the following: *The Wealth of Information: A Profile of the Post Industrial Society*, by Tom Stonier; *Future Shock*, by Alvin Toffler; or *Megatrends*, by John Naisbitt. Then, as an antidote, we suggest Theodore Roszak, *The Cult of Information*, which argues that the significance of the Information Revolution, if indeed one exists at all, has been greatly exaggerated.

Fritz Schumacher's hugely influential book, *Small is Beautiful*, is essential reading for those wishing to widen their knowledge of the philosophy of 'intermediate technology'.

Information on the Channel Tunnel project can be obtained from the Eurotunnel Information Centre (see *Appendix III*).

Finally, we suggest that students use the conceptual framework for analysing the effect of technology on society described in this chapter on a variety of technological projects and innovations. This can be done individually or as a group exercise using the resources of a good library.

Chapter 4

Energy Sources and the Environment

Concern about the potentially harmful effects of technology on the environment is not a new phenomenon. The ancient Chinese and Greeks had legislation to protect the soil, while in thirteenth-century London measures were taken to control air pollution by limiting coal burning. However, it is only since the 1950s and 1960s that a wider awareness of the long-term and unsustainable damage being caused to the environment has emerged.

The effects of some forms of pollution have been limited, while others seem to have got out of control. In addition, new forms of pollution have emerged with implications beyond national frontiers. For this reason environmental issues are now being tackled at an international level, particularly by the European Economic Community (European Document, 1987).

The EEC proclaimed the need for a Community Environmental Policy at its 1972 Summit and began the first of four action programmes in 1973. The importance the EEC attaches to the environment is demonstrated by the designation of one year (21st March 1987 - first day of Spring - to March 1988) as *European Year of the Environment* (EYE). When EYE was launched, the European Commissioner for the Environment warned that the environmental damage to the earth, air and water threaten the basic resources on which we depend. He went on to say that urban decay, abuse of the countryside, the destruction of the forests and the pollution of the rivers and seas, diminishes the quality of our lives and may even be irreversible.

There are hopeful signs that the momentum established by EYE will continue in Britain: green issues are rising nearer to the top of the political agenda and all the major parties now profess a deep concern for the environment. Prime Minister Thatcher accepted the importance of reconciling technology and the environment in a speech in Brighton on 14th October 1988: 'The choice facing us is not industrial development or a clean environment. To survive we need both. No generation has a freehold on this Earth. All we have is a life tenancy with a full repairing lease.'

Professional engineers must be sensitive to the full effects on the environment of the technology with which they are inextricably linked. And if engineers are to gain the full recognition in society they aspire to, they must play a leading role in the search for solutions to the problem of environmental pollution.

Technology's almost insatiable demand for energy is at the root of some of the most intractable and controversial environmental issues of the past decade. Let us now explore aspects of the engineer's responsibility for protecting the environment by focusing on the major environmental issues associated with the two most widely used sources of energy in the advanced industrial nations: *fossil fuels* and *nuclear fission*. And then we shall examine one of the main hopes for environmentally pure energy creation in the future: *nuclear fusion*.

Fossil fuels

Converting fossil fuel into energy leads to air and water pollution and the creation of solid wastes which cause land disruption and aesthetic degradation. There are also 'upstream' and 'downstream' effects to be considered. For example, the extraction and processing of fossil fuels often leads to environmental disruption in areas far removed from the place where the energy is actually used. The transportation phase, particularly where oil is concerned, may present serious pollution problems. Oil spills can damage the aquatic environment especially if they occur near shore. And, in the case of electrical energy, 'downstream' effects include the siting of transmission lines and even the eventual disposal of the end-use appliances such as televisions, refrigerators and washing machines.

Until comparatively recently all electricity in the UK was generated by fossil means. Today approximately 80 per cent is produced by burning either coal or oil to raise steam. Electricity generation eats up nearly 80 million tonnes of coal every year - more than 60 per cent of the UK's total production. Although natural gas is classified as a fossil fuel it accounts for less than 1 per cent of generated power.

Since 1980 the UK has been in the fortunate position of being totally self-sufficient in energy, due largely to off-shore oil production, and this self-sufficiency should be maintained for a number of years. Coal is still abundant and proven recoverable reserves are in excess of 4,600 million tonnes. But there are two major environmental problems which must be solved if there is to be any further expansion in fossil fuel generating capacity:

1. combustion of coal and oil leads to high atmospheric emissions of sulphur dioxide and nitrogen oxides, and both these gases can lead to the formation of *acid rain*

2. carbon dioxide, a by-product of all combustion processes, has recently been implicated as a cause of global warming, more commonly known as the *greenhouse effect*.

We will now consider these two major environmental issues in turn.

Acid rain

Until the 1950s air pollution was a problem associated with industrial towns and cities (for example, the London smog). The sources of the pollutants were local and could be readily identified. Control of these emissions through clean-air legislation led to dramatic improvements in air quality; and subsequent historical changes in patterns of fuel usage (from coal to oil and gas and eventually to nuclear power) have further helped to reduce the concentration of these pollutants.

However, confidence that the environmental problems associated with the burning of fossil fuels had been solved was shaken during the 1960s when evidence emerged which suggested that sulphur dioxide, a gaseous pollutant produced in combustion, could be transported great distances in the atmosphere. At the same time, concern was growing in Scandinavia about the acidification of lakes and rivers and the disappearance of fish in them. Long-range transport of pollutants from Western and Central Europe was identified as the cause of the excess acidity in the rain (see *Figure 4.1*) and, in turn, of the acidification of surface water. Over the ensuing decades acid rain has become an important international political issue, souring relations between the polluter and polluted, especially between the UK and Scandinavia.

As a result of this concern, the Central Electricity Generating Board (CEGB) and Government bodies in Norway and Sweden initiated major research programmes to assess the full environmental impact of acid rain (CEGB Research, 1987). In the process, some early, rather simplistic, per-

Figure 4.1
Facts on acid rain (*New Scientist*, 5th November 1987)

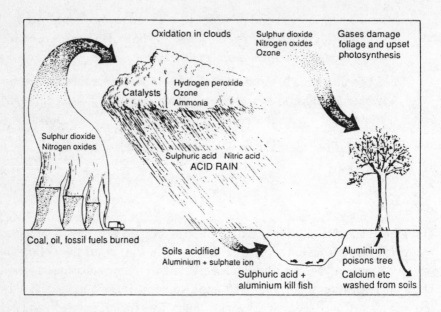

The term 'acid rain' was first used in 1872 to describe the atmospheric chemical processes whereby sulphur dioxide, emitted when coal is burnt, falls as sulphuric acid in rain. Today it is used to describe acid deposition, wet, dry, or as mists caused by a number of pollutants when fossil fuels are burnt.

These pollutants may be: sulphur dioxide, nitrogen oxides, or hydrocarbons (these are primary pollutants) or their atmospheric oxidation reaction products, namely sulphuric acid, nitric acid and ozone.

The resulting cocktail of gases and acids can be transported hundreds of miles in the atmosphere before being deposited in rain.

In the UK the CEGB is the biggest producer of sulphur dioxide, contributing about 60 per cent of the whole, while about 40 per cent of atmospheric nitrogen oxides are emitted from power stations and about 40 per cent from motor vehicles.

ceptions were modified and a number of new and important concepts regarding the atmospheric chemistry of acid rain were discovered. The research confirmed that the pollutants and their reaction products could be transported for thousands of miles. But perhaps the greatest advance has been in the understanding of the importance of soil chemistry in the water-acidification process. Acid rain can leach out massive amounts of aluminium from certain soils and this has been shown to be the real toxin that kills fish. The mobilisation of aluminium has now been implicated as the main reason for the marked decline of forestation observed in Central Europe.

Reports on acid rain and industrial air pollution have been published in the UK by Select Committees of both Houses of Parliament. The report by the House of Lords found that 'the magnitude of damage resulting from air pollution makes it necessary to implement a preventive programme now despite the scientific uncertainties - to do otherwise would be foolish and dangerous.'

Other influential reports have come from the Royal Society, the Watt Committee on Energy and, most recently, the Fellowship of Engineering. In addition, the environmental pressure group Greenpeace has continued to run an active public-awareness campaign.

Flue-gas desulphurisers

After much political and scientific debate, the CEGB decided, in 1986, to implement a programme to reduce emissions from three of its largest power stations (representing about 6000 Megawatts of coal-fired generating capacity): Drax A and B (Aire Valley, Yorkshire) and Fiddlers Ferry (Merseyside) power stations.

The aim of this ten-year programme is to install flue-gas desulphurisers which will be capable of reducing sulphur dioxide levels by up to 90 per cent (the removal of indigenous sulphur by washing before the coal is burnt was considered uneconomic) (CEGB, 1988). The two new tentatively planned stations at Fawley B (Hampshire) and West Burton (Nottinghamshire) will also be fitted with similar desulphurisers. In parallel, the nitrogen oxides will be reduced by installing special burners and possibly catalytic converters.

This limited programme is unlikely to satisfy the European Commission which is proposing legislation to enforce reductions of 60 per cent and 40 per cent in sulphur dioxide and nitrogen oxide respectively by the year 2003 (compared with 1980 levels). To achieve such a dramatic reduction the UK electricity industry would have to fit 12 existing coal-fired stations with desulphurisation equipment at a cost of up to £200 million per installation (and subsequent operating costs of £35 million per year per station) and make major modifications to boilers to reduce nitrogen oxides. As a consequence electricity prices for the consumer would rise by up to 5 per cent.

Flue-gas desulphurisers were first used at Battersea Power Station in 1933. However, the waste products from the power station were dumped into the River Thames with dire environmental consequences, and the new technology was not developed any further. This mistake effectively lost many millions of pounds for the UK in export business. Desulphurisation equipment is now widely used in West Germany, the USA and Japan.

Instead the British Government decided to site new stations away from the main centres of population and, although particulates were mostly removed, it agreed to let sulphur dioxide spread on the winds from chimneys up to 300 metres tall.

Engineers and chemists have now devised over 100 processes to enable the removal of sulphur dioxide from flue-gases. The two most widely used flue-gas desulphurisation methods today are the limestone/gypsum process and the regenerative process.

The *limestone/gypsum wet scrubbing process* is the simplest system. It works by bringing the waste flue-gases into countercurrent contact with a fine spray of limestone to absorb the sulphur dioxide. The limestone (calcium carbonate) combines with the sulphur to make calcium sulphate, which can then be oxidised to make gypsum, a valuable raw material for the plaster board and cement industries. It is hoped that any gypsum surplus to market needs could be used for landfill and reclamation, although eventually the disposal of this material may become a problem. This process has been chosen as the 'most environmentally appropriate' for the 4,000 MW Drax power station; it will use about 600,000 tonnes of limestone and produce about one million tonnes of gypsum per year.

Engineers still have to solve two problems at Drax. Firstly, British coal contains ten times more chlorine than coal found in most other countries, and the high levels of chlorine gases must be removed from the emissions before going through the desulphurisation process. Secondly, difficulties exist in choosing a source of limestone that does not itself contain dangerous trace elements that would further pollute the environment.

In the alternative *regenerative process* the chemicals which remove the sulphur dioxide from the flue-gases are recirculated. The best example is the

Figure 4.2
Summary of possible remedial strategies for ameliorating the effect of acid rain levels (Watt Committee, 1984)

1. DIRECT ACTION ON REDUCING SULPHUR OXIDE
   Sulphur Reducing Technologies:
   before combustion - coal washing
   during combustion - Pressurised Fluidised Bed Combustion
   after combustion - various flue gas desulphurisation devices

2. REDUCE SIDE EFFECTS (e.g. liming of lakes)

3. REDUCE OTHER EMISSIONS (e.g. nitrogen oxides

4. FUEL SUBSTITUTION (e.g. nuclear power)

5. ENERGY CONSERVATION

Note:
The *Watt Committee on Energy*, named after the engineer James Watt (1736-1819), was established in 1976. It is a voluntary body with membership drawn from 62 British professional institutions including the major engineering institutes. Its objectives are to present independent and unbiased assessments of the facts on various energy-related subjects in a manner commanding professional respect and in a form that the media and the public can readily assimilate. Some of the topics recently studied include acid rain and the environment, the Chernobyl accident and its implications for the UK, the disposal of energy wastes and renewable energy sources.

Wellman-Lord system where circulating sodium sulphite is used to capture the dilute sulphur dioxide and regenerate it into a concentrated stream of sulphur dioxide. The sulphur dioxide is then converted into sulphuric acid or sulphur, depending on the design of plant. Typically 300,000 tonnes of sulphuric acid could be produced from a 2,000 MW station. It is expected that the retro-fit at Fiddlers Ferry will use this process as there is a ready chemical market for the sulphuric acid produced.

Pressurised Fluidised Bed Combustion Furnaces

An alternative engineering solution to flue-gas desulphurisation after combustion is to limit the primary pollutants causing acid rain during the combustion process itself, by using Pressurised Fluidised Bed Combustion Furnaces (PFBC). These highly efficient furnaces burn fine particles of coal suspended in a bed of their own ash. An upward flow of air keeps the whole bed in motion. Pressurising the bed produces a stream of hot gases which can drive a turbine. As they burn coal at comparatively low temperatures, the amount of nitrogen oxides are reduced, and if limestone is added it will capture sulphur from the coal as it burns simultaneously. Early experimental research using these devices at Grimethorpe (South Yorkshire) power station has shown promise. However, there may be long-term problems associated with effluent waste disposal.

Postscript

The widespread use of these various processes (see *Figure 4.2*) would undoubtedly have a beneficial effect on the ambient environment. However, there will be no immediate improvements in the lakes of Scandinavia and the forests of West Germany as the soils there contain vast stores of acidic compounds and sulphur, a cumulative result of emissions since the start of the Industrial Revolution. As a palliative measure, the Scandinavians are currently adding limestone and other base elements to many of their inland waters so as to counteract the acidification and precipitate out the aluminium, albeit at a huge cost.

Unfortunately, reducing emissions from power stations will not be enough on its own to eliminate the precipitation of acid rain. The motor car remains another major source of emissions. There is an urgent need to reduce nitrogen oxide emissions from petrol engines by the use of catalysts and lean-burn engines. The introduction of strict standards for vehicle emission (already established in the USA and Japan) will eventually have to be introduced in the UK.

Although a start has at last been made to solving some of the engineering and scientific problems relating to acid rain, there is still a need to continue with a well-balanced programme of international research on air pollutants, their effects and the technology for their control.

The Greenhouse Effect

The Earth's atmosphere acts like glass in a greenhouse: heat is trapped from the sun, creating conditions necessary for life. About 35 to 50 per cent is reflected back into space; 10 to 20 per cent is absorbed by the atmosphere and 45 to 50 per cent reaches the surface of the earth. If all solar heat was re-

Figure 4.3
The various types of greenhouse gas (Davies, 1988)

Over 30 gases have been identified that can contribute to global warming. The principal gases include:

Carbon Dioxide
This is a good absorber of infrared radiation that would otherwise escape from earth.

Atmospheric proportion:	350 parts per million (ppm)
Annual growth rate:	0.5%
Residence time:	3 to 4 years
Warming contribution:	50%

Chlorofluorocarbons (CFCs)
Extremely powerful infrared absorbers, 10,000 times more efficient than CO_2. Also destroys the ozone layer.

Atmospheric proportion:	0.3 parts per billion (ppb)
Annual growth rate:	2.5%
Residence time:	100 years
Warming contribution:	10-20%

Nitrous Oxide
Accumulates in the lower atmosphere and promotes ozonation damage.

Atmospheric proportion:	300 ppb
Annual growth rate:	0.25%
Residence time:	150 years
Warming contribution:	5-10%

Methane
May be independent of energy use.

Atmospheric proportion:	1.5 ppm
Annual growth rate:	1.5%
Residence time:	10 years
Annual contribution:	15-20%

flected back into space the Earth would be too cold to support life; if all the heat was absorbed, the Earth would be too hot. Some absorption by the atmosphere is necessary, as without this 'greenhouse effect' there would be no life.

The amount of carbon dioxide (CO_2) in the atmosphere affects the amount of solar heat reflected back into space. CO_2 is transparent to incoming short-wave solar radiation but it absorbs long-wave infra red radiation reflected from the Earth, warming the lower levels of the atmosphere.

The profligate use of fossil fuels for electricity generation has caused an increase of between 15 per cent and 25 per cent of CO_2 in the atmosphere since the onset of the industrial age. Coal combustion produces 75 times more CO_2 than sulphur dioxide; and for each tonne of coal consumed there will be between three to four tonnes of CO_2 emitted into the atmosphere. The continuing increase in energy consumption (currently about two per cent per annum) will double the levels of CO_2 which existed in the atmosphere before the Industrial Revolution and contribute to a four-degree global warming by early next century. To illustrate the scale of this change, an equivalent temperature rise signalled the end of the last Ice Age, 11,000 years ago.

The potential consequences of this global warming could be devastating. Wind, rainfall and oceanic circulation patterns could be altered; and delicate ecosystems and life cycles could be disrupted by a shift in high rainfall zones. Most worrying of all, some scientists believe that the polar ice caps could begin to melt. If this happens there would be a rise in the level of the world's oceans by several metres, which could put most low-lying coastal areas under water.

CO_2 is not the only greenhouse gas. Other trace gases, such as nitrous oxide, the chlorofluorocarbons (CFCs), methane and tropospheric ozone, act in a similar way (see *Figure 4.3*). The atmospheric concentrations of these gases, too, have been rising, and at present they are responsible for about 50 per cent of the total effect. These gases also have high atmospheric residence times, some in excess of 100 years.

The global warming hypothesis has not been proved beyond all doubt, but the United Nations and other international agencies have embarked on ambitious research programmes to monitor CO_2 changes in the atmosphere. Suggestions for limiting these effects in advance of irrefutable proof and before the need for binding legislation include:

1. increasing the momentum towards improved energy efficiency

2. limiting deforestation - particularly the destruction of tropical rain forests

3. increasing the non fossil fuel component in the total energy mix

4. reducing the levels of CFC's emitted into the atmosphere.

Energy efficiency and alternative energy sources

There are, of course, many reasons for increasing energy efficiency apart from the CO_2 issue. That lesson was learnt in 1973 with the first oil price rise shock, but there are substantial possibilities for further improvements. During 1987 the EEC committed itself in principle to a vigorous energy saving policy, with at least a 20 per cent improvement in efficiency by 1995. A 10 per cent reduction in the Community's energy requirement would reduce oil consumption by almost one million barrels a day. Environmental benefits, apart from the reduction of CO_2, would mean 125,000 tonnes a year less sulphur dioxide and a reduction of 200,000 tonnes a year of nitrogen oxides (Johnson, 1988).

The use of alternative energy sources such as hydropower, geothermal, wind and solar power could in theory help to cut the use of fossil fuels, but in reality their potential for providing enough energy for an advanced industrial society is extremely limited.

Reversing deforestation

The Earth's tropical forests absorb large quantities of CO_2 and thus stabilise the world's weather patterns. Large-scale deforestation in the tropics (for cattle ranching and agriculture) is causing about one fifth of the CO_2 build-up in the atmosphere. To absorb the predicted increase in CO_2 emissions, a complete halt to deforestation is not enough: a new forest, equivalent in area to the *sub-continent of India*, would have to be planted. The prospects of re-forestation on such a scale is remote. However, an American company has agreed to plant 52 million trees in Guatemala to absorb the equivalent amount of waste CO_2 emitted from its new generating station under construction in the USA (Davies, 1988).

Reducing CFC emission

Plans to reduce the levels of CFCs emitted into the atmosphere are already in progress. These non-toxic gases not only contribute to the 'greenhouse effect' but have also been implicated in damaging the ozone layer which lies some 10 to 30 km above the Earth and protects it from the sun's harmful ultraviolet rays. Studies recently carried out by NASA have shown large holes in the ozone layer above the polar ice caps caused by ozone destroying chlorine monoxide gas derived from the breakdown of CFCs in the stratosphere.

CFCs are used ubiquitously, as propellants for aerosols, as fire extinguishers, as solvents and as refrigerants (the freons). They are also used in the manufacture of foam packing materials. During 1987, under the Montreal Protocol, a 50 per cent reduction in the worldwide CFC production by the year 2000 was specified, although scientists predict it could take up to a century to repair the damage that has already occurred. In the UK, due to consumer and environmentalist demands, many manufacturers have stopped producing aerosols containing CFCs and by the end of 1989, 90 per cent should be free from these propellants. The chemical companies ICI and Du-Pont are both developing less harmful hydrofluorocarbon-based refrigerants to replace conventional CFCs. As the name suggests these compounds contain one molecule of hydrogen instead of ozone-damaging chlorine. Another major problem, however, is how to replace the 10,000 tonnes of CFCs already existing in UK refrigeration systems (Long, 1989).

Postscript

A picture has begun to emerge of a future global climate that will be radically warmer than anything hitherto experienced by humanity. This knowledge is tempered at present by the inability to say, unequivocally, that the greenhouse effect has been detected, or to say exactly how the climate will change in specific regions of the world. This frustrates attempts to formulate policies for dealing with the problem. It is, therefore, essential that further research work on an international level is carried out to sharpen our understanding of the greenhouse effect and its potential impact on the environment and society.

Nuclear power

Nuclear power provides about 16 per cent of the total electricity generated in the world. In France, it provides almost 60 per cent. Many, including Bri-

Figure 4.4
Summary of operational nuclear reactors in Europe in 1987 (*Atom*, 1988)

COUNTRY	REACTORS	POWER (MW)
Belgium	7	5477
Czechoslovakia	8	3207
Finland	4	2310
France	53	49378
Germany (Dem Rep)	5	1694
Germany (Fed Rep)	21	18947
Hungary	4	1645
Italy	3	1273
Spain	9	6529
Sweden	12	9646
Switzerland	5	2932
UK	38	10214
Yugoslavia	1	632

tain's Margaret Thatcher, see the expansion of nuclear power as an important means of combating the greenhouse effect.

The use of nuclear power does have many positive environmental benefits. It creates *no* sulphur dioxide, carbon dioxide, nitrogen oxides or particulate emissions. (By comparison, a 1,000 MW coal-fired station, consuming about three million tonnes of coal per year, produces seven million tonnes of CO_2, 120,000 tonnes of sulphur dioxide, 20,000 tonnes of nitrogen oxides and three-quarters of a million tonnes of ash). And each year nuclear power contributes to a worldwide saving of over 500 million tonnes of coal or 350 million tonnes of oil and saves the lives of about 250 miners (Jones, 1988).

But the growth of the nuclear power industry has been modest (McCormick, 1985). By 1987 some 26 countries generated electricity by nuclear means from a total of 417 plants (see *Figure 4.4*). Yet in the 1970s, at the time of the oil crisis, it was predicted that there would be 100 nuclear power stations built every year during the 1980s, many of them in the southern hemisphere. The UK generates a little under 20 per cent by atomic means and lies thirteenth in the world league, although this percentage will grow as several new stations come on stream in the 1990s.

There are several reasons why nuclear power has so far failed to fulfil its potential:

1. the fear of reactor accidents

2. the risks to human life by exposure to low levels of radiation

3. the environmental problems of dealing with radioactive waste

4. the military implications of nuclear programmes which may lead to the proliferation of nuclear weapons

5. the construction costs of nuclear plants which are much higher than conventional fossil fuel installations.

In the following sections we shall discuss three issues which have caused most concern about nuclear energy's effect on the environment: the *disposal of radioactive nuclear waste* and the *Three Mile Island* and *Chernobyl* disasters. These issues are so problematical that it seems likely that increasing the use of nuclear power as a means of reducing CO_2 emissions would just transfer the problem from one set of environmental hazards to another.

The disposal of nuclear waste

Radioactive wastes arise at all stages of the nuclear fuel cycle, from the mining and preparation of uranium ore as nuclear fuel, to its use and reprocessing in nuclear power stations. Engineers and scientists have to find a safe and environmentally acceptable means for the disposal of this material, which can occur in gaseous, liquid or solid forms, to ensure that there are no risks to present and future generations. In addition, they will soon have to consider the disposal of radioactive wastes originating from the decommissioning of obsolete nuclear reactors.

Gaseous and liquid nuclear wastes usually contain low levels of radioactivity and can be released, in accordance with Government legislation, directly into the atmosphere or sea, where they become quickly diluted. Even so, discharges of liquid waste from Sellafield into the Irish Sea have made that sea the most radioactively contaminated water in the world (Milne, 1986). These discharges are now being reduced.

Solid wastes fall into three classes of radioactivity: low, intermediate, and high level (see *Figure 4.5*). They are generally more radioactive than liquid or gas waste, and consequently greater care has to be taken over their dispo-

Figure 4.5
Levels of radioactivity in solid nuclear wastes (Saunders, 1987)

1. **Low level wastes**: these consist of items such as paper towels, protective cloth-
   ing, filters and laboratory glassware and contain various radionuclides with short
   half lives and trace quantities of radionuclides with long half lives. About 25,000
   cubic metres of low level waste is produced in the UK every year.

2. **Intermediate level wastes**: these consist of items such as contaminated equipment, concentrated sludges and resins from treatment processes and the metal
   cans which contained the nuclear fuel in the reactor. They contain larger quantities of fission products and actinides (elements with atomic numbers from 89
   to 103 - all radioactive) with long half lives. About 2,500 cubic metres of this
   waste is produced in the UK every year. Material from decommissioned nuclear
   power stations will significantly add to this figure in the future.

3. **High level wastes**: these consist essentially of heat-generating liquid produced
   during the reprocessing of used nuclear fuel. They contain most of the fission
   products and actinides from the fuel cycle and are converted into a solid matrix
   before disposal.

sal. About one million tonnes of solid waste will have been produced in the
UK by the end of the century.

In 1982 the Nuclear Industry Radioactive Waste Executive (NIREX, subsequently called UK NIREX Ltd) was set up by the UK electricity industry,
with Government agreement, to co-ordinate plans and develop facilities for
the management and safe disposal of low and intermediate level wastes
(NIREX, 1987).

Low level waste.

The practice of controlled dumping of low level waste (sealed in steel drums)
onto the Atlantic ocean floor was stopped under a 1982 moratorium - following pressure by Greenpeace and the National Union of Seamen. At present
low level short-lived waste is buried in trenches at a 300 acre site at Drigg
near Sellafield, where a natural layer of boulder clay isolates it from the
underlying sandstone. The waste is then backfilled by a two metre thick layer
of topsoil and granite chippings. As this site will be full by the turn of the century, NIREX recently examined four other possible waste disposal sites with
favourable clay formations (Elstow, Bedfordshire; South Killingholme,

Humberside; Bradwell, Essex; and Fulbeck, Lincolnshire). However, in May 1987 after a public outcry and on economic grounds a decision was made to abandon near-surface disposal and incorporate all low level waste with the intermediate types.

Intermediate level waste

Much of the material from fuel reprocessing operations falls into this category, which requires a period of isolation lasting possibly for thousands of years. After initial encapsulation in a solid matrix such as bitumen, plastic or cement the waste has to be buried underground to a depth of at least 100 metres (the German approach) or under the seabed accessed by tunnels from the shore (the Swedish approach) or from a sea-based rig. The hydrology of the host geological formation, normally clays, mudstones or evaporites, has to be studied carefully to ensure that the radionuclides cannot enter any ground water which may eventually reach the surface to enter drinking water or the food chain. Moreover, tunnelling in soft clay-bearing rocks causes civil engineering problems because of the possibility of cave-ins. However, the combination of the correct geological environment and engineered barriers should ensure that the wastes are kept safe until much of the radioactivity has decayed.

In the UK intermediate waste is currently stored in silos at the various nuclear sites (chiefly Sellafield, see *Figure 4.6*) awaiting a final recommendation by NIREX to the Government on the appropriate disposal method. Their decision on the best practicable environmental option is expected by the end of 1989, with the repositories being operational by the year 2002.

Whichever disposal method is adopted there will undoubtedly be formidable legal obstacles, as well as considerable political, public and diplomatic opposition. Favoured locations at present are Sellafield, the beleaguered UKAEA fast breeder reactor station at Dounreay, Caithness (both for undersea disposal reached by a land tunnel) and at Altanabreac near Dounreay (for land disposal).

High level waste

Over 95 per cent of the total radioactivity of all the waste produced in the UK is contained in the high level waste from fuel reprocessing operations. It requires sophisticated handling techniques.

Figure 4.6
Sellafield, Cumbria, nuclear fuel reprocessing operations (BNFL, 1987)

Sellafield is operated by British Nuclear Fuels PLC under a licence from the Health and Safety Executive and has been involved in reprocessing spent nuclear fuel since 1952. The Sellafield site, one of the largest in the world, is divided into two works:

Windscale includes the chemical reprocessing plants (primarily for fuel from Magnox reactors), effluent disposal and facilities for plutonium fuel fabrication and waste management.

Calder includes the Calder Hall power station, fuel receipt, storage and decanning plants.

A new thermal oxide reprocessing plant (THORP) to reprocess fuel from modern advanced gas-cooled and light water reactors is under construction at a cost in excess of £1500 million and is expected to be operational by the early 1990s.

Other buildings presently under construction include the Windscale high level waste vitrification plant, an encapsulation plant for intermediate level Magnox waste and an Enhanced Actinide Removal Plant (EARP) to reduce the activity level of liquid discharged into the Irish Sea.

Much criticism has been voiced on Sellafield's allegedly poor operational safety record - especially since:

the release of radioactive iodine into the atmosphere in October 1981

the accidental discharge of highly radioactive effluent into the Irish Sea in November 1983

and an unsatisfactory report on the Magnox fuel reprocessing building number 205 (HSE, 1987).

These techniques recover over 99.2 per cent of the uranium for use as new fuel and 0.3 per cent of the plutonium for use as fuel in fast reactors or for military applications. At present the heat-generating waste left after this recovery process (currently about 1,200 cubic metres) is stored at Sellafield as a concentrated, aqueous nitric acid solution, in nineteen high-integrity double-walled stainless steel tanks in concrete vaults. Overheating is prevented by a series of cooling coils. The intention is to vitrify this waste into large, metal-clad, borosilicate glass blocks to make handling safer, and then to put it into storage for at least 50 years in a pond or a naturally convected air store at Sellafield. It will take this long for the radioactivity to decay and the associated heat to disperse. This technique of vitrification and storage has been in use at Marcoule, France since 1978 and a similar plant should be operational in the UK by the mid 1990s (BNFL, 1983).

After 50 years the waste will be permanently buried in deep (typically 500 metres or more) geologically stable land- or ocean-based repositories similar to those used for the long-term disposal of intermediate level waste. Favourable geological rock structures include salt, granite and clay. Salt is attractive because it is dry. However, granite and clay, although wet, do have the capacity to absorb radionuclides.

The countries involved in the problem are co-operating in a major research programme to decide on the best type of repository. Solutions originally proposed, including removal from the earth by rocket, burial under the polar ice caps or transmutation of the long-lived radioactive components have now been discarded.

Decommissioning nuclear reactors

Over the next few years the UK, along with many other countries who use nuclear power, will have to begin to decommission their reactors and find a safe means of disposal for the waste this will produce. The first in the UK will be 18 ageing Magnox stations (such as those at Berkeley in Gloucestershire and Bradwell in Essex): the target is to close all 18 by the year 2000 at a cost of between £2 billion to £2.5 billion. Then, during the first 12 years or so of the twenty first century, the country's second type of nuclear plant, the Advanced Gas Cooled Reactors (AGRs), will reach the end of their working lives.

At present the major problem inhibiting decommissioning is the uncertainty about how the waste will be disposed of. No country has yet dismantled a commercial-sized plant, although work on small experimental stations in the USA and at Sellafield is currently taking place.

Decommissioning, after final shutdown, is generally agreed to be a three-stage process:

1. mothballing - removal of spent fuel and coolant from the reactor

2. entombment - removal of everything outside the biological shield

3. removal of everything else.

For a Magnox station it will take about five years to remove the nuclear fuel as there are not enough transport casks or sufficient handling capacity at Sellafield to do the work any faster. Another five years is likely to be spent on cutting away the external boilers from the main structure, which would then be sealed, weather-proofed and left for up to *130 years*. The boilers, which

can weigh up to 800 tonnes would also have to be sealed and placed in a pur-
pose-built on-site store for a similar period.

Scientists estimate that, after this length of time, radiation levels will have
decayed low enough to allow workers inside the core to dismantle it. A potential flaw in this plan is that the detailed engineering drawings of the plant
might be lost or accidentally destroyed in the intervening period. It is also to
be hoped that these drawings will still be intelligible to engineers in the year
2120. Furthermore the plan assumes that the CEGB and its successors would
still have the interest, money, and expertise to demolish the reactors. Similar problems, albeit on a smaller scale, will be encountered by the Ministry
of Defence when they eventually dismantle the Royal Navy's Polaris nuclear
submarine fleet.

Postscript

Regardless of the UK's future nuclear policy we are still faced with the problem of how to manage safely the existing radioactive wastes and contaminated
decommissioned equipment that we have accumulated over the past 40 years.
Technical solutions are now becoming available for the disposal of radioactive wastes presently in existence or being produced, as is the capability to
perform the risk assessments needed before decisions on final disposal methods are taken. The remaining dilemmas for the UK are those of choosing the
best of the available techniques and of finding locations for disposal sites.
These sites, like motorways, power stations and airports will undoubtedly
become emotive issues for the local communities and environmental groups.
The final choice will inevitably be a controversial political issue.

Although the UK was a pioneer in the development of nuclear power for
electricity production during the 1950s, in the late 1980s it is at least a decade
behind the USA and Europe in finding a permanent resting place for the
waste it produces.

Nuclear reactor accidents

There has long been public concern over the safety of nuclear power, and
these fears were reinforced by two serious nuclear reactor accidents: Three
Mile Island (TMI) and Chernobyl. Following the TMI accident one engineer
said: 'The engineering profession must take the lead to ensure that such ac-

cidents do not recur and restore the confidence of the public so that it will accept the increased use of nuclear power.'

Severe accidents are major system failures not foreseen by the designers and which result in such consequences as damage to the reactor, high risks to site personnel and, in the worst case, large releases of radioactivity into the environment. Because of their rarity, worldwide experience of such accidents is limited, but the large potential social impact of such events make their avoidance and control a matter of special concern.

Three Mile Island Nuclear Power Station accident, Harrisburg, USA, 1979

Shortly after 04:00 hours on Wednesday 28th March 1979, several water pumps stopped working in unit 2 of the pressurised water reactor (PWR) nuclear power station on TMI, ten miles south-east of Harrisburg, Pennsylvania. The reactor's core was seriously damaged, radioactive fission products escaped into the environment, and there was considerable public alarm. The cost of the accident to the nuclear power industry ran into billions of dollars.

The events leading to the accident were complex and are covered at length in the report of the President's Commission (TMI, 1979). The six-month investigation concluded that the fundamental reasons why the reactor failed were a combination of mechanical, human, and institutional errors (see *Figure 4.7*)

The reactor at TMI had been in commercial operation for only three months before the accident. The design was generally good, although problems had been experienced in shutting down a similar type of reactor at a station in Sacramento, California.

The first major fault at TMI occurred when water pumps supplying the steam generators stopped working. The safety system came into operation: the turbine was tripped and three emergency pumps started up. But during routine maintenance operators had incorrectly shut the discharge valves from the pumps to the steam generator. Control room instrumentation showed the emergency pumps were functioning but the operators did not notice warning lights telling them that the feed lines were closed.

With no flow of feed water the steam generator rapidly dried out and there was no water available to cool the reactor's primary water circuit. The pressure and temperature in the primary circuit rose until the reactor automatically shut down. As less heat was now being generated in the core the pressure began to fall. A pressure relief valve should have closed but it did not do so.

Figure 4.7
Conclusions from TMI Inquiry (Collier and Davies, 1980)

POOR CONTROL OF MAINTENANCE PROCEDURES:
   closed emergency feedwater valves

MALFUNCTIONING EQUIPMENT LEADING TO SMALL LOSS OF COOL-
ANT:
   a pressurised relief valve stuck open

AMBIGUOUS INADEQUATE AND BADLY SET-OUT INSTRUMENTATION
AND ALARM SYSTEMS

HUMAN ERROR:
   inadequate training of operators, misinterpretation, poor judgement leading to inappropriate responses

INSTITUTIONAL FAILURE:
   US Nuclear Regulatory Commission failed to set acceptable safety levels in the nuclear industry.

A light on the control panel indicated that the electrical power to the valve had been cut off, making the operators believe that the valve was shut. In fact the valve was stuck open and remained so for over two hours.

During these first few minutes more than 100 alarms went off in the control room. Some key alarms were on the back of the control panel and were completely overlooked. Furthermore, there was no system for suppressing the unimportant alarms so that operators could concentrate only on the significant ones. The fact that information was not presented to the operators in a clear and understandable form led to further operator errors.

The loss of coolant (and pressure) continued until the plant's high pressure safety injection system automatically triggered, injecting fresh cooling water into the primary system. Fearing that the reactor was 'going solid' (filled rigid with water) the operators cut the cooling water flowrate. They did not appreciate that large amounts of steam were now being generated in the system because the reduced cooling effect of the primary coolant was not sufficient to remove the core's decay heat. The reduction in cooling led to damage of the fuel elements. A bubble of hydrogen formed in the primary circuit from a chemical reaction of the steam with the zirconium fuel cladding. Some fission products, principally krypton-85 and xenon-133 and traces of iodine-131 escaped to the atmosphere and there was a hydrogen burn, but unlike the later accident at Chernobyl the building's concrete containment wall was strong enough to stem this.

From these events it is clear that although there were mechanical problems with the reactor, operator error was a major contributing factor to the accident. Yet, judged on their Nuclear Regulatory Commission examination performances, the operators at TMI were among the best in the USA. All four of the licensed operators on duty at the time of the accident had considerable experience with commercial reactors. The Presidential Inquiry concluded that the operators were adequately trained to cope with large-scale problems (where the safety equipment would react automatically in any case) but not for small-scale incidents such as the initial loss of coolant at TMI. It concluded that operators needed more training in all the possible circumstances giving rise to such incidents.

At the time of the accident, evacuation of the area surrounding the site was considered and the authorities recommended that expectant mothers and children should leave. Fortunately, exposure of the public to radioactivity was very small, and the future consequences in terms of additional cancer deaths are calculated to be undetectable in the surrounding population (less than one in 200,000 such deaths over the next 30 years). The major health effect was severe mental stress.

The station was rebuilt and started operating again in 1985. However there is much anxiety within the local community; some people still suffer from depression, hostility and other psychological disorders. These symptoms are similar to those experienced by victims of terrorist hijacks, shipwrecks and car crashes. Many local people remain unconvinced by assurances that the installation is now safe, and feel powerless to protect their interests.

Chernobyl Nuclear Reactor accident, USSR, 1986

Reactor unit No. 4 at the Chernobyl Power Station exploded at 01:20 hours on Saturday 26th April 1986. The explosion severely damaged the core and containment building and discharged fission products, principally the noble gases *xenon* and *krypton* followed by *iodine-131* (half life eight days) and *caesium-137* (half life 30 years), into the atmosphere. This release corresponded to 3.5 per cent of the total fission product inventory - some six to seven tonnes of material (Gittus et al, 1987; Collier and Davies, 1986).

Two operators were killed instantly by falling debris and a further 31 people, primarily those involved in fire fighting, died subsequently from massive doses of radiation. The Russian authorities ordered the evacuation of 135,000 people from a 30 km decontamination zone around the plant which is located on the Pripyat River, 60 miles north of Kiev, Ukraine.

In the days following the accident a radioactive cloud spread across Western and Central Europe, and rain deposited relatively high levels of caesium-137 in parts of Wales, Cumbria and Scotland (CEGB, 1987; *New Scientist*, 1987).

Before the disaster, there were four operational 1,000 MW RBMK reactors (boiling water, pressure tube, graphite-moderated direct cycle reactors of a type developed by, and unique to, the USSR) on the Chernobyl site (see *Figure 4.8*).

One inherently weak design characteristic of the RBMK reactor is its 'positive void coefficient'. This means that if the power from the fuel increases or the flow of water decreases (or both) the amount of steam in the fuel channels increases. Neutrons, which are absorbed by water, pass more easily through the steam, causing additional fissions in the uranium fuel. This can occur when the reactor is operating at about 20 per cent of full power and can cause the reactor to become unstable.

The immediate cause of the disaster was an experiment carried out by the operators, the objective of which was to 'check experimentally the possibility of using the mechanical energy (inertia) of the turbine generator, isolated from its steam supply and the grid, to maintain the output of the unit station auxiliary machines.' The experiment required the reactor to be run at about 25 per cent of full power.

At 01.00 hours on 25th April, 24 hours before the explosion, the operators began to reduce power from 3,200 MW. At 14.00 hours, in accordance with the experimental plan, the emergency core cooling system was disconnected. However, the grid controller requested the unit to continue to generate power to the grid until 23.10 hours. Operation was continued but, in violation of regulations, the core cooling system was still switched off.

The experiment was restarted and power was reduced to obtain test conditions of 700-1,000 MW. During this staged reduction, the power momentarily fell to 30 MW, which could be corrected only by withdrawing the control rods farther out of the core than authorised limits. Eventually the power was stabilised at 200 MW, well below the proposed experimental level. Additional reactor coolant pumps were started up as planned but this resulted in

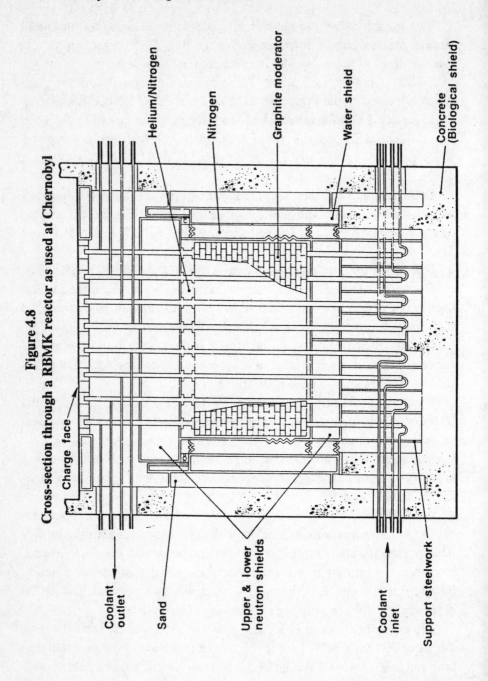

Figure 4.8
Cross-section through a RBMK reactor as used at Chernobyl

a water flow higher than allowed for the conditions prevailing, which had to be compensated for by farther withdrawal of the control rods.

By 01.22 hours the operators concluded that the reactor had restabilised at a reasonable power level and switched off the turbine. In fact the reactor was far from stable. Steam started to form in the core. This simultaneously added reactivity and raised the power output. Because the reactor had a positive-void coefficient more steam was formed in the fuel channels and this further increased the power. The operators realised that something was wrong and activated the manual trip, sending the control rods into the core. But because the rods were in a near fully withdrawn position a delay of about 10 seconds occurred before they took effect. In this time a 'prompt critical' power excursion was experienced. A few seconds later there were two explosions, the first resulting from the interaction between fuel and coolant; the second caused by hot hydrogen and carbon monoxide mixing with air, the explosion causing damage to the reactor's containment vault. The temperatures reached were high enough for the graphite moderator blocks to catch fire. Remarkably the three other units at the station were not damaged and continued to generate.

During the next two weeks the Russians, in an attempt to stem the release of fission products, covered the reactor with 5,000 tonnes of lead, boron, clay sand and dolomite dropped by helicopter. Compressed nitrogen was also used to cool the core. Eventually the core was stabilised and has since been completely entombed in a one metre thick concrete sarcophagus.

The Russian Government inquiry into the disaster concluded that there were several shortcomings in the concept and design of the RBMK reactor:

1. the positive-void coefficient

2. inadequate and slow shut down system

3. inadequate instrumentation and alarms

4. scope for operator interference with safeguards (reactor did not fail safe)

5. the reactor could still be operated with safeguards disabled or degraded (inherent safety not built in)

6. inadequate containment building.

The design shortcomings of the RMBK reactor were magnified by serious violations carried out by the operators. In effect the operators took premeditated action to override the protection devices provided for safe operation of the reactor. The reactor had been designed to 'handle mistakes' but not these deliberate acts. The Russians admitted that operator training was inadequate; they did not have enough simulators to give trainees 'hands on' experience of how to deal with a real emergency (only two simulators for RBMK and one for PWR designs). Poor plant management was also considered a contributory factor and since the accident a number of local and central Government staff have been sacked.

Following Chernobyl, many countries with nuclear power programmes are reviewing their own safety procedures and co-ordinating comprehensive emergency plans for dealing with similar events. The EEC is setting up a new system of accident reporting and improved environmental monitoring and plans to impose tolerance limits for any contaminated foodstuffs in the event of a nuclear accident. In the UK the Health and Safety Executive are appointing 20 more nuclear inspectors to review the safety of existing reactors, and to monitor the new generation of Pressurised Water Reactors.

Nuclear fusion - energy for the next century?

Although the long-term future of nuclear *fission* now hangs in the balance - primarily because of environmental issues - there is the exciting possibility of commercially generated electricity from nuclear *fusion* by the year 2040. Using fusion energy, the same energy of the sun and the stars, it is theoretically possible for a mere 130 tonnes of deuterium fuel (which is virtually limitless anyway) to supply the earth's electrical energy requirements for one year. This would represent a saving equivalent to 1,700 million tonnes of coal a year at current energy consumption rates.

While nuclear fission generates energy by breaking the nuclei of heavy elements apart, fusion generates energy by joining light elements together. About 30 different energy-releasing fusion reactions are theoretically possible, but only those involving the hydrogen isotopes deuterium and tritium and the common metal lithium are of practical interest.

When two deuterium atoms combine, they form helium and release energy, or form tritium and hydrogen, which also releases energy. The tritium in turn combines with deuterium, again forming a helium isotope and releasing an energetic neutron. If lithium is introduced it yields helium and tritium, releasing energy and the tritium fuses with deuterium. All of the radioactive components are 'consumed' and the final products are helium, hydrogen and energy. As, however, there is a neutron released in the reaction, the containment vessel and exposed equipment would become radioactive, although probably not to the same extent as in a fission device.

Research has shown that fusion between nuclei will occur only at temperatures greater than 100 million degrees centigrade - a temperature hotter than the centre of the sun (although there are claims, as yet unsubtantiated, that the conditions for fusion to take place can be created at room temperatures - the so called 'cold fusion' technique). At these temperatures a sufficient density of deuterium and tritium nuclei, now in the form of a plasma, must be confined in a strong magnetic field before the liberated neutron energy can be captured and used to raise steam as in a conventional power station.

Several experimental reactors have been constructed over the past 20 years. Most use a toroidal or ring-shaped device called a 'Tokomak'. Three of the largest reactors outside the USSR are the TFTR at Princeton University, USA, the JT-60 in Japan and the Joint European Torus (JET) at Culham, Oxfordshire, UK. Considerable international collaboration exists between these centres under the auspices of the International Atomic Energy Agency (Johnstone, 1987).

The JET, established in 1978, is a collaborative project involving 14 European countries. It employs some 650 people at a cost of about £750 million. The project is considered an outstanding example of scientific and engineering international co-operation.

The reactor has overall dimensions of approximately 15 metres in diameter and 12 metres in height. At its heart is the toroidal-shaped vacuum vessel three metres in radius with a 'D' shaped cross-section where the fusion takes place (JET, 1987; 1988). All of the preconditions for fusion have been produced at JET, which in itself is a major technological achievement, but so far not at the same time.

The high temperatures required have been achieved by pulsing 1.5 per cent of the electricity available from the National Grid for a few seconds, supplemented by radio frequency and neutron beam heating. When all the conditions are right it is hoped that a 'break-even' point, where as much energy is extracted as is put in, will be reached. The fusion experiments take place behind three metre thick concrete walls,which have been specially lined with boron to absorb neutron radiation when tritium is eventually introduced, making the whole apparatus radioactive. Special remote handling equipment has been designed to cater for all aspects of running, replacement, maintenance and eventually decommissioning of the reactor after 1992. The inherent safety risks are considered to be lower than with a fission device, especially as the amount of fuel in the reactor at any one time will only be enough for a few seconds of operation.

JET can be regarded as the first stage of a much greater investment if fusion is eventually to be successfully harnessed, and plans are already under way to build NET (Next European Torus), probably in West Germany. The ultimate cost of building a fusion reactor for the commercial production of electricity is virtually impossible to calculate at present, but it will undoubtedly be very expensive. At the moment, however, there is no other energy source to match the potential of nuclear fusion. However, we will have to wait for about 50 years into the next century to see if these dreams become a reality. In the meantime the fusion experiments engineers and scientists are performing today are having valuable spin-offs in other fields of technology.

Postscript - the privatisation of the UK electricity industry

During 1988 the Conservative Government, in keeping with an election promise, announced plans to privatise the electricity supply industry. Under this plan, the CEGB will be divided into two generating boards, National Power and Power Generation which will produce the electricity, while 12 distribution boards will pass it on to consumers. National Power will take over the running of nuclear plants. To date, however, there have been few proposals regarding the environmental implications of privatisation.

Potentially, environmental issues are as fraught as any of the technical problems surrounding attempts to recast the industry in a more competitive mould. As we have seen, some of the most controversial and intractable environmental issues of the past decade - acid rain, disposal of radioactive waste, and the greenhouse effect - are all related to the generation of electricity.

If stricter European controls on acid rain are enforced in the UK, the huge cost of these measures would make the reshaped CEGB less inviting to investors. Furthermore as Britain's coal is expensive and contains high levels of indigenous sulphur, private companies may have to look overseas for cheaper, 'cleaner' coal sources, with the loss of jobs for the home miners. A

Government so keen on competition could hardly refuse the opportunity to buy abroad.

A partial solution would be to expand the nuclear capacity but the high construction costs and safety risks would somehow have to be reduced. In the USA no new atomic energy plants have been built for a decade as these two factors have proved unacceptable to private utility companies. In addition, as we have seen, there are the huge problems (and costs) associated with decommissioning and radioactive waste disposal.

Some environmentalists have argued that the further development of nuclear power will be an immediate casualty of privatisation.

It is expected, however, that for political reasons the Government will insist that about 20 per cent of Britain's power must be generated by non-fossil means, and may introduce a levy system to make this economically viable. Another solution would be to use natural gas for electricity generation, but wasting this important natural resource has serious implications for future fuel policy.

Under privatisation we may see a re-emergence of smaller, more flexible local power stations similar to those in existence before the nationalisation of the electricity supply industry in 1948. These could provide a better return for the investor (and hopefully, the consumer) with 'mini heat' and power schemes; and the supplementary use of wind, water and the burning of rubbish to generate power. A proliferation of such schemes would partially reduce levels of atmospheric pollution.

Suggestions for further study

The controversies surrounding the major environmental issues discussed - acid rain, the greenhouse effect, the safety of nuclear reactors and the disposal of nuclear waste - show no sign of fading away. It is essential that student engineers follow the latest developments in these issues in the quality newspapers and such journals as *New Scientist*. In addition, there is currently considerable interest in the claims of leading scientists from the Universities of Southampton and Utah to have created the conditions for 'cold fusion' to take place under laboratory conditions. Students should closely follow these developments.

Chapter 5

Issues in Engineering Safety

It is part of the professional responsibility of engineers to be constantly aware that their actions might cause injury or death. They must always be on guard against complacency - the feeling that, 'it can't happen to me' - and must study the causes of accidents to prevent them recurring. Unfortunately, as Petroski (1985) has argued, 'to engineer is human', and history shows that many accidents are repeated after a lapse of a few years. Petroski suggests that periods of prolonged technological success encourage over-confidence and the acceptance of lower margins of safety, which, in time, leads to disaster. Failure leads to greater safety margins and a new period of success and progress, before over-confidence leads inexorably to further disaster.

But it is morally indefensible for engineers to argue that the loss of human life is a price which has to be paid for progress. The engineering institutions recognise this and build a firm statement of principle into their codes of conduct. For example the Institution of Electrical Engineers' code states that 'a member shall at all times take care to ensure that his work and the products of his work shall constitute no avoidable danger of death or injury or ill health to any person.'

Engineers can be expelled from their professional institute for a serious breach of its code (although, as we discussed in *Chapter 1*, this rarely happens and will not prevent them from continuing in employment and describing themselves as engineers).

Codes of conduct can help engineers attain a measure of independence from their employers in relation to the vital issue of safety. Where there is a potential danger to life and limb, engineers have a professional responsibility to put the interests of the general public or other employees above the short-term interests of their employers.

Engineers employed in the UK also have a well-defined legal responsibility to give adequate consideration to safety matters under the statutes embodied in the Health and Safety at Work Act.

The Health and Safety at Work Act, 1974

In the early 1970s, the UK Government recognised that existing health and safety laws were not keeping pace with changes in modern technology. The Robens Committee was set up to investigate these problems and its recommendations formed the basis of the Health and Safety at Work Act 1974 (which has been in operation since 1st April 1975). The Act superimposed a comprehensive new legal structure in some 31 Acts, on existing foundations (principally the Factories Act, 1961) and is one of the most important statutes for both industry and commerce.

The Act provides sweeping powers with the aim of reducing death and injury caused by industrial and commercial accidents and affects employers, employees (from the boardroom to the shop floor) and the self-employed, wherever they work. Maximum penalties for breach of some of the rules are two years imprisonment and/or an unlimited fine. Directors, managers and supervisors are personally (and criminally) responsible if a breach of the Act occurs due to their neglect or with their consent or connivance. Any employee who fails to co-operate with safety arrangements is also liable to prosecution.

Before the Act, an accident could lead to a civil action for negligence, but rarely to a criminal prosecution. Today there is no need to wait for an accident to happen, as failure to provide adequate safety precautions can result in a prosecution. With such a heavy responsibility resting on management, engineers and workers alike, it is vital that they all know the rules.

The Act is enforced by the Health and Safety Executive (under the direction of the Health and Safety Commission). The Executive itself co-ordinates the work of various inspectorates: for example, the Factory Inspectorate, the Alkali Mines and Quarries Inspectorate, and the Nuclear Inspectorate. It also provides medical, legal and research services, a Hazardous Substances Group (dealing with explosives, fire and toxic hazards) and a Major Hazards Branch. In addition, the Executive has access to the various Government research and consultancy establishments.

Under the Act the inspectorates have a positive means of enforcement. If their Inspectors consider an article or substance poses a risk of serious per-

Figure 5.1
Some major technological accidents and disasters, 1974-88

LOCATION AND OUTLINE DESCRIPTION OF EVENTS	DATE	ESTIMATED DEATHS
Piper Alpha Oil Drilling Platform: Massive gas explosion on board rig, North Sea	6.7.88	167
* King's Cross Underground: Smoke and fire emanating from a burning escalator, London, UK	16.11.87	31
*** Sandoz Chemical Plant: 1,300 tonnes of Toxic Chemicals washed into River Rhine after a fire in a warehouse, Basle,Switzerland	1.11.87	
* *Herald of Free Enterprise*: Ferry capsized after ingress of water through open bow doors, Zeebrugge, Belgium	6.3.87	193
** Chernobyl Nuclear Reactor: Experiment carried out by plant operators caused reactor to go critical and release radioactive material into the atmosphere, Kiev, USSR	15.4.86	33
*Challenger **Space Shuttle:** Blew up after launch due to fuel leak, Cape Canaveral, USA	28.1.86	7
* Union Carbide Factory: Escape into atmosphere of 30 tonnes of highly toxic methylisocynate, Bhopal, Mahdya-Pradesh, India	2/3.12.84	+ 2500
Pemex Liquid Petroleum Gas: Fuel pipe leak causing massive liquified petroleum gas explosion, San Juan Installation, Ixhuatepec, New Mexico	19.11.84	+ 550
Abbeystead Water Works: Methane gas explosion in an underground tunnel, Lancashire Fells, UK	23.5.84	16

Sellafield Nuclear Plant:	11.11.83	***
Radioactive waste accidentally flushed into the Irish Sea, Cumbria, UK		
Hyatt Regency Hotel:	17.7.81	113
Collapse of overhead skywalks Kansas City, USA		
* ICMESA Trichlorophenol Plant:	10.7.79	***
Release of 2.5kg of dioxin in the form of a cloud which drifted over the area surrounding the plant, Seveso, Italy		
** Three Mile Island Nuclear Power Station:	28.3.79	***
Leak of radioactivity caused by a series of reactor, mechanical and operational faults, Harrisburg, USA		
* Nypro (UK) Works:	1.6.74	28
Pipe failure liberated a cloud of cyclohexane which subsequently ignited,		

* These incidents are described in detail in this chapter.
** These incidents are described in detail in Chapter 4.
***Although no fatalities were recorded during the incident itself, the effects of exposure to radiation or highly toxic chemicals may cause deaths in the long term.

sonal injury, they can seize, neutralise or destroy it. Inspectors can also issue improvement and prohibition notices and can bring prosecutions in the courts for contravention of the relevant statutory provisions.

The most important duties for engineers and managers are covered in Section 2 of the Act (Mitchell, 1977). These duties include:

1. provision and maintenance of safe plant and safe systems of work

2. arrangements for ensuring safety in connection with the use, handling, storage and transport of articles and substances

3. provision of all necessary information on safety matters including instruction, training, and supervision

4. provision and maintenance of a safe place of work and working environment.

The legislation also requires engineers involved in the manufacture, design or supply of plant, machinery, components or substances for use at work, to carry out proper inspection, testing or examination and supply adequate information, in order to avoid any risk to health and safety.

Unfortunately, despite the Act, 330 people still died and 161,000 were injured in industrial accidents in the UK in 1987 (Hooper, 1988). And in recent years there have been some terrible accidents involving the use of advanced technology (see *Figure 5.1*).

We shall now describe six infamous accidents which have occurred within the past 15 years. They have been selected as salutary examples, where engineers and managers can learn from other people's mistakes; not as accidents causing the largest amount of damage or the greatest loss of life. These accidents are generally known as the Flixborough, Seveso, Bhopal, *Challenger*, Zeebrugge and King's Cross disasters.

Explosion at Nypro (UK) Ltd factory, Flixborough, 1974

At about 17:00 hours on the afternoon of the 1st June 1974, the Nypro factory at Flixborough near Scunthorpe was virtually demolished by an explosion equivalent to about 30 tonnes of TNT. Twenty-eight people were killed and many others injured, but if the explosion had occurred on a weekday instead of on a Saturday afternoon the death toll would have been much higher. The area surrounding the works was devastated.

The huge explosion was the result of the ignition of an unconfined vapour cloud of cyclohexane. This escaped under pressure from a section of the caprolactum plant devoted to the oxidation of cyclohexanone and cyclohexanol, for use in the manufacture of nylon. It was not the first vapour cloud explosion to have occurred in the world, but it was one of the most serious, and the first in the UK.

A full-scale inquiry was initiated by the Factory Inspectorate (Flixborough, 1975). Within a few days two possible causes of the leak of cyclohexane emerged:

1. The rupture of a 20 inch diameter 'dog-leg' pipe which had been installed as a temporary by-pass assembly following the removal of one of a train of oxidation reactors. The reactor had been removed because it was found to be leaking from an extensive crack and it was necessary to join the two adjacent reactors for production purposes

2. A 50 inch split and severe cracking in an 8 inch pipe running between two separators in the oxidation plant. Could the rupture in this pipe

have released enough cyclohexane to initiate the larger explosion,
or was the damage caused by the fire subsequent to the main explosion?

The inquiry found it difficult to establish which of these was the principal
cause of the disaster. Eventually, the 8 inch pipe theory was discounted. Although superficially credible, it was found on detailed examination to be
based on an improbable sequence of coincidences. So the Inquiry concluded
that the disaster resulted from the failure of the 20 inch pipe assembly (Flixborough, 1975).

There were many lessons to be learned regarding the failure of both pipes
and the safety of the plant in general. The installation of the bridging pipe
between the reactors destroyed the integrity of the otherwise well designed
and constructed plant. The design of the bridging pipe presented several engineering problems which were not appreciated by the plant's management
at the time, partly because the key post of the works engineer, who would
have advised on the construction of the line, was vacant. As a result there was
no proper design study and the only drawing was a full-scale sketch in chalk
on the workshop floor. Furthermore, there was no proper consideration of
the need for a supporting structure, no safety testing, and no reference to the
relevant British Standard and codes of practice. Once installed, the assembly was liable to rupture at pressures well below safety valve pressure, and at
or below the operating temperature, thus proving the old adage that a chain
is only as strong as its weakest link. Disaster might have occurred at any time
after the installation of the bridging pipe (as was admitted later by Nypro).

The accident occurred shortly before the implementation of the Health
and Safety at Work Act (1974). A Health and Safety Inspector who spotted
the makeshift pipe could now use his powers to issue a prohibition notice
(under Sections 22 and 23 of the Act) which would have enforced an immediate shut down of the works. The Act also imposes a statutory duty (Section
6) on those who design any articles for use at work to 'ensure, so far as is rea-
sonably practicable, that the article is so designed as to be safe when properly used (and) to carry out any necessary research ...'

The explosion produced several metallurgical phenomena which were
not widely known to chemical engineers at the time and which set alarm bells
ringing throughout the chemical and process industries. Investigations revealed that:

    1. Water treated or contaminated with nitrates can cause corrosion of
       pressure vessels. The original cracked reactor which had initiated

Figure 5.2
**Some lessons learnt by the engineering profession following
the Flixborough disaster**

- Hazardous installations should be sited away from densely populated areas
- local authorities should be responsible for licensing the storage of hazardous materials
- safety should be given equal priority to production
- hazardous plant inventories should be limited
- control rooms and other buildings should be located away from hazardous plant areas
- management systems for operating hazardous plants should be improved
- standards and codes of practice should be used for designing equipment
- adequate control of plant and process modifications
- problems in restarting the plant after discovering defects
- emergency plans should be co-ordinated with police, fire brigade and hospitals
- dangers of unconfined vapour cloud explosions

the sequence which led to the disaster had suffered from nitrate stress corrosion

2. During the extreme heat of a fire, stainless steel pressure plant can, if in contact with a small source of zinc (e.g. from galvanised walkways), undergo rapid zinc embrittlement, leading to cracking

3. Creep cavitation fractures in stainless steel can be produced within minutes in a small fierce fire. This phenomenon probably led to the failure of the 8 inch line.

A summary of the lessons learnt from the Flixborough disaster is shown in *Figure 5.2.*

Release of dioxin from ICMESA plant, Seveso, Italy, 1976

Another serious accident involving the chemical manufacturing industry occurred on Saturday, 10th July 1976, when up to 2.5 kg of dioxin was accidentally released from the Industrie Chemiche Meda S.A. (ICMESA) factory in the north Italian town of Seveso near Milan. The dioxin drifted out of the factory as a cloud and deposited white flakes on the town of Seveso and surrounding downwind areas. Although no deaths were directly linked to the disaster, the misunderstanding and confusion that followed led 90 women to have abortions. In addition, the chemicals released caused widespread *chloroacne* (an acne-like skin condition which may persist for several years); it is estimated that up to 30,000 people may suffer long-term exposure effects.

The plant's parent company was Hoffman-la-Roche and it was used to make *2,4,5-trichlorophenol* (TCP) which is the essential raw material of the antibiotic *hexachlorophene*. Unfortunately the manufacture of TCP from 1,2,4,5-tetrachlorobenzene (TCB) and caustic soda can, under certain operating conditions, simultaneously produce the undesired by-product 2,3,7,8-tetrachlorodibenzo-p-dioxin, one of the most toxic substances known to man, having carcinogenic, mutagenic and teratogenic properties.

ICMESA had a poor record in relation to health and safety laws ever since it started TCP production at Seveso in 1970. Although no major incidents had occurred previously, a series of design errors and bad operating practices culminated in the 1976 disaster.

After the accident the owners of the plant said that the disaster could not have been foreseen and was the result of some 'hitherto unknown or unexpected chemical reaction'. But it emerged later that an operator had failed to add water to the reactor (a simple fifteen minute operation) as the production shift finished work on the Saturday morning. Thus the chemical reaction producing TCP was left unfinished and uncooled.

As a result, the reactor's contents spontaneously over-heated, expanded, blew the rupture-discs (metal plates that give way at a set pressure) and emptied the contents of the cauldron into the atmosphere. To make matters worse, on the day of the accident only one of the two site workers (neither of whom was fully trained in how to run the plant anyway) was present to shut it down.

In fact, very few of the personnel employed by ICMESA were aware of the potential dangers of the process they operated. They were not issued with any information regarding the possible risks, even though TCP reactions had been known to cause explosions before. Similarly, the people living nearby were completely ignorant of the dangerous nature of the plant.

Technical experts also asked how so much TCB could have remained in the reactor, as this should have been removed by a process known as *vacuum distillation*. Loose pipe connections were found on the equipment, indicating that there was perhaps insufficient vacuum to complete the removal of the chemical. The melting of TCB deposited on a condenser above the reactor, which eventually flowed back to start the reaction anew, was also pinpointed as a possible cause.

Another concern was the modifications carried out to the original plant design, especially the incorporation of rupture-discs on the vents above the reactor. There was unfortunately no provision allowed for a containment chamber above the discs to trap the escaping gases just in case the reactor did explode. These discs were retro-fitted by the parent company because 'they were fashionable on all their equipment at the time'. Unlike conventional safety valves (which close after the initial high pressure is dissipated) rupture-discs simply open and let all the pressure escape. The use of safety valves on the reactor would have minimised the eventual dioxin pollution caused to the area surrounding the plant.

The inquiry into the accident took until 1983 to reach its conclusions. Afterwards, four technicians and managers were given prison sentences for negligently causing the disaster and wilfully neglecting to equip the plant with the necessary safety devices. These sentences were, however, partially over-turned on appeal in 1985. Today many people living in the Seveso area are still suffering various health problems allegedly caused by dioxin poisoning.

One useful consequence of this accident was the setting up by the European Economic Community of the so-called *Seveso Directive*, which requires all hazardous installations to be designed and operated safely, and insists that local hospitals, fire and police departments formulate emergency contingency plans to deal with such accidents. The guidelines of this original directive have subsequently been revised and extended in the UK and are included in the Control of Industrial Major Accident Hazards Regulations 1984 (CIMAH, 1985), Notification of Installations Handling Hazardous Substances Regulations (NIHHS), and in amendments to the Town and Country Planning Act 1971.

Release of methyl isocyanate from the Union Carbide Corporation plant, Bhopal, India, 1984

On the night of 3rd December 1984 an underground tank of methyl isocyanate (MIC) at the Union Carbide plant at Bhopal, Mahdya-Pradesh, India, exploded and released a cloud of 40 tonnes of lethal toxic gas. The cloud soon covered 40 square km of the city of Bhopal and caused thousands of casualties. The exact number killed and injured will never be known, but at least 2,500 people lost their lives and more than 100,000 were injured. The accident was the worst industrial disaster in history. It also raised serious questions about the moral responsibilities of multi-national companies who operate advanced technology in developing countries (Marshall, 1987; Lihou, 1985).

Union Carbide had made MIC at Bhopal since 1980. MIC is used as an intermediate in the manufacture of plastics, drugs, and pesticides; at Bhopal its primary use was to make the insecticide *Carbaryl*. Small chemical leaks, one of which resulted in a fatality, had occurred at the plant before.

As MIC is a highly volatile and reactive liquid it is kept under pressure and refrigerated by heat exchange with cooled chloroform. The storage tank at Bhopal was equipped with three additional safety devices. The first was a pipe leading from the tank which contained a safety valve set to rupture when the pressure inside the vessel exceeded 40 pounds per square inch. After the valve there were two other devices: a 30 metre flare tower to burn escaping gas and a counter-current absorption or 'scrubbing tower' where any vapour could be saponified to sodium isocyanate by reacting with sodium hydroxide, before being released into the atmosphere.

Why did this safety system fail on that December evening? Was it the design and operation of the plant which was at fault or was the failure due to unforeseen circumstances? At the inquiry Union Carbide said that 'the accident was the result of a unique combination of unusual events'. Some of these events are detailed below.

After the accident, concrete cladding surrounding MIC tank number 610 was found to be damaged and cracked. This suggested that a pressure rise had occurred which was so rapid that the rupture valve in the vessel could not act quickly enough to release the pressure, thus resulting in a 'run-away' reaction. This conclusion was supported by the fact that all 40 tonnes of MIC were released into the atmosphere within 40 minutes.

Evidence from the similar Union Carbide pesticide plant at West Virginia, USA, before the accident had shown that run-away reactions take place if MIC comes into contact with water. But this vital finding was never relayed to the management at Bhopal, where water could easily have entered the tank through a 'jumper pipe' on the outlet. This pipe was washed out with water a few hours before the accident, and the only valve between it and the MIC was found to be faulty. The trainee supervisor in charge of this washing procedure subsequently admitted knowing the line was not sealed off correctly, but decided it was not his job to do anything about it.

Once water was in the vessel, a self-generating and heat-releasing reaction took place with the MIC. This resulted in the whole of the contents being propelled through the safety vents into the scrubbing tower at high pressure. The scrubber was completely overwhelmed by the massive flow of vapour and boiling liquid (analogous to a bottle of champagne having its cork rapidly removed) making the sodium hydroxide saponification process ineffective. Thus the gas which emerged from the tower was essentially unchanged MIC. The tower was originally designed to handle only gases (as are most scrubbers used on chemical plants) and could not cope with this mixed phase flow (MacKenzie, 1985; 1986). Furthermore, the vapour could not be burnt off in the flare tower as this was shut for maintenance and there was no provision for a back-up system.

The incorporation of a simple 'knock-out pot' before the scrubber where the liquid and gaseous phases could separate would have prevented the accident. The technology to make the plant safe was therefore available but was not used, as the plant was not designed for the 'worst case' accident. The adequacy of emergency relief systems is obviously crucial in relation to the safe operation of chemical plants, yet it remains one of the least understood aspects of engineering design.

An even simpler solution would have been to use a plant design which did not necessitate the on-site storage of such large quantities of hazardous material (the highly toxic MIC in the tank that exploded had not been used for two months because of changing market requirements). Quite simply 'what you don't have, can't leak'. During 1988, the Health and Safety Commission in the UK drew up proposals to reduce the quantities of MIC to be used in process activities. These proposals will be implemented under amendments to the European Seveso Directive and the CIMAH regulations.

There were also weaknesses in the management of the plant at the time of the accident. Most of the original managers had left and were replaced by others whose experience was in the manufacture of batteries. In fact, there had been eight different managers in charge of the plant in fifteen years (Kletz, 1988).

Although the Union Carbide Corporation must take the blame for the poor design and operation of the plant, the Indian Government also has much to answer for. They had known about deficiencies in the equipment at the Bhopal works following the completion of a report by American inspectors in 1982. However, the State authorities did not ensure that any remedial action was taken (Vaidyanathan, 1985). Even worse, the plant was never properly checked by the local Health and Safety Inspectors: they simply signed the necessary paperwork without carrying out a proper inspection of the factory and, as they were mechanical engineers, they had little knowledge of the potential chemical hazards in the plant. Furthermore, as the local authorities had never been advised of the dangerous nature of the plant, they had made no plans for coping with an emergency.

Finally, the question must be asked: why did the Indian Government allow Union Carbide to operate a potentially dangerous plant in such a densely populated area? Were commercial reasons the prime motive with the health and safety of employees and the population surrounding the plant coming second? In the UK and many other countries strict zoning laws exist to ensure, as far as possible, that housing developments do not take place near major, hazardous installations.

In December 1987 the Indian Government brought criminal proceedings against nine officials of the Union Carbide Corporation. The charges laid included culpable homicide, causing grievous injury, causing simple injury, and maiming and killing animals. The accused face a maximum penalty of life imprisonment. Meanwhile an independent investigation carried out on behalf of the Corporation has alleged that the explosion was caused by an act of sabotage by a disgruntled operator (IChemE, 1988a, 1988b).

In February 1989, the Indian Government and Union Carbide agreed to a final settlement of $470 million to compensate victims of the disaster.

'Challenger' space shuttle explosion, Cape Canaveral, USA (1986)

Disaster struck the NASA space programme on 28th January 1986 when the shuttle *Challenger* exploded 73 seconds after take off. All seven crew members were killed and, although the loss of life was not large compared, say, to Bhopal or Ixhuatepac, the impact of this accident was magnified as the whole tragedy was captured on film and witnessed by millions throughout the world. The accident demonstrated the vulnerability of advanced machines and technology to poor design and human error and it undermined American confidence in a programme which had been seen as a major achievement for the engineering profession.

An independent commission was appointed by the President of the USA to investigate the causes of the accident. Their reconstruction of events established that there was a fuel leak in the right-hand solid-rocket booster which emanated from a faulty seal. These seals, or 'O' rings, were manufactured from vulcanised rubber - 7 millimetres thick and 5 metres long - and stretched like rubber bands around special grooves machined into the individual booster segments. Each 'O' ring was classed as a *criticality one* item: a single point failure component with no back-up, that would result in loss of life and of the mission if it failed (Joyce, 1986; Baker, 1986).

Morton Thiokol, the company which made the boosters, was working jointly with NASA on ways to improve the 'O' ring design when the accident happened. Before the accident there had been numerous memoranda circulating within NASA warning that the seals could fail with catastrophic consequences. On 23 out of the 24 flights before the accident the seals were found to have suffered varying degrees of erosion when the booster rockets had been recovered from the ocean; yet the Administration continued to fly shuttles in response to intense political, military and commercial pressures to reach their goal of 24 flights a year.

On the evening before the shuttle took off, engineers from Morton Thiokol warned that the rubber of which the 'O' rings was made could lose its resilience in the below freezing temperatures expected at the Cape and that the seals would therefore not seat properly (Kolcum, 1986). There was evidence of significant seal erosion before a launch on 24th January 1985, when temperatures were similarly low. But that launch had been successful, which meant that the burden of proof for safety was on those who wanted to stop the flight. Consequently NASA decided to overrule the Thiokol engineers and continue with the launch.

The Commission concluded that fatigue may have contributed to the bad management decisions made on the morning of the fatal launch.

Working long shifts over extended periods was commonplace at NASA and at many of their major suppliers, such as Lockheed and Morton Thiokol. A willingness of employees to work long and irregular hours may be laudable but it does raise serious questions when it jeopardises job performance: particularly when critical decisions regarding safety are at stake.

The Commission also criticised the way NASA management classified the criticality of components simply on whether their failure would result in the need to abort the mission, or lead to the total destruction of the craft. Risk assessment was also fragmented and subjective with no quantitative data available regarding hazards, principally because NASA lacked engineers trained in statistical sciences.

Figure 5.3

Comparison of old and new designs of booster rocket joints for the space shuttle programme.

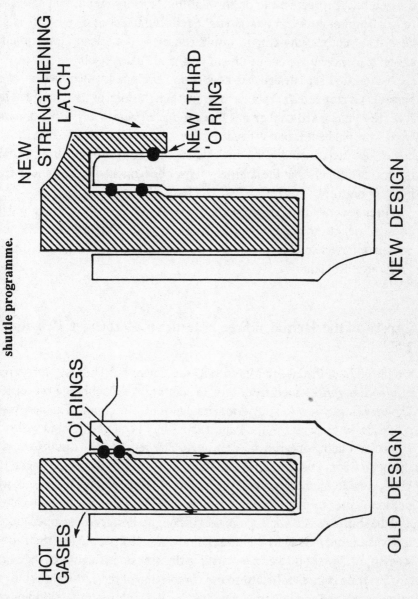

Since the accident, management procedures have been completely re-examined, with staff given clearer mandates and the appointment of contractors' representatives to safety committees. The agency, however, is in danger of sinking under the resultant morass of bureaucracy and paperwork. For instance, it now requires almost 100 signatures to authorise the replacement of a single heat protective tile on the shuttle. This has meant that the launch rate of 24 missions a year has had to be reduced to about seven. Officials believe that another catastrophe would cause the American Government to cancel the whole programme or even disband NASA itself.

A modified seal design has now been developed which incorporates a back-up 'O' ring and a new latch to strengthen the joint as a whole (see *Figure 5.3*). The vulcanised rubber has been replaced with a *nitrile polybutadiene* type. External heater bands have also been installed to ensure that the seals do not lose their flexibility if launch-pad temperatures should drop; although it is highly unlikely that the shuttle will ever be launched again at near-freezing temperatures.

After several unsuccessful experimental test firings of the redesigned booster rockets, the space shuttle *Discovery* took off from Florida on 29th September 1988 and completed its mission safely, some 32 months after the *Challenger* accident.

Capsize of the 'Herald of Free Enterprise', Zeebrugge, Belgium, 1987

On the night of Friday 6th March 1987 the Townsend Thoresen ferry *Herald of Free Enterprise* sailed from the Belgian port of Zeebrugge on route for Dover with her bow loading doors inadvertently left open. The bow was already low in the water as the ballast tanks had been partly filled with water to aid the loading of cargo at Zeebrugge. This reduced the distance between the open doors and the sea level. Then, as the vessel increased speed to 16 knots outside the harbour and the height of her bow wave increased, water began to enter through the open bow doors. The water flooded the car deck and the ship capsized almost at once. Although a heroic rescue operation was launched immediately by the local authorities, 193 people lost their lives. It was Britain's worst peacetime maritime disaster since the loss of the *Titanic*.

The time from the first list to the completion of the capsize was only four minutes, but the escape arrangements, based on international shipping regulations, had assumed that the vessel would remain afloat for at least 30 minutes. Further lives were lost because emergency lighting was inadequate, there was a shortage of rope ladders, and many of the ship's life jackets were locked away to prevent vandalism. Fortunately the ship capsized onto a sandbank which prevented her from inverting completely. If the capsize had occurred in deeper water, many more lives would have been lost.

The capsize of the *Herald of Free Enterprise* focused attention on the long running problem of the safety of 'roll on, roll off' (ro-ro) ferries, which have been a popular and commercially successful means of transport since the 1950s.

The first ro-ro disaster occurred in 1953 when the *Princess Victoria* capsized in the Irish Sea with the loss of 133 lives. The subsequent inquiry revealed that the ferry's inadequate stern door yielded to the stress of the seas, thus allowing influx of water into the car space. In 1982 the *European Gateway* capsized after a collision, but fortunately, like the *Herald of Free Enterprise*, she capsized on to a sandbank. Furthermore, she was almost empty at the time and so only six people were killed. The worst ever ro-ro ferry accident happened during 1981 in the Java Sea when 431 passengers were killed. In total more than thirty separate accidents involving ro-ro ferries have been recorded.

The problem with ro-ro ferries like the *Herald of Free Enterprise* is that they are designed to have a large, open, car deck, close to the water line, which runs the entire length of the ship so as to enable the rapid loading and unloading of vehicles. This makes them particularly vulnerable to flooding if they are holed at, or below, water level. Once a volume of water enters the car deck it is free to slop from side to side: 'the free water effect'. Eventually the water will collect on one side of the ship forming a wedge-shaped cross-section. Once this happens the vessel's stability is destroyed and rapid capsize becomes inevitable.

The solution to this fundamental design problem has been known to engineers for many years. It is to install either permanent or portable longitudinal and lateral bulkheads to sub-divide the deck and prevent water from flowing the complete length of the ship. In fact, when ro-ro ferries were requisitioned by the Ministry of Defence for the Falklands War in 1982, the Ministry insisted, on safety grounds, that the vessels were fitted with such bulkheads before being passed for service in the South Atlantic. And for the same reason passenger-only ships are required by law to have completely subdivided hulls.

But this simple engineering solution has been resisted by the ferry operators on commercial grounds. They argue that the installation of bulkheads would undermine the profitablity of ro-ro ferries by slowing loading and unloading operations and increasing turnaround times in port. This was the reasoning behind the decision to remove the bulkheads on the ro-ro ferries returning from South Atlantic duties when they resumed commercial service. Immediately after the accident the British Government seemed to accept the argument that the design of ro-ro ferries was intrinsically unsafe. A few days later, however, a spokesman back-pedalled, claiming that the accident was caused by the failure to shut the bow doors and that there was no evidence to suggest that there was anything wrong with the design of ro-ro ferries. Nevertheless the Department of Transport has since commissioned a three-year research programme into ro-ro ferry design and safety.

However, the Royal Institution of Naval Architects fears that lives may be lost while the industry waits for the results of this research and has stated that 'The current design of ro-ro passenger ships now in service makes them unacceptably vulnerable. Technical solutions to the fundamental problems of rapid capsize are available and they should be adopted immediately.'

The judicial inquiry into the accident did not make a judgement on the basic design of ro-ro ferries, but it did find many faults in the management and operation of Townsend Thoresen (MV *Herald of Free Enterprise*, 1987).

The immediate cause of the accident was not a subject of controversy: the inner and outer bow cargo loading doors had been left open because the assistant bosun, whose job it was to close these water-tight doors, was asleep when the ferry set sail. The inquiry concluded that a general feeling of complacency existed among the crew and management, who were operating what was 'little more than a bus service across the Channel'. The fact that the *Herald* was allowed to leave port with the double bow doors open was principally a fault of the on-board running procedure. A negative reporting system was used whereby the ship's master assumed that the doors were closed unless he was told otherwise. There was no back-up or fail-safe system that told the crew on the bridge that the doors were closed. The idea of installing bridge warning lights had been suggested by one experienced captain in a memorandum to senior Townsend Thoresen managers, but had been dismissed as unnecessary. One company official is reported to have written: 'do they need an indicator to tell them whether the deck storekeeper is awake and sober?'

Operational problems had been made worse by staff cuts which meant that the loading officer who was supposed to supervise closing of the bow

Figure 5.4
Short-term proposals for improvement of ferry safety suggested by the
Herald of Free Enterprise **inquiry.**

- Fitting of bridge indicator lights to all superstructure doors. The circuit for these lights should be designed to be fail safe.
- Closed-circuit television surveillance of all doors, decks, engine rooms, etc.
- If a ship cannot leave a berth with the doors shut then alterations should be made to the berth.
- A reliable procedure is needed to ascertain the weight of cargoes.
- Improved self-contained emergency lighting facilities.
- Fitting of suitable draught gauges to all vessels.

[Since March 1988 all passengers have been issued with boarding passes and it became illegal for a ship to proceed to sea with its loading doors open.]

doors was, at the same time, supposed to be on the bridge. If the officer had waited to ensure that the doors were closed and then gone to the bridge, sailing would have been delayed by about four minutes.

During the inquiry many serious operational malpractices were uncovered. Principally these included:

1. fictitious entries in the official log book regarding the ship's draught when leaving port

2. captains were often unaware of the exact number of passengers on board

3. vessels were frequently overloaded when they set sail - the *Herald* was probably overloaded by 100 tonnes on the night of the accident, but ironically this may have saved lives; if the ferry had been lighter it could have travelled farther and capsized completely in deeper water (Hammer, 1987).

After receiving a wealth of evidence the wreck commissioner concluded that the capsize resulted from serious negligence, not only by some of the crew on board ship at the time, but also by Townsend Thoresen management. He said that 'from top to bottom the body corporate was infected with the disease of sloppiness'. The master's Certificate of Competency was suspended and some crew members may face criminal proceedings.

An extensive list of recommendations, divided into three classes, was also given. Many of the short-term recommendations (see *Figure 5.4*) were carried out voluntarily by ferry operators immediately after the accident.

Improvements to operational procedures were also recommended by the Court, who emphasised a particular need for:

1. clear and concise orders

2. strict discipline

3. attention at all times to matters affecting the safety of the ship and those on board - there must be no 'cutting of corners'

4. the maintenance of proper channels of communication between the ship and shore for the receipt and dissemination of information

5. a clear and firm management and command structure.

The King's Cross Underground fire, London, UK, 1987

The fire safety record of the London Underground was ruined on the evening of 18th November 1987 when a fire at King's Cross underground station killed 31 people and injured 50. Seventeen people died from cyanide poisoning, one from burns, and 13 from carbon monoxide inhalation. Previously there had only been one fatality due to fire on the Underground since the Second World War.

The King's Cross fire began on the wooden wheel tracks of escalator number 4 which carried passengers upwards from the Piccadilly line into the station's booking hall (see *Figure 5.5*). Although wiring underneath the stairway was found to be in a poor condition, it was not implicated as the cause of the fire. The source of ignition was a lighted match, carelessly discarded by a smoker, which fell through a gap between the tread of the escalator and the skirting board.

Smoking was officially banned on the Underground, but a previous internal investigation into a fire had noted that smokers frequently lit cigarettes on the escalator before leaving stations. The escalator was 50 years old and had a tendency to move erratically from side to side, creating gaps of up to fifteen millimetres. Moreover, about a third of the angle cleats (small metal rims designed to catch matches, cigarette ends etc) on the treads of the esca-

Figure 5.5
Layout of the King's Cross Underground Station showing the spread of the fire from the escalator to the booking hall (*New Scientist*, 7th July 1988)

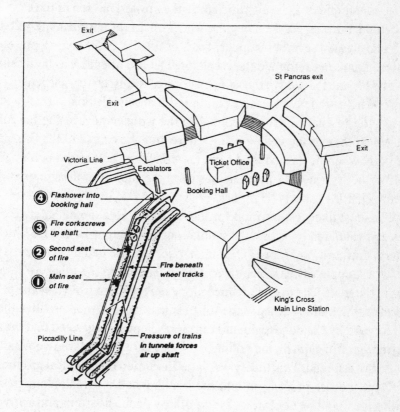

lator were missing, thereby allowing an easy passage for debris to fall underneath.

After ignition, the fire was fuelled by an accumulation of lubricating grease on the wheel tracks which had gathered wood-dust and fluff. Subsequent tests revealed that there was up to one third of a ton of grease and detritus on the escalator tracks, which effectively acted as a giant fire-lighter. There was also evidence that 18 smaller fires had occurred previously, but had miraculously burnt themselves out. The fire burnt unseen on the grease for up to ten minutes, during which time the upward motion of the escalator spread the burning grease along the wheel tracks for approximately 20 metres, and created several secondary seats of fire. At 19:30 hours a passenger noticed flames and stopped the escalator. The fire brigade was then called.

The fire next moved to the wooden parts of the escalator, particularly the plywood balustrades which were painted with unsuitable boat varnish and offered little resistance. It later spread to the wooden advertising hoardings above and then to the ceiling paint. Thereafter the course of the fire, up to the point where it flashed over from the escalator shaft to the booking hall at 19:45 hours, was less clear and has been the subject of disagreement between scientific experts (Hammer, 1988).

The most likely explanation (proposed by the Health and Safety Executive and validated by computer simulations carried out by the UK Atomic Energy Authority at Harwell), was that, once the fire had moved across one tread, it set up a vortex which spread the flames on to the other two escalators in the shaft. The fire was fanned along the escalator trough by the piston effect of trains still running in the tube tunnels below. An alternative theory put forward by London Regional Transport scientists suggested that the special anti-graffiti paint on the ceiling of the escalator shaft played a crucial role in the fire's spread. This theory was later discarded on technical grounds.

Once the fire progressed into the booking hall it spread along painted ceiling tiles, igniting ticket rolls, a temporary wooden hoarding and a plywood store, and eventually the ticket office itself. The hoarding was painted with 'Broflame': a type of fire-resistant paint not approved by London Underground's code of practice because it gave off dense smoke when burnt. In addition the hoarding had been given a second coat of another unapproved paint, thereby upsetting its fire resistance. About 0.75 tonnes of fuel was consumed by the fire in the booking hall and the temperature reached 600 degrees Centigrade.

Figure 5.6
Some of the principal conclusions and recommendations of the King's
Cross Underground inquiry

Conclusions

- London Underground's approach to safety was seriously flawed. Senior management tended towards a 'dangerous, blinkered self sufficiency' and general unwillingness to take advice or accept criticism.
- Staff were 'uncoordinated, haphazard, and untrained.'
- The Railway Inspectorate failed to discharge its duty for the safety of the Underground as required by the Health and Safety Act.
- The fire was caused by a lighted match.
- The flashover could not have been predicted.

Recommendations

- Removal of wood from escalators.
- Installation of heat detectors, sprinklers and closed-circuit television.
- The appointment of a director with special responsibility for safety.
- An injection of new talent and professional advice leading to a cultural change in management attitudes
- A total ban on all smoking and sale of smoking materials anywhere on the Underground system.
- Closer monitoring of incidents, more specialist staff, below ground radio communications, and closer liaison with the Fire Brigade.

The 91-day, £4 million public inquiry into the accident, conducted by Desmond Fennell QC, exposed London Regional Transport's poor maintenance procedures, ineffective staff training and sloppy management (see *Figure 5.6*) (Fennell, 1988).

The report criticised top management for a fatalistic attitude towards fires: managers seemed to believe that fires were inevitable on a system as old as the London Underground. Furthermore the report found that financial matters were strictly monitored at the highest levels in the organisation, in stark contrast to safety matters, which were never discussed at board level. Although specialist safety staff were employed, they were mainly in junior positions and no one person was charged with overall responsibility for the safety of the Underground. Although directors believed they were responsible for the safety of staff in their respective divisions, they did not believe that this responsibility extended to passengers. The operations director passed responsibility for the safety of lifts and escalators to the engineering department. This lack of accountability for safety meant that station staff at King's Cross were simply not trained or equipped to handle an emergency on the scale of the fire on 18th November 1987.

After the fire, London Regional Transport produced a list of over 100 actions designed to prevent another tragedy and costing some £37 million. Ironically many of these safeguards had already been suggested in 1985 by an independent watchdog group who studied the Underground's safety standards. One of their recommendations was that the escalator wheel tracks should be cleaned more frequently to remove grease. The Underground's rules at the time stated that this should be carried out every eight months; in practice at King's Cross they were cleaned only every eleven months because of staff cut backs. Moreover, inadequate cleaning methods employed by the 'fluffer teams' meant it was virtually impossible to remove all the grease from the escalators. Half-empty oil drums, greasy rags, paint tins and bags of rubbish were also allowed to gather under the stairwells.

Automatic sprinkler systems and heat sensors are now being fitted under the stairways throughout the Underground system. Although sprinklers were installed at King's Cross they were not used. They would in any case have been totally ineffectual in stopping the inferno, as the pipework was completely undersized and lacked any regular maintenance. (Of the 58 sprinkler nozzles fitted, only 40 were found to be operational). Furthermore, the Underground staff were inadequately trained in the operation of the sprinkler system.

To make matters worse, fire extinguishers were hidden away and water buckets had remained empty for years. There was no practised plan for the emergency evacuation of passengers in the event of a fire. Of the dozen or so staff working at the station on the night of the fire, nobody knew what to do, and practically everybody did the wrong thing.

In future, the wooden panels on the escalators are to be replaced with metal panels, and only wooden treads and step risers will remain. A similar recommendation was made in 1985 following a fire at Manor House Station, but was rejected by management as too expensive. The idea of removing wood from Underground stations was first recommended in *1904*, following a fire on the Paris Metro in which 83 people died.

Immediately before the Fennell Report into the fire was published, the Chairman of London Regional Transport, and the Chief Executive of its subsidiary, London Underground, resigned (*Guardian*, 1988).

The lessons learned

The case studies in this chapter demonstrate that accidents can be caused by poor engineering design or management error, or a combination of both. Engineers must be constantly aware of these factors, especially when they are given responsibility to design or manage any potentially hazardous piece of apparatus. Safety should be of concern to all those in positions of responsibility and not only to specialists.

Safety in design

In order to design safer and more reliable equipment and installations, the engineer must:

1. recognise the specific possibilities that can cause safety or operating problems
2. determine which of these need to be guarded against
3. decide on an appropriate course of action.

Various qualitative and quantitative techniques have been developed to assess safety criteria by the chemical, nuclear and aeronautical engineering professions. These techniques can help engineers to decide on measures which can reduce risks to acceptable levels and to compare the effectiveness of alternative safety strategies (IChemE, 1981). In the UK all undergraduate chemical engineers must be now trained in such techniques before they are admitted to membership of the Institution of Chemical Engineers.

Safety should first be considered at the inception or research stage of a project. This allows hazards to be eliminated at their source, rather than trying to compensate at a later stage by the incorporation of complex control and protection systems. For example, in the chemical industry it is better to develop a manufacturing process where operating conditions are not unduly difficult, which uses reactions that are easily controllable, and where the raw materials themselves present the minimum hazard (in terms of their toxicity, flammability etc.). Furthermore, the reduction of hazards must be considered in the context of the life of a particular item of plant or machine. This should therefore include: construction, transport, installation, commissioning, operation, start-up, shut-down, maintenance, decommissioning and final disposal.

Inherent safety principles should also be applied during the design stage of a project where equipment and other materials are specified and selected so as to minimise the risk of failure. In many cases codes of practice and British or international standards exist and these are a natural starting point for any new design. Designers must be aware of the professional responsibility they carry for safety; they must ensure that the design is sound and that measures are taken to deal adequately with any hazards previously identified in the research stage. Careful design can often eliminate or reduce the need for additional costly complex protection equipment. Where critical components or operations are involved, however, it is essential to have multiple levels of safety so that a single-level failure cannot lead to catastrophic consequences. Secondary and tertiary back-up systems must be used and regularly maintained.

A key factor in reducing hazards is the reliability of the equipment specified. This is directly related to plant safety and overall performance. Any failure, however small, can result in an accident. A vast amount of data has been assembled on the reliability of standard items, especially for electrical and electronic components. The UK Atomic Energy Authority has a separate Safety and Reliability Directorate based at Culcheth, Warrington to assess the performance of parts for use in nuclear installations where their failure could have dire consequences. Many firms now employ their own reliability engineers.

Once the design has been completed, hazard and operability studies should be carried out to show, in a systematic manner, where possible failures can occur. These techniques can also be applied when equipment is operational or when modifications to it are made.

The two most widely used analytical procedures are *Hazop* and *Hazan*, and both have proved to be of particular value in improving the safety of chemical manufacturing plants (Kletz,1984). The Flixborough disaster could have been foreseen and avoided if these procedures had been used.

Hazop

Hazop (HAZard and OPerability) is a fault-tree type of analysis in which a series of standard 'what-if' questions are asked at each stage of a process, to identify all deviations from the intended design that could produce undesirable effects on safety and operability. For example, what if the coolant leaked? What if the pump failed? What if more catalyst is added? These fault trees use the same techniques as decision trees in business decision-making.

However, the accident at Bhopal illustrates the limitations of hazard assessment techniques. If asked before the accident to estimate the probability of a leak of MIC, most analysts could have calculated the probable failure rates of the refrigeration, scrubbing, and flare systems easily enough. But it would be highly unlikely that any of them would have considered the possibility that all these systems might have been switched off.

Where thousands of factors are present it is easy for the special significance of an item to be missed. The selection of personnel to provide the necessary skill and experience to carry out these studies is therefore critical, as the technique will not make up for any gaps in their knowledge. Furthermore, these people should report directly to senior management and have sufficient delegated authority to implement any actions they decide are necessary. There must also be constant monitoring to ensure any recommendations made have been fully carried out.

Hazan

The Hazan procedure is similar to Hazop, but is more quantitative. A probability of failure is assigned to each hazardous stage of a process; these are then combined to give an accumulative overall failure prediction. These numerical predictions can help to produce a safer design. However, a major difficulty is in quantifying human error which is a major factor in many accidents.

Recently computer-based models have been developed by the Health and Safety Executive to quantify risks associated with chlorine and liquidified petroleum gas installations sited above ground. By taking account of various plant-failure scenarios, wind directions and surrounding population densities the technique enables an overall risk factor to society at large to be estimated.

Human factors in safety

People will always make mistakes. Estimates attribute about 45 per cent of critical incidents at nuclear plants, 60 per cent of aircraft accidents and 80 per cent of marine accidents to human error. Some errors are the result of an aberration or a moment's forgetfulness; others are the result of errors of judgement, inadequate training or supervision. Very few accidents are the result of negligence.

Managers

Errors by management affecting the safe operation of equipment are often hidden within the management structure as a whole, and it is only after a major incident occurs, and an external investigation takes place that these faults are brought to light.

A journalist who sat through the King's Cross and Zeebrugge inquiries identified the same symptoms of sloppy management in both cases. He heard witnesses talking of low morale, tired and listless workers and bad safety procedures; of long-serving seamen and railway workers who were made redundant to save money, and whose specialist knowledge and experience had been lost to their industries; and of managers who knew everything about balance sheets and cost efficiency but knew little about running ships and railways (*Independent*, 1988).

A similar managerial culture was evident at Bhopal and Seveso. And we saw how, in the *Challenger* disaster, the professional advice of the engineers who wanted to cancel the launch was overruled by managers who were responding to commercial and political pressures. Some commentators have suggested that operating at the frontiers of science with complex technology inevitably multiplies the opportunities for human mismanagement and misjudgement.

If accidents like those described in this chapter are not to be repeated in the future, engineers must act as 'risk managers' who take on special responsibility for identifying risks and pressing the case for safety at all times at the highest levels in the organisations they work for or advise.

Safety considerations should be prominent at boardroom level, and directors and accountants need to recognise that expenditure on safety cannot be subject to the normal terms of financial rate of return on investment (it has been estimated that 15 per cent to 30 per cent of the capital costs of a process plant represents equipment and instrumentation relating to safety, environmental enhancement, and anti-pollution measures). Unfortunately, it is all too common for companies to postpone investment in safety. There is often also the mistaken notion that safety is different from any other management function, such as marketing or finance and it is therefore not included in the main flow of management information systems.

Supervisors

Having established the fact that top managers have the ultimate responsibility, we should not forget that the enforcement of safety in the workplace is usually the job of supervisors or foremen. They have a key role in accident prevention because:

1. they represent management on the spot, and should be well acquainted with local hazards and rules
2. they are responsible for staff training and can pick suitable individuals to go on relevant safety courses
3. they know the culture and language of their own workforce and can 'suggest' rather than 'order'.

Since the King's Cross Underground fire, London Regional Transport have appointed new supervisors who will act as 'landlords', responsible for all safety activities at their particular station or groups of smaller stations. Consequently junior managers themselves have to be trained with respect to safety and must be required to go on refresher courses periodically. Education and training must be continuous (Kharbanda and Stallworthy, 1988).

Operators

Another aspect of the human factor in safety is mistakes made by operators. This was illustrated by the Zeebrugge and Bhopal accidents and the Three Mile Island and Chernobyl disasters described in *Chapter 4*.

Consequently we need to understand how operators make mistakes in order to reduce the risks of a disaster. The reasons are interwoven with logic, cognitive psychology and ergonomics (the study of interaction between man and machines). Reason and Mycielska (1982) believe that people make three different kinds of mistake: those concerning routine tasks, those involving a familiar problem and those that occur when a new problem appears. These are respectively called *skill-based*, *rule-based* and *knowledge-based* errors.

Skill-based errors happen at the intuitive, or automatic, levels of thought before the mind is conscious of the mistake. Once the operator is conscious of the error, it then becomes rule-based and can be solved only by applying the lessons of past experience (this is why it is essential to train operators on equipment simulators). If experience cannot correct the mistake, then it is knowledge-based, and requires time to work out. The disaster at Three Mile Island was initiated by a knowledge-based error where the operators could not decide what was going on until it was too late. Complex mechanisms and processes should be designed to keep human errors at the intuitive or skill-based level as these are the least dangerous.

Occasionally accidents occur simply because people decide not to carry out instructions or to disobey them. This was a primary cause of the Chernobyl nuclear reactor explosion, where operators deliberately overrode the safety systems. As a consequence automatic safety systems are being considered for some nuclear power installations (Sizewell B in the UK). It is hoped these would limit human error by making it difficult for operators to take manual control of a reactor for 30 minutes after an accident begins. The 30-minute period is intended to ensure that operators do not make an accident worse by taking precipitate action under the stress of an emergency. Controversy however surrounds the use of such systems as they are good only for coping with 'designer expected' incidents.

Likewise 'the man-machine' interface must be carefully designed to present factual information correctly if people are to act on it. This may be thought of as an imaginary surface across which information passes from the system to the operator by means of displays, and from the operator to the system by the controls. The efficiency of information transfer depends on the visibility, legibility and intelligibility of the displays, i.e. the ease with which they can be seen, read and understood. Furthermore it also depends upon the size, colour and ease of operation of individual knobs and switches. Therefore displays and controls should be arranged in an orderly manner and incorporate release catches (that cause a pause for thought).

Current thinking suggests a simplification of control-room instrumentation whereby large numbers of lights and read-outs are replaced by a single screen display that indicates relative status of equipment as a bar diagram or as segments of a pie diagram. Such seemingly trivial details make a considerable difference to operators' work loads and hence to the operability of a system. They have a profound effect on their chances of committing a fatal error especially when under stress.

The selection, training, aptitude or motivation of individual operators is also important. Computerised psychological tests can help to match operators to job and particularly to exclude those whose character traits could add a hazard. A typical test has 500 or so questions to be answered and has the advantage of removing bias that can arise in personal interviews.

Suggestions for further study

Since *Chapter 5* was written major avoidable accidents have continued to plague the industrial world: the Piper Alpha explosion, the Clapham rail disaster, the M1 air crash and the Hillsborough football disaster. Student engineers should study the technical and human issues raised by such disasters by reading the relevant articles in the quality press and journals. They should also acquire, or consult, copies of the official reports into these accidents as they are published. In their study of eye-witness accounts and evidence presented students should try to develop an empathy with the engineers involved and ask themselves the question - how would I react if it happened to me?

Part II

The Organisation of Engineering Activities

Chapter 6

The Pioneers of Management Thought

The practice of management has been around ever since someone was placed in a superior position over someone else to achieve a predetermined goal. Early civil engineering triumphs, such as Stonehenge and the Great Pyramids, suggest that the ancient civilisations had an impressive understanding of the principles involved in organising large numbers of people.

The problems of organisation have also been around for a long time. The Roman, Gaius Petronius Arbiter wrote in AD 66:

'No sooner did we form into groups than we reorganised. I was to learn later in life that we tend to meet any new situation by reorganising, and what a wonderful method it can be for creating the illusion of progress while producing confusion, inefficiency and demoralisation.'

Many modern management principles were first developed in the only large-scale organisation to exist before the Industrial Revolution: the army. Most notably the Roman Legions and the reformed European armies of the sixteenth century gave clues to the efficient control and mobilisation of large groups of people. Later, in the eighteenth century, Frederick II of Prussia drew on these classic military principles to create an army which became the most feared in Europe.

Morgan (1986) describes some of the organisational principles which were introduced into the Prussian army during Frederick's reign (1740-86). They included:

1. a strict hierarchy of control formalised by ranks and uniforms

2. the extensive and consistent use of rules and regulations

3. specialisation or division of work

4. the appointment of specialist advisers (staff officers) outside the line of command to undertake planning activities

5. the decentralisation of certain controls to lower levels of the hierarchy to encourage flexibility and speed of response in combat situations.

These basic principles are still applied in military and many civilian organisations today. But to sharpen our understanding of the organisation of engineering activities today, we need to examine the development of organisation and management theories in the twentieth century.

After the Industrial Revolution, new industrial organisations began to spring up throughout Europe and the USA. In the early days these organisations were run by their owners in an informal and paternalistic style with a management philosophy based largely on hunch and intuition. But by the beginning of the twentieth century, the growth in size and complexity of companies through amalgamation and takeover meant that a new and more rational approach to the management of organisations was needed.

One solution was found by drawing on the principles of military organisation described above. A second major influence on the management of the emerging industrial organisations was the unchallenged success of science and engineering. The proponents of a new 'scientific' approach to management believed that they could transfer this success to the running of human organisations and run them with the efficiency of a smoothly oiled machine. They looked at the way in which a machine operated as a collection of interlocking parts arranged to operate in a specific sequence and with maximum precision, and they attempted to design organisations to similar specifications.

The mechanical metaphor, in which the running of organisations is compared with the running of machines, also underpins militaristic organisation. An efficient army, or even an individual soldier, is often referred to as a 'fighting machine'. Thus both mechanistic and militaristic principles are reflected in the work of the early pioneers of management.

The modern development of organisation and management theories is closely linked to the development of engineering. Indeed three engineers, working independently, can claim to have pioneered management as we know it today. The three are: Frederick W. Taylor and Alfred P. Sloan of the USA, and Henri Fayol of France.

Scientific management ('Taylorism')

Frederick Winslow Taylor (1856-1915) was a flamboyant, self-made engineer whose original ideas on the practice of 'scientific management' (or 'Taylorism' as it is often known) generated considerable controversy in his own lifetime and afterwards.

Taylor started his career at the Midvale Steel Works in Pennsylvania as a labourer and he worked his way up to be foreman and, later, chief engineer. He then transferred to the Bethlehem Steel Company where he had greater freedom to try out his new approach to management. For the last part of his career he was a consultant for other companies and spent his time as a proselyte for scientific management.

Taylor's approach is best illustrated by describing his attempts to transform the shovelling of coke into the blast furnaces at the Bethlehem Steel Company into a 'science'. Taylor personally selected two shovellers who were particularly good at their job and whom he described as 'first class men'. After a long and patronising lecture from Taylor which included a mixture of flattery, promises of double wages and veiled threats, the men agreed to take part in a series of experiments conducted by Taylor's team. Over a period of months the men were carefully timed by stop watch to see how much coke they could shovel in a day using different sizes of shovel. Taylor used the findings from these painstakingly conducted experiments to devise a new method of working in the yard. Instead of bringing their own shovels to work, the men were issued with a company shovel suited to the precise task they were to do on a particular day. In addition, a 'labour office' was built to plan and co-ordinate the work of the several hundred men in the yard (the whole operation was carried out like a military operation, with large maps of the yard on the walls). Finally, and most importantly, the men were paid a carefully calculated wage incentive which meant that those who met their daily production targets were able to earn up to 60 per cent more in wages than workers in other comparable, but 'unscientifically' organised, companies.

Taylor was able to boast that after three years of the new system a streamlined work-force of 140 men were shovelling as much material (amounting to several million tons a year) as a workforce of 500 had done under the old system. Furthermore, despite the costs of the bureaucracy needed to run the new system (such as new clerical procedures, a telephone system for moving men around the yard, the employment of instructors and supervisors, and the building and running of the labour office) and the dramatic increase in wages

Figure 6.1
The keynotes of scientific management

- Scientific analysis, not 'rule of thumb' should be applied to all aspects of work organisation

- there is always 'one best way' to organise work; it is management's responsibility to find that best way and the workforce's job to implement it

- the work of all operatives should be planned and organised by management so that the former do not have to waste any time or energy on 'brainwork'

- workers should be scientifically selected to suit the particular tasks they are to carry out and thereafter should be carefully trained and monitored

- in order to achieve maximum efficiency, any complex job should be reduced to its basic components and divided between specialised but unskilled workers; precision would be achieved by constant repetition

- carefully calculated wage incentives linked to production would ensure that 'first class men' could earn high wages with no artificial ceiling, while failure to meet targets would be penalised by loss of earnings

- co-operation between management and work force could be achieved by the recognition by both sides that company profits and individual earnings are inextricably linked and that both could be dramatically boosted by the scientific approach.

paid to the workforce, Taylor reported that the cost to the company of handling a ton of material had been halved (Taylor, 1912).

Today, Frederick Taylor is acknowledged as the father of time and motion study. His ideas spread like wildfire throughout the industrial world and became a major influence on the running of organisations in Europe and Japan as well as the USA (see *Figure 6.1*).

The principles of administration (Fayol)

Like Taylor, Henri Fayol (1861-1925) established his reputation by taking over the management of an ailing company and masterminding a dramatic turnaround in its fortunes. In 1850 Fayol joined a large mining and metallurgy company in the Auvergne region of Central France, as a young and

Figure 6.2
Fayol's five key functions of management

1. TO PLAN: devise a corporate plan which attempts to look ahead and forecast events

2. TO ORGANISE: design a logical organisational structure; introduce effective systems for recruitment and training of the human resources of the company; build or acquire the necessary physical resources

3. TO COMMAND: motivate staff to put all their energies into organisational objectives (managers can achieve this by 'leading by example' and by applying their superior technical knowledge and overview of the organisation)

4. TO CO-ORDINATE: ensure that there is no unnecessary duplication of effort or wasteful competition between different departments (to be achieved by constant circulation of information and regular meetings)

5. TO CONTROL: monitor all aspects of corporate performance against specified rules and procedures (Fayol recommended that independent and impartial 'staff' departments should be set up to inspect the work of 'operational' departments).

newly qualified mining engineer. He worked his way up the management ladder to become managing director in 1888, only to find the company in poor financial and organisational condition. But within a few years Fayol had transformed its performance and, when he retired in 1918, he left a successful and financially secure enterprise behind him.

After his retirement Fayol founded a centre for management studies in France and acted as a consultant for various private sector companies and the French post office, army and navy. But his ideas were not widely known in America and Britain until the translation of his major work, *Administration Industrielle et General*, into English in 1949 (Fayol, 1916).

Fayol is widely acknowledged as being the first to attempt a comprehensive definition of management. He suggested that managers have five key functions or responsibilities to carry out (see *Figure 6.2*). This five-fold definition of management is still taught today on training courses and has been used as a starting point for later writers attempting to produce their own definitions of management.

Fayol's second major contribution to the development of organisation and management theory was to codify a set of 14 'universal' principles which

Figure 6.3
Fayol's Principles for Organisational Structure

UNITY OF COMMAND:

   an employee should receive direct orders from only one superior (the same principle is expressed in the biblical 'no man can serve two masters: for either he will hate the one, and love the other, or else he will hold to the one and despise the other', Matthew 6:24)

SMALL SPANS OF CONTROL:

   the number of employees reporting to one manager or supervisor should be limited to a small number so that communication and co-ordination problems are kept to a minimum (the ideal span of control was never successfully defined by Fayol or later writers in the same tradition, but 3-6 subordinates reporting to one superior would fit the theory)

LINE OR CHAIN OF COMMAND:

   hierarchical lines of authority should be established to run from the managing director, through 'line' managers and supervisors, down to the operatives on the shop floor. Each employee should be in one, clearly defined, line of command and all communications and orders to him should be channeled through this line (to ensure that 'unity of command' is adhered to)

DIVISION OF WORK:

   like Taylor, Fayol believed that specialisation was the most efficient way of organising the work of individuals and departments (but note that the nineteenth century economist Adam Smith is credited with first promulgating this concept)

AUTHORITY AND RESPONSIBILITY:

   Fayol believed that these two principles should be equal: for example it is pointless to hold a manager 'responsible' (or accountable) for a budget if he does not have full 'authority' or control over every item of spending within it. Later writers used this principle to define a fundamental principle of delegation: a manager should delegate authority to carry out a task but not responsibility (i.e. the manager remains accountable for the success or failure of that task)

he argued could be applied to any organisation. From a modern perspective, some of these now look like platitudes: for example, he argued that there should be 'discipline', 'order', 'subordination of the individual interest to the general interest' and *'esprit de corps'* (principles which are easier to espouse than to achieve). However, some of his other principles, in particular those relating to organisational structure, have withstood the test of time and are still employed by some consultants or internal management services departments (see *Figure 6.3*). Other writers who have developed a similar approach to that of Fayol are the American F.W. Mooney and the Englishman Col. Lyndal Urwick.

Alfred Sloan and General Motors

The third pioneer was Alfred P. Sloan (1875-1966) who built his reputation in General Motors, the largest manufacturer of motor vehicles in the world.

The General Motors Company was formed in 1908 by Billy Durant, a manufacturer of horse-drawn carriages and wagons who saw the shape of things to come and switched to the horseless variety. In 1906 he acquired ownership of the floundering Buick Motor Car Company and, within a year, had acquired three other car manufacturers (Oldsmobile, Cadillac and Pontiac) thus forming four of the main General Motors car divisions. Numerous other acquisitions of smaller companies, mainly in the automobile parts and accessories business followed in rapid succession.

Although Durant had an entrepreneurial flair for taking over companies, his abilities as an administrator were limited and, by 1910, he had overreached himself. General Motors was faced with its first financial crisis but was saved by a massive cash injection by a group of investment bankers. As part of the deal, Durant relinquished the management of the company.

Undaunted, Durant teamed up with a brilliant inventor, Louis Chevrolet and formed the Chevrolet Motor Company. By trading Chevrolet stock for General Motor shares, Durant slowly worked his way back into the company, and by 1916 he was ensconced as president and chief executive of General Motors and Chevrolet became the fifth major car division.

As a leader Billy Durant had inspirational, although often infuriating, qualities. He ran the total General Motors operation, massive as it was, on a mixture of intuition and guesswork. Large parts of the organisation were left to run themselves as Durant did not have time to pay attention to them. He perceived subordinates with ability as potential threats to his own leadership and treated them capriciously and rudely. One of them, Walter Chrysler, resigned in frustration, and formed his own company which was to become a major competitor of General Motors; another, Alfred Sloan, swallowed his pride and continued to work as best as he could in difficult circumstances (Sloan, 1965).

Unsurprisingly, given Durant's erratic style of leadership, General Motors was in serious financial trouble again in 1920 and Durant was forced to resign for the second, and final, time. As the company was floundering, Sloan studied its problems and prepared his 'Organisational Study': a corporate plan designed to turn around the company's fortunes. Sloan's plan was implemented by the acting president during the confusion following Durant's resignation. Within three years the company had been restored to financial viability, largely due to the 'Organisational Study' and, in recognition of this fact, Sloan was appointed as the new president of General Motors in 1923. Sloan was to become the epitome of a new generation of professional managers.

Under Durant, the numerous companies brought within the General Motors empire had continued to run themselves without much reference to the corporate headquarters staff based in Detroit. There were advantages in this system in that managers based in the constituent parts of the organisation could make decisions quickly and close to the facts. However, there were major disadvantages such as the lack of central control over cash flow: an accounting failure which was to be a major contribution to the financial crisis faced by the company (Sloan describes how headquarters accountants had to bargain with the operating divisions for the release of money for payment of central dividends and taxes). In contrast, the secret of Sloan's success in reviving the fortunes of the company was his formulation of the principle of 'co-ordinated decentralisation': a management philosophy which reconciled the need to retain firm control by headquarters staff over issues vital to the future of the organisation as a corporate body, with the need to allow managers in distant parts of the empire to make day-to-day operational decisions without too much interference from Detroit.

Sloan's influence on General Motors was all-pervasive and was to continue past his retirement in 1956. John DeLorean (who was a top executive and engineer with General Motors in the 1960s and 1970s) has described how various power factions within the corporation argued over the 'true' interpretation of Sloan's original organisational plan in the years after his retirement. In DeLorean's opinion, the delicate division of power at the top of the organisation between the 'finance' and 'executive' committees established by Sloan was lost, and, by the early 1970s the corporation was effectively being run by a new breed of financial experts rather than the engineers who had traditionally exerted a major influence on both policy and operational affairs. DeLorean attributed the relative decline of General Motors, in the face of

Figure 6.4
Some integrating themes of classical management theory

- The constant search for rationality or the 'one best way' as measured by efficiency criteria

- The high degree of specification of written policies, rules and regulations

- The firm belief in hierarchy and a policy-making process which is conducted by top management and then communicated to subordinates (a 'top down' approach)

- The belief that employees act in rational and predictable ways and are motivated at work by money ('economic man')

- The belief that organisations and machines are analogous and that organisations be made to function as smoothly as machines; and a corresponding disregard for the human and social aspects of organisation

- The attempt to mould people and their work to the needs of the organisation rather than the other way round

fierce competition from Japanese and European car manufacturers in the early 1970s, to bad decisions made by financial experts who lacked an intimate knowledge of the business of making cars (Wright, 1980).

However, the sheer size of General Motors allowed it to ride out such fluctuations in the market and Sloan's concept of 'co-ordinated decentralisation' still survives today. Note, for example, how the British companies Vauxhall and Bedford, although part of the General Motors empire and firmly controlled from Detroit, are allowed to keep their corporate names and identity.

Postscript

The work of Taylor and Fayol in particular, together with the work of later writers in the same tradition, is usually linked under the generic term *classical management*. The term is appropriate because, like classical music or poetry, classical management theory is long established (or old) and bound by a clear set of conventions or rules.

The effect of classical management on the standard of living enjoyed by the advanced industrial nations has been immense. The classical managers were at least partly responsible for the phenomenal increase in levels of production which occurred in the early part of the twentieth century. Ironically, the temporary hiccup of the Great Depression was partly attributable to the success of the new methods of production as the world's market and distribution systems could not accommodate the deluge of manufactured goods produced. Moreover the influence of classical management can still be seen in many British and American industrial organisations today. Modern management techniques such as operational research, materials requirements planning, and financial planning and budgeting are all underpinned by the ruthless, restless search for the 'one best way' of doing things started by the classical managers; or in more modern jargon, the search for the *optimum solution*.

However, many of the themes underlying classical management (see *Figure 6.4*) have been challenged by modern organisation theorists. We shall explore some of these criticisms next, with special reference to the organisation of engineering activities in British manufacturing industry.

Modern criticisms of the pioneers of management

Modern organisation theorists have four main criticisms of the pioneers of management. They argue that the widespread application of classical management ideas has led to:

1. inhuman working conditions and poor industrial relations

2. over-specialisation and restrictive working practices

3. bureaucratic organisational structures

4. inward-looking organisational structures.

Inhuman working conditions and poor industrial relations

The philosophy underlying classical management and scientific management, or 'Taylorism', in particular has long been attacked for the way in which it de-skills work and treats human beings like machines. A leader in the *Engineer* on 19th May 1911 complained that 'There are fair and unfair ways of diminishing labour costs. We do not hesitate to say that Taylorism is inhuman.'

Consequently, the introduction of Taylorism was often associated with industrial strife and poor labour relations. Skilled craftsmen perceived Taylorism as a direct attack on the autonomy and power they had traditionally enjoyed under more informal methods of organisation. Taylor claimed, with justification, that the introduction of his techniques to the Bethlehem Steel Company was trouble free and that the workforce actively welcomed his new approach. But this may have been due, in part, to the feeble position of the unions in the American iron and steel industry in the aftermath of the 1892 Homestead strike. In this major confrontation between management and unions, Andrew Carnegie, owner of the Homestead works in Taylor's home state of Pennsylvania, comprehensively defeated the Amalgamated Association of Ironworkers. This strike is notorious in American labour history for the role played by operatives of the Pinkerton detective agency, who were hired by Carnegie to infiltrate the ranks of the strikers, and the violent way in which it was brought to an end by the state militia.

However, there were serious industrial problems when Taylor's methods were introduced to a US Government arsenal. These were so bad that Taylor was summoned to explain the principles of scientific management to a special committee of the House of Representatives. Ironically, the publicity gained from reports of the proceedings of this committee served to make scientific management famous and hasten the spread of Taylorism to other American and European companies.

In Britain, too, the introduction of Taylorism caused problems. Price (1986) describes how, in the early 1900s, the London engineering firm of Thorneycrofts introduced a number of changes based on scientific management principles. Feed and speed charts were devised using work-study techniques and monitored by special supervisors. The old lax methods of clocking in were replaced by time clocks which allowed a two-minute grace period; and 'discipline men' marched around to see that work began as soon as the factory hooter sounded. The sharpening and grinding functions were hived off into a separate department according to the principle of specialisation. Visits to the lavatory were limited to seven minutes and the doors were taken off to discourage malingering.

The immediate result of these changes was passive resistance, sabotage and violence. Feed and speed charts were lost, the rules about access to the grinding department by workers were continually broken, work was spoiled when speed-ups were ordered and supervisors were harassed, bullied and sometimes assaulted. Yet this reaction came from what had previously been a deferential and respectable workforce. Eventually management was forced to back down, and although parts of the scheme dealing with the systematising of production were retained (and were to last for many years) its more repressive features were withdrawn.

The British motor industry provides an extended history of the negative aspects of scientific management and the tyranny of mass production (Overy and Pagnamenta, 1984). The British excelled in the production of beautifully engineered cars in small numbers at the beginning of the century. Then in 1911, Henry Ford built a new factory in Trafford Park, Manchester and introduced scientific management techniques to Britain. His British rivals were forced to compete and leaders of the industry such as William Morris travelled to the USA to study the new American management techniques. By the end of the 1920s the five main British manufacturers - Morris, Austin, Vauxhall, Rootes and Standard - had diluted the traditional craft skills of the industry and introduced job specialisation and flow production techniques. The industry paid little heed to the human cost of these changes, and prospered - albeit protected from the worst effects of American competition by protective trade tariffs.

In 1931 Ford built another new factory - this time a massive integrated production facility in Dagenham, Essex. This factory introduced the continuously moving production line to Britain. This was an innovation which created even more inhuman working conditions: an increase in noise, more pressure on workers as they struggled to keep up with the pace of the line, and more monotony and less skill. Ford also tightened up its already harsh autocratic management procedures. Security men and foremen patrolled the line making sure that company rules were enforced. Ford of Britain was exempt from the protective tariff and the home companies responded to the increase in competition by adopting similar techniques.

In the boom years after the Second World War the industry continued to prosper and the workers were compensated for the continuing monotony of their jobs by higher wage incentives. But job security was low and workers were laid off at will in response to fluctuations in the market. The industry's lack of concern for the human aspects of organisation was storing up industrial relations trouble for later years. The turning point occurred in the 1950s.

In 1952 the two biggest companies - Austin and Morris - merged to create the British Motor Corporation (BMC). Then, in 1956, BMC announced large-scale layoffs at the Morris factory in Cowley (Oxford) and the Austin factory at Longbridge (Birmingham). The men came out on strike and, although the company won in the short term, it was forced to concede many negotiating points to the unions. Chief among these was the introduction of 'closed shop' arrangements whereby only union members were allowed to work on certain jobs in the factory. From that point on, the company had effectively lost its 'right to manage'. The result was industrial anarchy in the 1960s as the company was plagued by poor relations between management and workforce and beset by industrial disputes. Looking back, we can see that classical management - and scientific management in particular - has contributed to a poor image of engineering activities.

Looking forward, new technology and robotics offer the opportunity for humanising work by taking over the most boring and uncomfortable jobs. This is certainly the route taken by Austin Rover - the nationalised company which has evolved, via several name changes, from BMC and which has invested millions in computer-controlled robots.

Over-specialisation and restrictive working practices

The long-term decline of the British shipbuilding industry can be attributed to the pushing of one of the central principles of classical management - specialisation or division of work - to extreme limits.

In the period 1900-14, British shipyards produced six out of ten of all the new ships in the world, based on frugal management and a specialised 'squad' system which would have delighted Taylor. Under this system, managers could employ, as and when needed, precisely the right number of men with the right skills from the thousands who lived in the back-to-back houses next to the yards along the great shipbuilding rivers of the Tyne, Mersey and Clyde. When the men had finished the specific task they had been hired for, they were laid off until they were needed again or could find work in another yard.

The extent of the specialisation practised by the squads is illustrated by the method adopted to rivet the steel plates from which the ships were constructed. First, a *plater* shaped the plate. Next, a *shipwright* filed it. Then a *heater* heated a rivet in a small coke fire before tossing the rivet to a *holder up* who bumped the rivet into the prepared hole in the plate and held it there with a long tool. Finally, two *riveters* - one left handed and one right handed - hammered the rivet in from opposite sides. The employment of two different-handed riveters was a brilliant, Taylorist solution to the challenge of finding the 'one best way' of operation: one riveter would have been able to work at only half the speed and two right handed riveters would have got in each other's way.

The squad system worked well within the limitations of existing technology. But there were problems when the management wanted to introduce new techniques and working practices. Firstly, chronic job insecurity prevented the men from identifying with the firm; instead they developed fierce group loyalty to their trade. This developed into a form of class warfare:

> 'Each trade seemed to have its own particular pride, and seemed to be very clannish. Electrical engineers thought they were better than boilermakers, they were more highly skilled. Boilermakers used to think they were the salt of the earth, because they literally built the ship, and if they didn't build the ship the engineers couldn't finish it' (joiner, quoted in Overy and Pagnamenta, 1984).

Secondly, fear that work, once lost, would be gone for ever because there was no transferability of skills between trades, caused men to hold on to existing work practices and resist the introduction of new technology.

Consequently the British shipbuilding industry, along with other industries which adopted a classical management style, has been plagued by demarcation disputes between groups of workers over which group was entitled to do what task. These reached levels of absurdity in the shipbuilding industry with disputes over who had the right to drill holes in different materials and who should draw a chalk line on a metal plate to mark where it should be cut. Yet it took until 1965 for the workers in what was left of the industry to be offered a reasonable level of job security. And only in 1988 did Harland and Wolfe of Belfast reach an agreement which removed all demarcation lines between skilled, semi-skilled and unskilled workers.

Many people have blamed these symptoms of poor industrial relations on the unions. On the other hand, it must be remembered that it was the management side who first introduced the specialisation and rigid working practices which are at the root of the problem.

Bureaucratic organisational structures

The German sociologist Max Weber was an academic observer of the development of large-scale industrial organisation in the late nineteenth and early twentieth centuries. He coined the term *bureaucracy* (based on the French word *bureau* for 'office') and applied it to this emergent form of organisation. Weber was not an enthusiastic advocate of bureaucracy but he did see it as

Figure 6.5
A chain of command (Jaques, 1976)

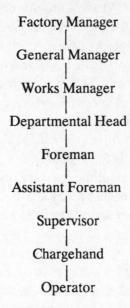

Factory Manager
|
General Manager
|
Works Manager
|
Departmental Head
|
Foreman
|
Assistant Foreman
|
Supervisor
|
Chargehand
|
Operator

the most rational way of organising and accepted it as part of an inevitable social trend.

Over the years classical management has become closely associated with bureaucracy and the two terms are often used synonymously. But few, if any, modern organisation-theorists would agree with Weber's conclusion that bureaucracy is the most rational, or the most efficient, way of organising. Today the term has mainly pejorative connotations.

One common criticism of bureaucratic organisations is their pathological tendency to develop tall organisational structures with long chains of command. To find out how this phenomenon occurs we need look no further than Fayol's principles of *span of control* and *unity of command*.

Management consultants brought up on Fayol's principles look for points in the organisational structure where spans of control are too wide - say a team of 12 workers reporting to one supervisor. According to the theory, a span of control of this size is too wide for the supervisor to monitor and control the work of his subordinates effectively. Typically, the solution recommended by the consultant would be to split the work group into two teams of six with one supervisor in charge of each team. In addition, to maintain the principle of unity of command he will need to recommend the creation of a new post of senior supervisor to supervise the work of the two supervisors.

There are two obvious and related disadvantages to this solution. Firstly, labour costs have gone up as 15 people are now employed where 13 were employed before (moreover, the two new posts created are more expensive, non-productive supervisory posts). Secondly, although unity of command has been preserved, the line of command has been lengthened and an extra layer in the hierarchy has been added. This process, repeated over and over again in countless organisations and over a period of many years has resulted in the inexorable growth of bureaucracy.

C. Northcote Parkinson (originator of Parkinson's Law that 'work expands to fill the time available for its completion') exposed the extent of this growth in British defence establishments. He discovered that the numbers employed in the Admiralty headquarters and dockyards expanded by 80 per cent in the period 1900-50 - a period when the number of ships and the officers and men who crewed them actually went down (Parkinson, 1965).

Many modern studies have drawn attention to the inefficiencies of bureaucratic structures and long lines of command. For example, Jaques (1976) describes an official chain of command in a factory with nine levels of hierarchy (see *Figure 6.5*). He was interested in finding out how this official chain worked in practice. So he posed the question: 'who is your manager?' to each individual in the chain. Jaques writes:

> 'if you ask the operator who is manager, he will probably ask if what you mean by his manager is his 'boss'. He will then want to know if you mean his 'boss' or his real 'boss'. The distinction here is between what the operator would call 'my real boss' - the one from whom he feels he stands a chance of getting a decision about himself - and the 'middlemen' or 'straw bosses' who are pushed in between him and his real boss, and through whom he must go if he wants to see his boss. The operator would then probably pick the assistant foreman or foreman as his real boss with the chargehand and supervisor (and possibly the assistant foreman) as middlemen or straw bosses.'

According to Jaques this is a classic situation where a bureaucracy has acquired too many hierarchical layers of organisation. He went on to identify a number of problems which are likely to occur as a result. These include poor communications between top and bottom, frequent 'by-passing' of the chain of command, lack of accountability ('passing the buck'), excessive 'red tape' and the stifling of discretion. Moreover, the extra layers of management lead to heavy administrative overheads (one recent study estimated that a manager's salary accounts for only about one third of his or her total employment costs).

Finally, tall bureaucratic structures and the consequent remoteness of management from shop floor has contributed to the pathological 'them and us' attitude in British industry:

'The tradition in the industry is of separate canteens, even separate toilets. It still exists today where on the toilet door you can see "Ladies" and "Gentlemen" on the staff side, and "Male" and "Female" on the shop floor. There are four canteens still today at British Aerospace, Manchester. There's a special mess for the directors, there's a mess for middle managers. Below them there's another mess for supervision, and ultimately the larger canteen on the shop floor. And yet when things go wrong the directors tell us we're all working for the same company. I can't square that circle' (supervisor in a Manchester aircraft factory, quoted in Overy and Pagnamenta, 1984).

Inward-looking organisation structures

The assertion that classical management theories neglect the interaction of organisations with the environment comes from the advocates of a 'systems theory' approach to the study of organisations.

A 'general systems theory' was first postulated by Von Bertalanffy in the 1960s. All engineers will be familiar with the second law of thermodynamics which states that 'it is impossible to make a machine which will continuously take heat from a heat source and, by itself, turn it all into an equivalent amount of mechanical work.'

This law means that all mechanical-based systems will eventually run out of energy and cease to function unless they are replenished or refuelled by an outside source. Yet this basic law of physics does not apply to biological or life processes. Living organisms, as long as they are in their correct environment, are able to replenish themselves by a process of constant interaction and interchange with their environment and thus become self-perpetuating.

Von Bertalanffy is credited with linking these conflicting laws of physics and biology by developing the concepts of 'closed' and 'open' systems. A closed system is one which is independent of its environment and where a steady state is achieved through chemical processes of degradation which can be explained by the laws of thermodynamics. When the system reaches its final steady state no further work can be obtained from it (an example of such a closed system is an electric battery which goes flat when the internal chemical reaction between acid and lead plates is completed). In contrast, an open system is continually in contact with its environment, importing energy, converting, and then exporting the transformed energy back to the environment. A steady state is still achieved but, unlike a closed system, continual change and adaptation is taking place and work is still carried out. One example of this phenomenon is the human cell which appears constant but is, in fact, continually renewing itself by importing appropriate chemicals from its environment - the bloodstream - and is always ready for any work required by the body (Von Bertalanffy, 1969).

General systems theory offered an attractive framework of thinking for the study of organisations. For example, it is clear that the classical management theorists treated organisations as closed, mechanical systems and consequently devoted most of their energies to the principles of internal design and control. They showed little, if any, concern for the relationship between the organisation and its environment. On the other hand, an open systems approach suggests that organisations should be sensitive to their environment. In particular companies need to be flexible and responsive in their direct interactions with customers, competitors, suppliers, financial institutions, the media, government agencies and so on. The top priority for management in these circumstances then becomes 'managing the boundary' between the organisation and its environment rather than internal matters.

The difference between open and closed systems can be illustrated by a comparison between British and Japanese industry. It has been suggested that the prime aim of most British manufacturing companies organised on classical management lines has been to reduce unit cost and improve internal efficiency. In contrast, manufacturers in Japan have traditionally emphasised other aims which are geared to the needs of the customer - such as product design, quality, reliability and prompt delivery. In other words, the British approach has been inward looking and symptomatic of a closed system while the Japanese approach has been outward looking and market driven - an open systems approach.

Systems theory tells us that the classical, closed system model can be effective as long as the environment - i.e. market conditions - is stable. And for many years, British industry was·in the fortunate position of operating in stable conditions with an assured market for its goods. In the first years after the Industrial Revolution there were no other industrialised countries and hence no competitors. Consequently, Britain's managers were able to do things their own way and concentrate on internal matters of production and control. But when Britain's competitors did arrive in the early twentieth century, they were much more aware of the external environment and of the importance of interaction with customers - in other words selling and marketing. However, British companies were able to shelter from competition behind the preferential agreements provided by the British Empire.

During the Great Depression of the 1930s the Government was forced to introduce tariffs to protect the home industry from the harsh reality of world markets. The Second World War arrived to save many British companies, and once again they were able to concentrate on all-out production without having to worry about a market for their goods. In the period immediately after the war the environment for manufacturing continued to be stable, as many of Britain's major rivals were temporarily out of action and there were extreme shortages of manufactured goods.

However, in the 1960s and 1970s the manufacturing environment changed. Britain's major rivals, including Germany and Japan, re-established their industrial bases and became even more competitive than before. In addition, the pace of technological change quickened and made the environment both more complex and more unpredictable.

In the 1980s manufacturing industry worldwide is facing increasingly fierce competition. Key material resources are becoming scarce and, as industrialisation spreads to the Third World, there are more manufacturers to compete for these resources. And while British Governments in the 1960s and 1970s had often intervened to prevent manufacturing companies from going bust (a policy of supporting so-called 'lame ducks'), the Conservative Government of the 1980s has pursued a strict policy of 'letting the market decide.' In these circumstances, few British manufacturing companies, apart from those left in a dwindling public sector or with secure defence contracts, are fortunate enough to operate in a stable environment with assured markets. Thus the closed-system, classical-management model of organisation is looking increasingly ill-adapted to the modern, turbulent environment.

The challenge for British industry in the 1980s and 1990s is to break away from bureaucratic forms of organisation into more organic forms based on a biological rather than a mechanistic metaphor. This is a conclusion that was shared by the Finniston Report (1980) which found that 'a common feature was a belief that the traditional hierarchical and compartmentalised organisations of companies was no longer appropriate for meeting marketing changes and other approaches to innovative activities in manufacturing were needed.' The report goes on to commend the various 'organic' types of team groupings which it found had replaced conventional organisation structures in some companies in the USA and Sweden.

Suggestions for further study

Most textbooks on management and organisation theory give detailed accounts of classical management theories. D. S. Pugh's edited collection of *Readings in Organisation Theory* is slightly different in that it gives extracts from the actual writings of such pioneers of classical management as Fayol and Taylor. Overy and Pagnamenta's book, *All Our Working Lives*, was written to support the BBC series of the same name. It charts the decline, and related industrial relations problems, of many major British industries in the twentieth century - often due to the unimaginative application of classical management principles. It is essential, if at times depressing, reading for engineers.

This chapter has been critical of many aspects of classical management. It is important that student engineers form their own opinions on this approach to management by evaluating the application of classical principles - such as span of control, unity of command, and specialisation - in organisations they work for or are familiar with.

Chapter 7

Modern Approaches to Organisational Design

The search for more organic models of organisation appropriate to the turbulent environment of today has led modern theorists to emphasise the importance of a concept linked to man's cultivation of the earth - *culture*. By culture we mean the rituals, values, ideas and laws which have been developed and shared by a whole society and which contribute to a general way of life. We can think of organisations as mini-societies which have their own distinctive patterns of *corporate culture*.

Modern theorists argue that bureaucratic organisations are fragmented and typically lack a unified corporate culture; rather they exhibit a series of sub-cultures built around different departments or professional groupings - often with conflicting goals. Thus it has been fashionable to argue that the main unifying feature of successful and non-bureaucratic organisations are strong corporate cultures. This assertion is backed up by evidence. Peters and Waterman (1982) carried out a survey of the most successful companies in America and concluded that they all placed great emphasis on 'getting the culture right'. Similarly, many commentators have attributed the phenomenal success of Japanese manufacturing industry in the 1970s and 1980s to strong national and corporate cultures.

The key to a strong culture is *simplicity*. The shared values which are at the root of a strong corporate culture must be easily understood if they are to influence the pattern of behaviour and thought of employees throughout the organisation. Peters and Waterman (1982) express this in their brash acronym KISS - 'Keep It Simple, Stupid.'

In this chapter we shall explore the theme of 'getting the culture right' with special reference to the much admired *Japanese Management Approach* and an idealised American model - *In Search of Excellence*. We shall then examine how these principles have been applied in some manufacturing companies in Europe and explore a new type of organisation - the *Federal Or-*

ganisation - which is emerging in response to harsh market conditions and the impact of information technology.

The Japanese management approach

Sayle (1982) has attributed much of the success of the Japanese style of management to a unique *national* culture. He argues that the focus of traditional Japanese village life has been the communal production of rice - a process which calls for intensive team spirit. Thus conformity and tradition have become important values at the heart of a 'rice culture' which has survived the transition to industrial society and accounts, in part, for the harmonious labour relations enjoyed by Japanese industry.

But if national culture were the only factor it would be impossible to transplant the Japanese approach into Western organisations. Japanese companies have opened factories in Britain and America and achieved impressive results with indigenous workforces. For example the Sony factory in San Diego, California has productivity and efficiency levels comparable to its Japanese counterparts. In 1986 General Motors cancelled orders for $80 million worth of robots and automation because their joint venture factory with Toyota, based in California, achieved twice the productivity of their other plants without using robots (*Financial Times*, 1987). In Britain, Japanese companies have successfully settled in Wales (Aiwa, Hitachi, Sony and Matsushita) and North East England (Nissan and Komatsu).

Takeo Fujiswawa, one of the founders of the Honda Motor Company has been quoted as saying 'Japanese and American management is 95% the same and differs in all important aspects' (Parker, in Pascale and Athos, 1986). One interpretation of this enigmatic statement is that while the techniques and technologies are basically the same in the two countries, the philosophy underlying their application is qualitatively different.

While Western companies rarely look beyond the end-of-year balance sheet presented to the shareholders, Japanese companies take a wider perspective. Pascale and Athos (1986) suggest that the outward-looking nature of the massive Matsushita Electric Company is linked to the company philosophy as articulated by its founder, Konosuke Matsushita:

'A business should quickly stand on its own based on the service it provides to society. Profits should not be a reflection of corporate greed but a vote of confidence from society that what is offered by the firm is valued.'

An emphasis on style, quality and service to the customer flows naturally from this philosophy.

The orientation to service is illustrated by the company's 'followship' strategy. From the outset, Matsushita has been more concerned with following its competitors (and out-performing them with higher quality and lower priced products) than originating products. Pascale and Athos (1986) describe the company's concept of Research and Development as 'analysing competing products and figuring out how to do better'. And the company channels massive resources into this activity. Take the battle for dominance in the world video cassette recorder market.

Sony pioneered this technology and established the brand name *Betamax* as the industry standard for tapes. Their position looked unassailable. But Matsushita's market surveys indicated that consumers wanted longer (4-6 hour) tapes rather than the 2-hour Betamax tapes. After intensive research and development Matsushita designed a compact recorder which met this need, was highly reliable, and was priced 10 per cent to 15 per cent below its competitor. Today Matsushita, selling under the *Panasonic* and *RCA* labels, manufactures two out of every three videos sold throughout the world, and consumers who bought Betamax machines find it increasingly difficult to find compatible tapes for their machines.

Another theme of Japanese management is simplicity. A Japanese metaphor for the production process is a river in flood (Open University 1988a). On the river bed are the business problems causing waste and hold-ups, such as long machine set-up times, poor quality, and long manufacturing lead times. But these problems are not apparent because of the depth of the water. In the analogy, the water is the stock of raw materials (inventory) held 'just in case' (a common Western practice). The rocks must be exposed before they can be removed and so the level of water in the river must be lowered. Thus the Japanese aim to keep the level of inventory as low as possible in order to make any problems on the production line apparent. Production then has to be on a 'just in time' process (JIT) with supplies delivered just before they are needed - Nissan keeps only just over a day's stock throughout its system and schedules its supplies by computer link to arrive every 20 minutes. JIT means that set-up times must be kept short, queues eliminated, zero defects demanded from suppliers and equipment maintenance must be constant and effective. Thus the Japanese have invested less in complex planning and control systems than Western companies and opted instead for simple, flexible systems that respond quickly to demand fluctuations.

The Japanese have also applied the principle of simplicity to the design of organisational structures. They have achieved this by indoctrination and socialisation processes which are geared to creating a strong corporate culture. This culture binds management and workers together and allows management to operate with much wider spans of control and flatter organisational structures than equivalent Western companies.

The companies achieve a strong culture by creaming off the best applicants (as measured by their moderate views and harmonious personality as much as by their technical ability or intelligence) from the thousands of young school and college leavers who are attracted by the status of working for a major company and the guarantee of life-time employment. The new employee will never have worked for another company and will almost certainly be male. He does not expect and will not get early promotion; instead the new employee will gain experience in a variety of different departments over a period of years rather than months.

This practice offers the company two main advantages. Firstly, the extended apprenticeship gives plenty of time for the employee to become indoctrinated to company norms and expectations. Secondly, the company will benefit later from the employee's flexibility - the ability to do a wide range of jobs and to fit into the work of other departments when necessary. Only later, after many years of loyal service, is the employee likely to be considered for promotion. His acceptance of this slow rate of promotion is encouraged by the fact that he has a life-time commitment to the company - thus the Western obsession with 'getting to the top' seems less pressing.

But a lesser known aspect of Japanese company life is that the much vaunted promise of life-time employment applies only to a core of trusted, male employees who are allowed within the company family. Outside the family, although still employed by the company, are large numbers of women and other peripheral workers who enjoy no security of employment and who can be sacked and re-employed according to the needs of production. Similarly, large Japanese companies sub-contract a lot of their work out to small companies whose workers enjoy little or no job security and suffer low wages and poor working conditions. When times are hard the large companies recall this work into the core and thus keep their life-time employees fully occupied.

But the privileged workers in the core must be prepared to be flexible. Pascale and Athos (1986) describe how assembly line workers in the Matsushita corporation had to leave the factory and start selling the company's products from door to door during a particularly severe recession in 1970.

'In search of excellence'

Peters and Waterman (1982) analysed the characteristics of a sample of American companies which had one factor in common: they were all highly successful in their particular market area - companies such as IBM, Delta Airlines, Du Pont (chemicals), McDonalds and Proctor and Gamble. From this analysis, they formulated a list of eight key attributes or principles which were characteristic of all these companies (see *Figure 7.1*).

The 'excellent' company, as constructed by Peters and Waterman, is an open system, organic model which is market driven and innovative. Recurring themes are simplicity and getting 'back to the basics'. Thus they argue that management's key role is to set the core values and direction which decide the corporate culture, rather than indulging in complicated and sophisticated planning and objective-setting exercises (which often go wrong anyway). If top management can 'get the culture right' then the correct objectives and targets will evolve naturally.

Computer integrated manufacturing

The European and American car manufacturing industries have been among those most affected by competition from Japan. Indeed a top executive with Ford of Europe has commented that in recent years 'the competitive threat from the Japanese has dominated our business life' (Open University, 1988b). Ford's response has been to combine the Peters and Waterman approach with the advantages of modern Computer Integrated Manufacturing (CIM) techniques.

Most manufacturing organisations consist of the five sub-systems of marketing, engineering and production, materials management, finance and accounting, and personnel. In a healthy organisation, the various sub-systems are connected by effective information and communication systems which, pursuing an organic metaphor, act as the 'nerves' of the organisation. In a small entrepreneurial organisation these connections are easily made. The

Figure 7.1
The eight key attributes of excellent companies (Peters and Waterman, 1982)

Bias for Action:
> an action orientation is helped by organisation fluidity, informal communications, acceptance of by-passing the chain of command, short-lived project teams and the willingness to move resources quickly to where they are needed to solve problems

Closeness to the Customer:
> all successful companies listen carefully to and involve their present and future customers

Autonomy and Entrepreneurship:
> 'champions' of new ideas are not seen as trouble makers but are given scope to take some risks (if a new idea does not work it can be dropped like a stone and something else tried) - innovation requires decentralised management systems and wide spans of control

Productivity through People:
> all the techniques of human relations (short of actual democracy) are employed to build employee involvement and initiative

Hands-on Value Driven:
> management should set and tightly control the core values and purposes of the organisation which set the culture (e.g. what business are we in?), and targets will then evolve naturally

Stick to the Knitting:
> do not take on extra functions which are not related to core values and purposes of the organisation

Simple Form-Lean Staff:
> structural arrangements and systems are simple, with small headquarters staff; complex structures like matrix or long chains of command should be avoided at all costs

Simultaneous Loose-Tight Properties:
> values and norms should be controlled centrally but operational decision decentralised; note that wide spans of control are possible if the culture is consistent - employees will know how to respond to different circumstances almost intuitively

organisational structure is simple and communications are informal and direct. But in large bureaucratic organisations the structure is typically complicated and inter-departmental barriers and 'red tape' can interrupt the free flow of information throughout the organisation, creating inefficiencies and dysfunctions. This situation has not been helped by the piecemeal introduction of new technology which has created 'islands of automation' in different departments in the factory. Thus the computer systems in the warehouse and offices are unconnected and are themselves incompatible with the computer-controlled machines and robots on the shop floor. CIM offers the exciting prospect of linking all these diverse sub-systems by providing an uninterrupted flow of electronic information throughout the organisation.

When executives at the Ford plant in Cologne considered the introduction of CIM in an attempt to boost efficiency levels to Japanese levels they started by defining three strategic 'visions' (Open University 1988b). These were that the company must:

1. bring a quality product to the market faster

2. be a high-quality, low-cost manufacturer

3. get much closer to the customer.

The concept of 'visions' was new and alien to a traditionally hard, mechanistic organisation like Ford. Sceptics within the company argued that the word vision was 'not a Ford expression'. However, CIM has allowed the concept to become reality.

Under the old system, ideas for new designs were modelled in clay by the Product Development Group and passed to the Manufacturing Department. The engineers in Manufacturing made engineering drawings of the model and then made more models to test the new design. In other words the design stages went from 3D to 2D and then back to 3D. The system was reactive and cumbersome.

Manufacturing would pass their comments on the design back to Product Development who would incorporate them into a revised design to be passed to manufacturing and so on. By using Computer Aided Design (CAD) as part of the overall CIM process, the new system can carry forward a geometric model in three dimensions which can be used to mill the surface of the vehicle automatically on to the dies without building intermediate models. The gains are both in quality (through the elimination of human interpretation errors) and time (the new system took three months out of the lead time from the design to the market place).

The company was not content with integrating just its internal operations. Computer links have been forged with its suppliers and dealers so that an order can be processed electronically by a dealer and passed automatically through sales scheduling to material requirements planning. Then the suppliers can be contacted electronically to tell them what parts are to be delivered 'just in time' (JIT) for production - thus eliminating the need for buffer stocks and inventory (note the similarity with Japanese practice). Finally, the electronic information is processed by the shop-floor computers so that the robots can be told which vehicle is coming along the line and which weld sequence is required.

The most startling feature of CIM is that a large engineering manufacturer can now adapt as quickly and flexibly as a small company. CIM also means that mass producers like Ford no longer need to dictate to their customers - as in Henry Ford's apocryphal quote: 'you can have any colour as long as it's black.' Instead CIM offers the prospect of 'bespoke engineering' to the mass consumer and enterprises which are truly 'close to the customer' and market driven.

The Jaguar turn-around

Another example of the 'back to the basics' approach is a success story of British engineering in the 1980s - the turn-around of *Jaguar Cars* (Goldsmith and Clutterbuck, 1985).

In 1975, as part of the nationalised Leyland Cars group, Jaguar had lost its identity. The Jaguar flags were removed from the factory entrance; and telephonists were prohibited from greeting callers with 'good morning, Jaguar Cars' (instead they had to say 'good morning, Leyland Cars - Large Assembly Plant Number One'). Furthermore, the two constituent Jaguar factories were reorganised into separate Leyland Divisions (the Power and Transmission and the Body and Assembly Divisions).

Sir Michael Edwardes, brought in by the Government to sort out Leyland, decided that the company had to bring back the famous marque names owned by Leyland (such as Jaguar, Rover, Land-Rover, Austin, and Morris) as a focus for employee and customer loyalty. Consequently he allowed John

Egan, chief executive at Jaguar, the freedom to recreate the corporate culture and ethos that had surrounded the Jaguar name before nationalisation.

One of the first things Egan did was to reinstate an old Jaguar tradition of holding family nights and open days so that friends and relatives of the workforce could feel involved with the company. He also set about improving communications by instituting a programme of company social events and arranging face-to-face meetings between shop floor and management at which videos highlighting the company's progress and problems were shown.

In line with the principle of 'closeness to the customer', samples of existing Jaguar customers, on both sides of the Atlantic, were followed up and interviewed to check their level of satisfaction with their car. These customer surveys highlighted the fact that poor quality was a major factor in the company's unsatisfactory performance at that time.

Egan decided that improving quality must become the overriding company concern. Thus strict standards of quality for employees and suppliers were laid down and enforced. Employees were encouraged to meet in small groups known as 'quality circles' to discuss and decide on ways of improving quality (see *Chapter 8*). Finally, Egan set up multi-disciplinary task forces, chaired by Jaguar directors, to cure the recurring faults (in line with an open systems approach, these task forces included representatives from suppliers as well as Jaguar employees). As a result of these measures, and a drastic programme of redundancies to cut overmanning, a transformation in the fortunes of the company was effected.

Contracting out

One way of achieving the simplicity which is a prerequisite for the creation of a strong corporate culture is holding firmly only to those activities which are essential to the company's main goals - 'sticking to the knitting' - and contracting out all the less essential activities. This process has been helped considerably by the advent of new information technology, which has made it cheaper and easier to move information around rather than people. Consequently, in the 1980s, we have seen the evolution of the ultimate open, organic system model in response to the turbulent environment of the times. This new organisational type has been described as the 'federal organisation' (Handy, 1985).

Traditionally, bureaucracies have set up prestigious head offices staffed with full-time specialists of almost every kind. In contrast, the federal organisation seeks to limit its full-time employees to the minimum 'core' of people directly needed to manage, provide and sell the company's products or services. Less directly important activities are relegated to the 'periphery' of the organisation and are given to temporary or part-time workers, or are sub-contracted to other companies or individuals (once again note the similarity with the Japanese style of management).

The main feature of the federal organisation is that it is no longer easy to define the line which delimits where the organisation begins, as many people who carry out the activities of the organisation are not directly employed by it. Peters (1988) has described this new type of organisation as 'fuzzy' around the edges.

The experience of being relegated to the periphery is not confined to unskilled and semi-skilled workers. Many companies now prefer to hire outside consultants when they need to call on professional expertise rather than have highly paid specialists available in house. Thus, personnel specialists, accountants, systems analysts, company lawyers, engineers and so on are likely to find themselves working on a self-employed basis or for a small firm of consultants.

The economic recession in Britain in 1981 and 1982 provided a major stimulus to the federal organisation. In these two years, British companies sacked thousands of full-time workers. When economic recovery came the companies were reluctant to take the risk of re-employing people on a full-time basis. Hence the massive growth in the peripheral or 'flexible' work force - part-time, temporary and self-employed workers. Hankin (1987) reports that in the three years from 1983 to 1986, the flexible workforce in Britain grew by almost one million jobs, or 13 per cent. Thus, in 1986 there were 8.2 million people working who were not in full-time permanent jobs compared with 15.6 million working full-time; in other words nearly one third of all workers are now in the flexible work force. Women make up nearly two thirds of this new 'breed' of worker (see *Figure 7.2*).

Admittedly, most of these new workers are in industries such as construction, retailing and catering where there is a tradition of part-time working and sub-contracting. But these patterns of working are now making a major impact in manufacturing industry - although the companies involved are reluctant to advertise this trend.

Figure 7.2
A comparison of female and male patterns of employment (*Employment Gazette*, 1987)

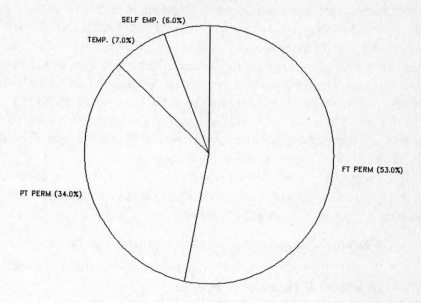

FEMALES

SELF EMP. (6.0%)

TEMP. (7.0%)

FT PERM (53.0%)

PT PERM (34.0%)

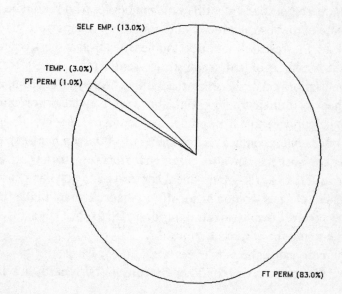

MALES

SELF EMP. (13.0%)

TEMP. (3.0%)
PT PERM (1.0%)

FT PERM (83.0%)

The federal organisation

The changes instituted in one plant of a major British company (which we shall call 'CGM Fibre Optics') are typical of the move to the federal organisation. In 1981, CGM employed 700 people in the manufacture of high-technology, high-value telecommunications equipment for foreign governments. The organisation structure was complicated and bureaucratic and labour relations were poor. In the economic climate of the time the plant management faced a stark choice: reorganise to produce a leaner and fitter structure or close the plant. The company decided on the first course of action and over the next two years 350 people were sacked as the company shrank to half its previous size. Those who were sacked received generous redundancy payments which lessened the pain and, more important from the company's point of view, neutralised opposition from the unions.

In deciding who to retain and who to sack, the company applied the federal model. Starting with a fundamental review of their business strategy the company posed three simple questions:

1. Who are the people who give us a competitive edge in our market?

2. Who are the people with skills specific to our company who would be difficult or expensive to replace?

3. Who are the people who could seriously damage our business if they joined a competitor?

The answers to these questions identified the employees who should be retained in the core of the restructured organisation. Two groups were identified straightaway: the research and development team and the sales and marketing team. Members of both teams were essential to the long-term future of the organisation and its success in the market. Moreover the company had invested heavily in their training. But, above all, they had information which would be highly valuable to a competitor: details of top secret designs and vital lists of customer contacts. Some members of the top management team and other key workers were also identified for inclusion in the core. All these staff were offered pay rises, permanent contracts, and 'top hat' pension schemes designed to act as 'golden handcuffs' to manacle them to the firm. In addition they received extensive retraining designed to hone key skills and indoctrinate them into the corporate culture.

Outside the core came the employees who did not have 'firm specific' skills and whom the company was confident of replacing fairly easily in a time of high unemployment. The 'first periphery' contained the production workers who were classed as semi-skilled. Most of these were sacked and then re-employed on a contract basis. The company compensated them for the erosion of their conditions of service by virtually doubling their pay. An important aim was to neutralise the unions, but the company also wanted a motivated and satisfied workforce and, because of the long term economies achieved by the restructuring, was prepared to pay for it. Also in the first periphery, were draughtsmen, clerical workers, computer operators and so on - all now employed on temporary contracts or working part-time.

In the 'second periphery' were workers who are now not even employed directly by the company. These included some chartered and technician engineers who had previously been laid off from the company but who now found themselves working in their old jobs but employed by an agency. Other staff employed by employment agencies are cleaners, caterers and additional clerical and computer staff.

Finally, in a 'third' periphery are the ranks of consultants who are called in from time to time to help the company: accountants, management consultants, training consultants, executive search agencies ('head hunters'), technical authors, public relations consultants, and so on.

The revised management structure of CGM exhibits Peters and Waterman's 'simple form, lean structure'. Only four department heads now report to the site controller. These are:

- Technical Manager (design and maintenance)
- Production Manager
- External Relations Manager (sales and marketing)
- Internal Relations Manager (personnel and administration).

The new structure has dramatically cut the company's employment costs and given it a new flexibility of response to changing environmental conditions. In times of economic recession the company can retract its boundary without incurring any redundancy costs, by sacking its part-time workers and not renewing the contracts of their contract staff and agency workers. If the recession is severe, the privileged workers in the core may have to accept retraining and redeployment, but in most cases their jobs are safe.

We have discussed the advantages to the management of CGM Fibre Optics of the revised structure. But how do the workers and ex-workers see the change to a federal organisation? It would be misleading to pretend that the changes pushed through by the company did not cause anguish and disruption in many people's lives, or to disguise the fact that many workers now find themselves with inferior conditions of work. Nevertheless there are advantages for workers - even in the less privileged periphery.

Production workers have lost job security but have been compensated by much higher wages. The job security which they enjoyed previously may have been illusory anyway - as many British workers in low-performing, bureaucratic companies have discovered. And many people, particularly women, welcome the opportunity that part-time working gives to combine paid employment and domestic work. This is confirmed by the results of a national survey (Hakim, 1987) which found that two-thirds of all part-time workers prefer part-time work, and only 10 per cent would prefer to have (and are available for) a full-time job. At higher levels, many workers, including male and female Chartered Engineers, enjoy the greater freedom and independence of working on a contract basis in a way which is more appropriate to their professional status. Working for fees rather than wages means that they can enjoy a more equal, 'adult to adult' relationship with the management of the company as opposed to the traditional superior to subordinate, 'parent to child' relationship. And some have been able to start up their own businesses or private practices to operate during the time when they are not contracted to the company.

Conclusion

A common feature of the new organisation types we have discussed has been the breaking down of departmental barriers and the overturning of bureaucracy. Peters (1988) has described this organisation of now and the future as: 'Flexible, porous, adapting, fleet of foot ... every person is "paid" to be obstreperous, a disrespector of formal boundaries, a hustler fully engaged in engendering swift action and constantly improving everything.'

Computer Integrated Manufacture also integrates people. Ford of Cologne now talks about 'simultaneous engineering' whereby multi-disciplinary teams of engineers work jointly on product design and manufacturing process design - with technology as the catalyst which brings them together. In Ford these teams cross national as well as departmental barriers.

In these new corporate structures and cultures a new style of leadership is needed which is less hierarchical and less autocratic than that practised by the pioneers of management whose work we examined in *Chapter 6*. The new approach emphasises the importance of flexibility, participation and effective team work.

Suggestions for further study

Peters and Waterman's *In Search of Excellence* was the best-selling book on management in the 1980s, but the key principles contained in it - such as 'closeness to the customer' and 'productivity through people' - show no sign of going out of date. We suggest that all student engineers measure the organisations they work for (or visit on work-experience placements) against Peters and Waterman's eight key attributes.

Pascale and Athos, *The Art of Japanese Management*, gives a fascinating insight into organisational life in the electronics giant Matsushita.

Not much has been written on the now emerging form of organisation, 'federal organisation' - partly because companies are reluctant to admit they are applying this approach. However, Charles Handy provides a useful description of it in *Understanding Organisations*. His earlier book, *The Future of Work*, is also relevant to this discussion.

Chapter 8

Team Leadership

An underlying theme of this book is that engineers must play a more prominent leadership role in the community and in the organisations they work for,
thus contributing to the raising of the status of engineering in society. But
what is leadership? And are good leaders born or made? The answers to these
questions are difficult to pin down, as successful leadership is multi-dimen-
sional. Let us examine here the key characteristics and skills of leadership
under four main headings:

    1. leadership motivation and team building

    2. the power of the group

    3. leadership style

    4. leadership and organisational structure

Leadership motivation and team building

An engineer's education and training provides an excellent foundation for
leadership. The Engineering Council has commented that:

> 'Engineers are taught to quantify and to measure, to appreciate the de-
> gree of accuracy of information, to understand that there often has to be
> a trade off between conflicting requirements. They know that decisions
> have to be taken to a time scale, that the product must be reliable, and
> meet the customer's needs and be at a price at which they will pay. The
> education and training of engineers provides a broad base on which to
> make judgements on a wide range of imprecise issues and with limited
> knowledge of all the facts. This provides a sound vocational base on which
> to build management and business skills' (Engineering Council, 1988d).

But engineers have no automatic right to become managers. They will only succeed if they develop basic leadership qualities in addition to their proven technical expertise and skills.

Job advertisements which attempt to define the personal qualities needed by a leader or manager usually include such words as:

Integrity	Drive	Enthusiasm
Ambition	Enterprise	Single-mindedness
Imagination	Courage	Sensitivity
Decisiveness	Sense of humour	Stamina
Good judgement	Intelligence	Presence.

If we find a leader with all or most of these qualities we might talk about someone who has *charisma* (a term derived from the Greek word meaning someone with 'godlike' qualities). However, there is no practical method for measuring this elusive quality and our judgements on whether someone has charisma remain largely intuitive.

Leadership motivation

We are on firmer ground when we talk about the sources of motivation which *drive* a good leader. McClelland (1961) argues that most people have three primary needs:

1. the need for *achievement*

2. the need for *affiliation*

3. the need for *power*.

The need for achievement is essential for the modern engineer as this is associated with an obsession with meeting standards of excellence and a desire to be successful in competition. According to Buchanan and Huczynski (1985), people who have a high need for achievement also tend to have the following characteristics:

1. they prefer jobs in which they get frequent and clear feedback on how well they are doing, to help them perform better

2. they prefer jobs that involve moderate risks of failure - low risk activities do not give them a challenge or an opportunity to demonstrate skill and ability

3. they have a good memory for unfinished tasks and do not like to leave things incomplete

4. they can be unfriendly and unsociable when they want to prevent others getting in the way of their performance

5. they have a sense of urgency, always appear to be in a hurry, and have an inability to relax.

However, people with a very high need for achievement may become too individualistic to be successful in modern engineering enterprises where team work and co-operation are essential. Thus good leaders, in this environment, have to temper their high need for achievement with a sensitivity towards others. The type of person most likely to have this ability is someone with a high need for affiliation.

Individuals with a high need for affiliation will tend to be more concerned with developing and maintaining relationships than with decision-making. These people are often regarded as well-meaning but ineffective, probably because they are not sufficiently task-orientated. Some need for affiliation is present in most people, but it is seldom dominant in successful leaders.

Finally, some degree of need for power combined with a high need for achievement and a reasonable need for affiliation, is essential for the successful leader. But, by itself, a high need for power can lead to an unimaginative and autocratic management style which is of little value in modern organisations.

Traditionally, psychologists have assumed that motives such as achievement, affiliation and power are developed only in childhood and, once formed, nothing much can be done to alter them. However, McClelland and his research group have had some success in running *achievement development* courses which include three primary goals (among others):

1. to teach participants how to think, talk and act like a person with high achievement

2. to stimulate participants to set higher, but carefully planned and realistic goals for themselves over the next two years

3. to give the participants knowledge about themselves.

These goals, of course, could form part of an engineer's programme of continued education and training (see *Chapter 2*).

Managing conflict and building effective teams

The well-known saying, 'too many Chiefs and not enough Indians', expresses the problems which are likely to face a group which contains too many people with high needs for achievement and power. Such a group is unlikely to function effectively as a team as it will be riven with internal conflicts. Johnson and Johnson (1982) argue that the relative importance of two fundamental drives dictates the way people behave in such situations. These drives are:

1. to achieve personal goals - conflicts occur because our individual goals conflict with another's; goals may be highly important to us, or they may be of little importance

2. to keep a good relationship with other people - we may need to be able to work with the same people in the future; relationships may be very important to us, or they may be of little importance.

Johnson and Johnson go on to suggest that four main personality types stem from the four possible combinations of the two drives.

1. Relationships - low importance
   Goals - low importance

This personality type gives up personal goals and relationships at the first sign of trouble and seeks to avoid conflict wherever possible. Johnson and Johnson describe them as *turtles* who withdraw into their shell at the first opportunity.

2. Relationships - high importance
   Goals - low importance

Personal relationships are more important to people of this type and they will readily give up their goals to placate others and smooth things over. Johnson and Johnson describe them as *teddy bears*.

3. Relationships - low importance
   Goals - high importance

This is a *shark*. A person who will ruthlessly pursue his or her own goals even if it means trampling on other people's ideas. These people do not mind courting unpopularity as personal relationships are unimportant to them.

4. Relationships - high importance
Goals - high importance

This type of person makes a good team leader. They see conflict as a problem to be solved and an opportunity to find a solution which achieves both their own goals and the goals of other people. Johnson and Johnson characterise them as *owls*.

An effective team is likely to contain all four types of person. Teddy bears and owls will help the leader build team spirit and good relationships within the group and sharks and owls will help focus the group on goals and tasks. Turtles are not much good to anyone but the good leader will want to encourage them to come out of their shells and make a contribution to the team's work.

All engineers who aspire to be good team leaders should subject themselves to a process of self, peer and mentor evaluation to assess their own position in Johnson and Johnson's classification and amend their behaviour accordingly. If they are sharks they will need to listen more carefully to other team members' ideas and be careful not to dismiss them out of hand. If they are teddy bears, they will need to be more assertive when putting their ideas across to other members of the team.

A more sophisticated version of Johnson and Johnson's classification of how people behave in teams is provided by Belbin (1981). He argues that variety is essential to teams working in an environment where rapid change is involved in the workforce, the technology, the market place or the product and has defined a list of eight team roles which are essential in such an environment (see *Figure 8.1*). In small teams, one person may have to perform more than one role; and in more stable environments, groups may be able to get by without the full set of roles. Belbin's model is a valuable tool for the team leader who is in the process of a putting a team together.

Action-centred leadership

The effective leader is driven by a balanced collection of motives. Adair (1988) has developed a model of leadership which encapsulates this principle and which has become known as Action-Centred Leadership. Adair argues that all teams have three areas of need:

1. to achieve the common task (task needs)

Figure 8.1
Eight roles in an effective team (Belbin, 1981)

The Chairperson

... presides over the team and co-ordinates its efforts. He is not necessarily brilliant or creative, but is disciplined and well organised, talks and listens well, and has good judgement. Constantly balances the needs of the group against the needs of the task and in this way shares the characteristics of Johnson and Johnson's owl.

The Shaper

... is highly strung, outgoing and dominant. He is the task leader and - given the chance - would take over the role of the chairperson (and might prove to be very good at it). His strength lies in his drive and his passion for work, and he is valuable as a spur to action. But he can be over-sensitive, irritable and impatient. Johnson and Johnson would call this person a shark.

The Plant

... is more introverted than the shaper but is intellectually dominant. Imaginative and the main source of original ideas and proposals in the group, he can however be careless of details and may resent criticism. This person needs to be drawn out or will switch off.

The Monitor Evaluator

... is also intelligent, but in an analytic rather than creative way. This person's contribution is the careful dissection of ideas and proposals and the ability to see the flaw in an argument. Dependable but can be tactless and cold. The character of Mr Spock in the classic TV series *Star Trek* is a good example of the monitor evaluator.

The Resource Investigator

... is a popular member of the team, who is extrovert, sociable and relaxed. He brings new contacts, ideas and developments to the group but is not original or forceful, and therefore needs the team to pick up his contribution.

The Company Worker

... is the organiser who converts ideas into practical tasks. He enjoys working on schedules, charts and plans, is no leader but is methodical and efficient.

The Team Worker

... holds the team together by being supportive to others. He is likeable, popular and uncompetitive; and the team does not feel right when this person is not there. He is Johnson and Johnson's teddy bear.

The Finisher

... without this person the team would miss important deadlines. He checks details, worries about schedules and instills a sense of urgency into the others. His role is important but sometimes resented by the others.

Figure 8.2
A leader's checklist (Adair, 1988)

1. Set the task of the team; put it across with enthusiasm and remind people of it

2. Instruct all leaders in the importance of the task, team, and individual. Make leaders accountable for teams of 4-15

3. Plan the work, pace its progress and design jobs to encourage the commitment of individuals and teams

4. Set individual targets after consulting, discuss progress with each person regularly but at least once a year

5. Delegate decisions to individuals. Consult those affected

6. Communicate the importance of each person's job; explain decisions to help people apply them; brief team monthly on progress, policy and people

7. Train and develop people, especially those under 25; gain support for the rules and procedures, set an example and 'have a go' at those who break them

8. Where unions are recognised, encourage joining attendance at meetings, standing for office and speaking up for what each person believes is in the interest of the task, team and individual

9. Care about the well-being of people in the team, improve working conditions, deal with grievances and attend functions

10. Monitor action; learn from successes and mistakes; regularly walk round each person's place of work, observe, listen and praise

2. to stay together and remain as a cohesive group (group maintenance needs)

3. to satisfy the individual needs of people in the group (individual needs).

If there is a failure to satisfy any one of these areas of needs, the group will become ineffective. If the group fails in its task, individuals will become dissatisfied and disillusioned and the group will begin to disintegrate. If there is a lack of unity or harmonious relationships within the group, progress towards the achievement of the task will be slow and individual needs will not be satisfied. Finally, if an individual feels frustrated and unhappy he will not be able to make a fully effective contribution to either the common task or to the life of the group.

Thus Adair argues that every leader has simultaneously to:

1. develop the individual

2. build and maintain the team

3. achieve the task.

All three activities overlap; none is more important than another. The model has stood the test of time and has been used as a basis for many training courses in 'group dynamics' and leadership skills. It also explains why, in the last analysis leadership is a lonely job. There must always be an area of social distance between the leader and the team because there will inevitably be occasions when the leader has to take tough decisions in the *task* area which will have a bad effect on *individual* and *group* motivation and temporarily lower the leader's popularity.

In order to help organisations as well as individuals develop more effective leadership, the *Industrial Society* has developed ten guidelines for the leader based on Adair's ideas (see *Figure 8.2*).

The power of the group

The army has long known of the importance of the power of the group as a means of motivating men. In answer to the question: 'what drives a man in battle?' General Sir John Hackett, has been quoted as saying, 'you can forget patriotism, loyalty to the regiment, pay and promotion - what counts is not letting his mates down'.

The first academic recognition of the power of the group as a source of motivation can be traced back to a series of studies conducted in the Hawthorne Plant of the Western Electric Company in Chicago in the 1930s. These studies were led by Elton Mayo of Harvard University and spawned a new approach to management which became known as the 'human relations' movement. Elton Mayo is widely acknowledged as the 'founding father' of this movement which set out to challenge the supremacy of the classical managers. Indeed, Mayo described the Taylorist or scientific management approach (see *Chapter 6*) as a 'rabble hypothesis'.

In one of the Hawthorne Studies, Mayo's researchers joined a gang of male workers in the 'Bank Wiring Room' and were accepted as co-workers.

The researchers were able to observe at first hand the internal workings of the gang and discovered that the workers had decided among themselves what constituted a 'proper day's work' - a level which fell well short of the production targets set by the time and motion officials. The workers paced themselves to achieve this level of production and no more, despite the fact that they were being paid individually on a piece rate basis. In other words, the workers were deliberately taking a cut in wages by not working flat out.

Significantly, the gang was a tightly knit social group as well as a work group - they got on well together and met socially outside normal working hours. The researchers discovered that members of the gang had two main rationalisations for voluntarily restricting their earnings:

1. fear of raising the targets - the workers were convinced (probably correctly) that if they reached the laid down targets for production, management would conclude that these were too easy and simply raise them

2. protection of the slower workers - the faster workers did not want to expose the slower workers to the risk of the sack by out-producing them by too much.

The group put powerful social pressure on members who refused to restrict production to the agreed level ('rate busters') or, conversely, on those who let the group down by working too slowly ('chisellers'). This pressure ranged from ridicule and name calling, to ostracism ('sending to Coventry') and, sometimes, physical intimidation. Faced with these sanctions, newcomers soon learnt to conform to the established group norms for production. Meanwhile, the management was blissfully unaware of what was going on.

The researchers' observations led Mayo to discount the classical management assumption that man was an economic animal who responded only to financial incentives. Instead he argued that social and group pressures were more powerful motivating forces in small work teams (Mayo, 1949).

The War Officer selection system

Psychologists working for the British Army during the Second World War were aware of this early American work on group motivation and used the findings to devise an improved system for selecting new entrants to the commissioned ranks.

The primary objective of the new system (the three-day 'War Officer Selection' system introduced in 1942) was to test each candidate's ability to work *in* a group *for* a group'. The core of this new selection process was a series of simulations in which a group of candidates had to achieve 'command tasks' such as moving a heavy drum from one side of an imaginary river to the other using only an assortment of ropes, pulleys and poles. Each member of the group was given an opportunity to lead the group through a different command task. Meanwhile observers assessed each leader's 'group-cohesiveness' - the ability to bind the team together in the achievement of a common task. The new selection system proved a great success and, over 40 years later, the same basic procedure is still used by the Army to select officers (Adair, 1988).

Creating cohesive teams

The ability to transform a collection of individuals into a cohesive team is at the heart of effective leadership. And the enlightened team leader can use a variety of human relations techniques to achieve this aim. For example, the team leader can:

1. allow social interaction at work - good results have been achieved by re-designing production lines to enable workers to communicate with each other

2. encourage social interaction outside work - works' parties and other social events can help build a sense of group identity

3. look for the unofficial leaders of the group and get them on their side - any attempt to alienate or treat 'ring leaders' as troublemakers can have a bad effect on group morale

4. encourage healthy competition with other groups in order to build team spirit - most groups will unite in the face of a threat from outside.

The Japanese style of management has used all these techniques, and more, to build team spirit to such an extent that a large Japanese firm, such as Matsushita or Nissan, can be thought of as a collection of teams rather than individuals (see *Figure 8.3*).

Figure 8.3
Some human relations aspects of the Japanese management style

- A family atmosphere is created by a range of communal social events including sports, parties, and holidays

- Tasks are assigned to groups instead of individuals; work groups are given considerable autonomy and responsibility for problem solving (e.g. quality circles)

- Hierarchical differences are less obvious than in Western companies. For example, managers and workers wear the same company uniform and share the same canteen; and workers are not required to 'clock on'

- Work spaces are open and few managers have private offices. Thus foremen and senior plant managers are often seen on the shop floor examining problems, discussing work improvements and instructing less experienced employees

- 'Acceptance time' is built into many decisions. New ideas are initiated at middle management level and discussed at length by the shop floor, before being referred back to top management. As a result, although slow in coming, decisions once made can enjoy widespread support quickly. In contrast, decisions in Western companies are often made quickly at the top and then managers face the time-consuming slow process of trying to secure subordinate support

Leadership style

The pioneers of classical management did not seriously address the issue of leadership style. They took it for granted that managers would make all the decisions and assumed that an autocratic style of leadership was the only way to run industrial organisations. The classical managers also had a limited and unimaginative view of what motivated individuals. They believed that motivation was simply a matter of reinforcing wage incentives with the threat of punishment and dismissal. McGregor (1960) neatly summarised the assumptions underlying classical management in his 'Theory X':

1. the average human being has an inherent dislike of work and will avoid it if he can

2. therefore, most people must be coerced, controlled, directed, and threatened with punishment to get them to work hard

3. the average human being prefers being directed, wishes to avoid responsibility, has little ambition and, above all, wants security.

The problem with Theory X is that it may be a self-fulfilling prophecy. No doubt there are organisations with workforces who behave in the way described above. But is this due to a collective weakness of character in the workforce? Or could it be that they are merely responding to an autocratic style of leadership which assumes that they have these characteristics?

Writers in the 'human relations' movement argued that a more imaginative and participative style was the key to effective leadership. McGregor summarised the assumptions underlying this approach in his 'theory Y':

1. the expenditure of physical and mental effort in work is as natural as play or rest

2. external control and threat of punishment are not the only ways to make people work hard; employees will exercise self control in the service of objectives to which they feel committed

3. commitment to objectives is linked to the rewards of their achievement and the feeling of 'a job well done'.

Participative styles

Early evidence of the superiority of a participative style was provided by an experiment carried out at the Iowa Child Welfare Research Station and supervised by Kurt Lewin (a pioneer of the human relations movement whose influence ranks second only to that of Mayo). The subject of the experiment was four boy's clubs which met after school to engage in various group activities. The researchers trained club leaders to work in one of three styles, *autocratic*, *democratic* and *laissez faire*, and rotated leaders every six weeks. The researchers then observed the boys' individual and group behaviour under the different styles of leadership.

The results were striking. Under the autocratic and laissez faire styles, the boys became aggressive or sullen and apathetic; while under the democratic style they were enthusiastic and motivated. Lewin interpreted these findings as conclusive proof of the superiority of a participative style of leadership (Lewin, Lippet and White, 1939).

Lewin was able to test his ideas on industry in a factory run by the Harwood Manufacturing Company in Virginia. The factory made pyjamas and was staffed mainly by young and inexperienced female workers. At the time of the experiment, production rates in the factory were well below management expectations. Lewin advised the company to introduce a participative style of management whereby small groups of workers decided their own hourly pace of work. Shortly after the introduction of this approach, production rose by over 30 per cent and stabilised at this new level.

After Lewin's death, further experiments were carried out at the company. These experiments measured workers' resistance to organisational changes against three levels of participation:

1. no participation by employees (they were simply informed of the changes)

2. participation through elected worker representatives

3. total participation with all group members designing the change.

The results, measured over a period of 30 days, provided more evidence of the superiority of the participative style:

1. Non-participation group - there were expressions of resistance and hostility, deliberate restriction of output, and 17 per cent of the group resigned

2. Worker representatives group - good and co-operative relationships were established, previous output levels achieved within fourteen days of the original changes

3. Total participation group - the best results of all were achieved. The previous output level was achieved within two days of the change and output subsequently rose to a level 14 per cent higher than previous output (Coch and French, 1948).

These new ideas had a major influence on the running of industrial organisations throughout the world. This influence reached a peak in the 1960s and early 1970s - a time when worker participation was fashionable.

One notable example was the Swedish motor industry. Volvo plants at Kalmar and Skövde broke away from the conventional production line and re-organised so that the workers were formed into small, semi-autonomous work groups. Instead of the workers having to run to keep up with the production line, automatic carriers for cars and engines were installed so that the work now came to them. Moreover, the teams of workers had the power to control the speed of the carriers and could thus determine their own targets for production. The changes were popular with the workers and the company benefited from a dramatic increase in the quality of cars produced.

More recently, Peters and Waterman (1982) have advocated a *participative* style of management which achieves 'productivity through people'. And Buchanan and Huczynski (1985) have listed four generally agreed advantages of a participative style. They argue that employees are likely to respond by:

1. accepting the legitimacy of decisions reached with their help
2. accepting change based on these decisions
3. trusting the managers who have to implement decisions
4. volunteering new and creative ideas and solutions of their own.

Quality circles

The advantages of a participative style are reflected in the success of *quality circles* as a means of boosting employee involvement and the quality of what they make.

According to Handy (1985) quality circles were invented in the United States in the 1950s and then exported to Japan, where they have been a huge success. They are now being re-imported to Europe and the USA.

Others have given the credit for inventing the quality circle to Kaoru Ishikawa, the leading Japanese management scientist who died in 1989. In the 1950s, Ishikawa recognised that the Taylorist management techniques were alien to Japanese culture, and recommended that a blend of management techniques combining the best of American concepts with the best of Japanese and European experience might provide the most desirable option. Ishikawa's quality circles were first tested in Japan in 1962 at the Nippon Telegraph and Cable Company. After that the concept swept through Japan. Currently there are 2 million Japanese quality circles involving 20 million workers (*Independent*, 1989).

A quality circle is a *voluntary group* of workers with a shared area of responsibility. They meet together, usually weekly, in company time on company premises to discuss ways of improving quality and production. They analyse problems and suggest solutions.

The process of setting up quality circles is not automatic. Training courses in communication skills, measurement techniques and problem-solving strategies are essential (see *Figure 8.4*). But the results justify the effort. Bryant and Kearns (1982) studied quality circles at work in an American naval dockyard and concluded that they saved the company over $200,000 a year.

Figure 8.4
Problem-solving strategies in quality circles (Industrial Society, 1988)

Quality circles, team briefings and consultative committees are three essential components in an effective structure for management-workforce communications

Consultative committees discuss issues raised by management and feedback opinions. Management feeds information to the workforce in *team briefings*

Quality circles discuss issues, problems, and solutions and make recommendations to management. They must not discuss pay and people as this could interfere with management-union negotiations and agreements

The main skills required are:
- working effectively in groups and teams
- brainstorming techniques
- problem-solving techniques
- report writing
- oral presentations

A five stage plan for effective quality circles
1. Clarify the problem
2. The investigation - cause-effect analysis using the 4 Ms:
   - Manpower
   - Machinery
   - Methods
   - Materials
3. The real solution
4. The benefits and costs (both tangible and intangible)
5. Implementation

The dockyard scheme was introduced under the slogan: 'it makes sense to reap from workers' brains as well as their bodies'.

The circles gave themselves names like *Wild Bunch*, *Sparkers*, *Red Eye Express*, and *Supply Storm Troopers*, and made recommendations for:

1. better tools and equipment.
2. more effective waste disposal.
3. savings in workers' time and effort.

One worker at Jaguar, where quality circles have formed an essential element in the transformation in the company's fortunes (see *Chapter 7*), contrasted the new approach with the old. In the days when Jaguar was in decline, all suggestions had to be put through the 'appropriate channels' and it took weeks or months before an answer - usually negative - was obtained. Moreover, in those days, the directors were only names on a closed door to the workers. Today Jaguar workers, organised in quality circles, make regular presentations to directors and can expect decisions to be made on the spot or within a few days (BBC, 1988).

Jaguar is one British company which seems to have made the change successfully from a Theory X to a Theory Y organisation.

Contingency leadership

While modern studies continue to stress the importance of the participative style of decision making, they also accept that other styles are appropriate in certain situations. This approach has become known as a *contingency* or *functional* approach to leadership. Put more simply this approach can be described as adopting 'different horses for different courses'. For any team leader there are disadvantages in lapsing into one, stereotyped style of decision making. For example, an over-democratic leader runs the risk of being accused of never making a decision himself; while the leader who always adopts the style of an autocrat is likely to stifle his subordinates' initiative and job satisfaction. A comparison of some of the advantages and disadvantages of the two extremes of decision making can be found in *Figure 8.5*.

The Figure does illustrate one advantage of the autocratic decision-making style - speed. This is why the armed forces continue to use an autocratic style. Once the bullets start flying there is no time to call a meeting to discuss the best course of action - the officer in charge has to make instant decisions.

Vroom (1974) suggests that three main criteria should be applied to any situation in order to decide which decision style is best:

1. the required quality of the decision.
2. the degree of group acceptance required of the decision.
3. the amount of time available to make the decision.

Decision quality can be assessed by asking the simple question: does it matter what the decision is? If there are a number of solutions which are equally acceptable then a high-quality decision is not required and the leader can make a quick, autocratic decision and move on to more important matters. A good example here is the stream of routine problems which arrive in an in-

Figure 8.5
A comparison between autocratic and participative
decision-making styles

AUTOCRATIC	PARTICIPATIVE
Quick - one person can make a decision in an instant	Slow - consultation and discussion always take a long time
One person is more likely to miss an important option or idea - this may result in a less than optimum decision	Group decision makes it more likely that all possible options and ideas are considered and that experts can contribute specialist knowledge; collective 'brain storming' can take place.
People affected by the decision are likely to be reluctant to accept it - particularly if problems arise later	People affected by the decision are more likely to accept it with enthusiasm if they have been involved in making the decision - even if problems arise later

tray every morning and which have to be dealt with quickly and efficiently before the more important tasks of the day can be addressed.

Conversely, if one solution is likely to be better than any other, then a high-quality decision is required. The next question the leader should ask is: do I have enough information or knowledge to make the decision alone?

If the answer is 'yes', then the leader should make the decision. If the answer is 'no', expert advice will be needed from colleagues individually or in a group problem-solving session. After taking individual advice or sharing the problem with the group, the leader should be in a good position to make the high-quality decision required. But this process takes time - in a crisis, where there is not enough time for consultation, the leader will have to revert to an autocratic style.

The degree of group acceptance required of a decision can be established by posing the question: how crucial is acceptance and commitment by the work group or team affected by the decision? Or, in other words: if the group is unhappy about the decision does it have the power or opportunity to under-

mine it? If the answers to these questions are 'very' and 'yes', then a participative style of decision-making stands the best chance of building involvement and commitment.

But if a high-quality decision is required, the group may not be capable
of making a satisfactory decision. Say, for example, there is likely to be disagreement over preferred solutions or some members of the group do not
share the goals and values of the organisation. In this case the leader will have
to impose a solution. Similarly, if speed is the most important factor then he
or she will have to make an autocratic decision. However, if the team is experienced, cohesive and well motivated, and time is not a major factor, then
a genuinely participative style is usually best.

To illustrate this point let us suppose a team leader has imposed an un-
popular decision on a work group. If things start to go wrong and the leader
goes back to the group to ask for their help - perhaps extra overtime working to cope with a crisis - he is likely to get a terse reply: 'That's your problem - it was your decision!' But if he had devoted some time to discussion and
negotiation with the group and forged a consensus decision, he would be
much more likely to gain their enthusiastic co-operation later in the project.

A consultative or decision-making style is essential in the introduction of
new technology to the workplace. It is clear that decisions associated with the
introduction of new technology are high quality ones which will have a long
term impact on the achievement of the organisation's goals - so it is wise to
draw on a variety of expert opinions. Next, it is vital to win the backing of the
work force for the proposed change - not least because the workers have the
capability to sabotage the introduction of the new technology. Thus consultation and negotiation between management and workforce is essential. An
autocratic style is ruled out because new technology should never be introduced in a hurry. If it is, the end result may be a long period of industrial action and drawn out negotiations while the newly installed machinery remains
covered by dust sheets.

Leadership and organisational structure

Any leader who concentrates on *style* and neglects the underlying structure
of power and authority relationships will soon run into problems. People in
organisations have a highly developed and intuitive sense of authority relationships and use this to decide which instructions from others they will ac-

cept, reject or ignore. And major problems can occur when there is a mismatch between the unofficial or informal structure - which exists in every organisation - and the formal structure based on the official organisation chart. These problems usually surface as personality clashes - but the underlying causes are structural. For example:

'How dare you go behind my back/over my head ...'

'Are you challenging my authority ...?'

'So and so is getting too big for his boots ...'

'You had no right to do that ...'

'It's more than my job's worth to ...'

'What authority have you to ...?'

'Why wasn't I consulted ...?'

To understand these problems, we first have to define our terms. A leader has *power* if he can make other people do what he wants them to do - even if they do not want to. He has *authority*, on the other hand, if people do things he wants them to do because they feel they 'ought to'. Weber, the German sociologist defined authority as *power plus legitimation*. He suggested that legitimation in industrial organisations was most commonly conferred on individuals by their technical knowledge or experience or by the fact that they had been 'legally' appointed to a position of authority.

Most conventional text books go on to describe two main types of authority (both of which draw on classic military principles of organisation):

1. *Line managers* - based on the principles of 'unity of command' and 'chain of command'

2. *Staff officers* - officers who are outside the line of command and act as advisers.

But if things are this simple why do organisations need so many different job titles to denote positions of authority? Consider the following list:

Manager	Managing	Executive	Director
Chief	Head	Senior	Principal
Co-ordinator	Supervisor	Foreman	Chargehand
Superintendent		Inspector	Controller
Deputy	Assistant	Vice	First

Area	Divisional	District	Department
Consultant	Analyst	Adviser	Officer
General	Acting	Designate	

The list can be lengthened by combining two or more of the titles - 'managing director', 'director general', 'assistant divisional controller' and so on. And the list would be almost endless if we included all the titles used in the armed forces and the church, for example.

To find our way through the proliferation of authority titles we need a model to guide us. Fortunately, researchers at the Brunel Institute of Organisation and Social Studies (BIOSS) have provided one. They argue that the real amount of authority accruing to a leader in an organisation can be judged by the answers to four key questions:

- Can he or she affect who is in a particular job?
- Can he or she change the shape of someone's job?
- Can he or she give straightforward task instructions?
- Can he or she check on results?

They have used these four questions to analyse authority relationships and to produce a list of seven definitions of the most common ones found in organisations (see *Figure 8.6*).

We can use these definitions of authority relationships to model the complex structure of a typical multi-disciplinary project team. In such a team the authority held by the team leader is most likely to fit the definition of a *co-ordinating* relationship. Note that the team leader is not the *main-line manager* of the team members. If the leader were to behave *like* a line manager, the team members would soon object and begin to complain that the person was 'exceeding his or her authority'. Thus a team leader in this situation has to work in a participative style and build consensus decisions wherever possible. Note also that, although we have broken the principle of 'unity of command', each member of the team still has only one main line manager. This modified application of the unity of command principle helps to resolve some of the uncertainty and conflict implicit in dual command situations.

Matrix organisation

A team leader is most likely to face challenges to his or her authority when leading a multi-disciplinary project team whose work cuts horizontally across vertical departmental structures. In such circumstances the classical manage-

Figure 8.6
BIOSS definitions of authority relationships (Rowbottom, 1987)

NB: The number of asterisks corresponds to the number of positive answers to the four questions posed in the text

**** **Main Line Managerial (MLM):** involves assigning duties and responsibilities, appraising performance and ability, and forwarding staff development; implies authority to join in selection of staff, to prescribe work in as much detail as may be required, and to initiate promotion, transfer or dismissal

** **Supervisory:** involves inducting, giving technical instruction, assigning tasks, checking performance, and helping with problems; unlike a managerial relationship, it does not imply authority to reallocate duties, or to initiate promotion, transfer or dismissal

** **Co-ordinating:** involves preparing and issuing detailed plans and programmes to forward agreed objectives, keeping informed of actual progress and attempting to overcome obstacles and setbacks; it implies authority to obtain information of progress and to decide what shall be done in positions of uncertainty. It does not imply authority to set new directions, to override sustained disagreements or to appraise personal ability or performance

** **Prescribing:** implies the right to set specific tasks to be carried out, and the right to check results, but no other right to manage, supervise or direct

* **Monitoring:** involves checking, or keeping informed of the effect of others' activity in some given area; warning of sustained or significant deficiencies, and advising corrective action; it does not imply authority to give instruction or to appraise personal ability or performance

Collateral: implies mutual dependence without any authority, one over the other. Sustained disagreements can only be resolved by referral to some higher authority, where one exists

Service: implies an obligation to respond to the stated needs of another, though in a manner and timing of choice

ment principle of 'unity of command' becomes impossible to maintain. Each member of the team has to report simultaneously to at least two superiors - their regular department head and their project team leader.

Knosuke Matsushita, founder of the massive Japanese electronics company of the same name, saw nothing wrong with this situation. He once remarked that we all grow up under two bosses - a mother and a father - and that it is the nature of life to have to juggle with the complexities that arise

Figure 8.7
Matrix organisation in the Matsushita Corporation

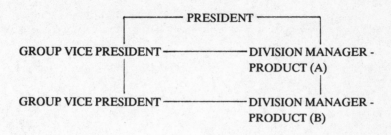

from such arrangements (Pascale and Athos, 1961). Thus the Matsushita Corporation had a matrix organisational structure as early as 1954 - some ten years before such structures became fashionable in the American aerospace industry (see *Figure 8.7*).

Matrix structures are an attempt to reconcile the conflicting forces of centralisation and decentralisation. The vertical axis in the Figure represents decentralisation, with the divisional managers encouraged to operate as line managers of semi-autonomous business units. The horizontal axis represents centralisation: the vice presidents at headquarters are given responsibility for co-ordinating the work of the divisions for specific products or programmes.

Suggestions for further study

The British 'guru' on leadership and team building is John Adair. Two of his books, *Effective Leadership* and *Effective Team Building*, are particularly relevant to the content of this chapter and offer additional practical advice.

In addition, there are many useful books on 'organisational behaviour' which give insights into leadership and the way people behave in groups. We would particularly recommend Charles Handy's *Understanding Organisations*; Fred Luthans' *Organisational Behaviour*; and Buchanan and Huczynski's book - also entitled *Organisational Behaviour*.

However, there can be no real substitute for experience, and we recommend that student engineers put themselves forward for leadership positions wherever possible - at college or university, in their workplaces, or in clubs and societies.

Part III

Communication

Chapter 9

Face-to-Face Communication

If engineers are to achieve the aim of raising the profile of engineering in society, they will need a high level of communication skills. At the heart of these is the skill of persuading and influencing people in *face-to-face communication*.

Some people undoubtedly have a natural ability to communicate well. But the good news about face-to-face communication is that it is a skill and, as such, can be practised and improved. There are three types of face-to-face communication in which it will be particularly valuable for the ambitious engineer to acquire skill:

1. making a formal presentation
2. chairing a meeting
3. selection interviewing.

These skills are important for all engineers, not just those in management or supervisory positions. They are also vital to the engineer when he or she is playing a wider role in the community: for example giving a talk on careers in engineering to school children, or serving on the governing body of a school.

Making a formal presentation

For most engineers, and indeed most people, giving a formal presentation to a group of colleagues, customers or members of the public is one of the most stressful activities that they have to undertake in their working lives. A certain amount of stress is inevitable and even helpful: it serves to concentrate the mind and sharpen delivery. But if that stress develops into chronic anxiety or fear, it will undermine performance and waste an opportunity for persuading and influencing people.

Fear can come from two main sources: fear of the audience and fear of the unknown. The key to successful presentations is learning the techniques to overcome these fears. The required set of techniques centre on the concepts of inter-personal skills (to conquer the fear of the audience) and preparation (to conquer the fear of the unknown). Also important, are techniques for the actual delivery of the presentation.

Inter-personal skills

Psychologists have observed that babies deprived of handling over a long time will tend to sink into a physical decline and become more prone to disease even though their physical requirements in terms of food, water and warmth continue to be met. Similarly, adults deprived of social stimuli are liable to develop serious mental disturbances. And it is well known that, in prisons, an extended period of solitary confinement is a punishment more dreaded than physical brutality and torture. Thus we all need to receive emotional stimuli or attention from other people; and any stimulus, no matter how minimal or how low quality, is better than no stimulus at all.

In the jargon of a theory of social communication known as transactional analysis, the term 'stroke' is used to describe any kind of attention which one person gets from or gives to another person. This attention can be *physical*: in the way that adults will hug, pat or, literally stroke an infant or in the way that adults nod to each other in recognition of another's presence. Or it can be *verbal*: in the way that people express greetings, praise or appreciation to one another. Hence a stroke may be used as a fundamental unit of social action and an exchange of strokes constitutes a transaction, which is the unit of social intercourse (Berne, 1964.)

There are two types of stroke: positive and negative. Positive strokes are any kind of positive recognition, praise, gratitude, or admiration and can be expressed in words or by physical action or 'body language' (such as hugs, smiles, handshake, appreciative look). Naturally, positive strokes make us feel happy and important. On the other hand, negative strokes express such feelings as criticism, contempt, sarcasm, ridicule, and make us feel sad and resentful.

Superficially, the communication pattern during a presentation appears to be one way, with the presenter actively sending out information and the audience passively receiving it. At a deeper level, it is clear that the communication pattern is two way or interactive. In reality the audience is continually sending out a variety of non-verbal communications to which the presenter must be sensitive. If things are going well, the audience will be leaning forward in their seats and showing interest and enthusiasm. On other occasions, some of the audience may be expressing anger and hostility in their body language. This may develop into verbal expression of their frustration - 'heckling'.

However, even negative strokes are better than no strokes at all and skillful presenters can sometimes turn heckling to their own advantage (politicians are particularly adept at this). The worst scenario for the presenter is when the audience begins to express indifference by looking out of the window, falling asleep or even walking out.

So how can an appreciation of transactional analysis and the importance of strokes help the presenter overcome his fear of a hostile (or indifferent) audience? The lesson is that if you want to receive positive strokes from the audience in terms of interest, praise, and possibly applause you first have to give them positive strokes in exchange. Basically this means that you must make your audience feel relaxed, happy and, above all, important. Some ideas for achieving this aim are set out in *Figure 9.1*.

There is evidence to suggest that whenever people meet, they quickly form an emotion such as pleasure, interest, boredom, or dislike which becomes firmly rooted and difficult to change.

Thus, at the beginning of a presentation, the audience will be forming an 'instant impression' of the speaker. So what happens between presenter and audience in terms of strokes, words and body language in the first four minutes is absolutely vital.

Successful presenters pay great attention to making a good start and getting the audience on to their side in that first vital four minutes. The way to achieve this is to try to protect yourself from distractions in the minutes leading up to the presentation, to visualise yourself being successful and to rehearse your opening words silently. Then be sure to smile, stand up straight with hands relaxed or holding your notes, look at all of the audience, and introduce yourself properly. Once you have passed the four minute point, concentrate on not making any mistakes, do not talk for too long, and try to end on a high note. In other words, quit while you are ahead.

Figure 9.1
Social transactions between presenter and audience

Presenters can give their audience positive strokes by:
- smiling and showing enthusiasm
- looking at all the audience individually during the presentation
- showing a sensitive sense of humour
- paying them a compliment by looking smart
- expressing gratitude ('thank you for giving up your time to listen to me ...')
- praise ('of course, in a successful company like C.G.M. Engineering ...')
- keeping their presentations brief and to the point
- using visual aids
- welcoming questions from the audience and responding to them in an open and friendly way.

Presenters can give their audience negative strokes by:
- looking as if the whole exercise is an ordeal for them
- expressing ingratitude
- insensitive jokes
- being sarcastic or patronising ('if you'd listened more carefully, you would have understood what I was trying to say ...')
- expressing criticism ('I'm not surprised the present system is in a mess ...')
- waffling and getting off the point
- not giving their audience a chance to ask questions or responding to questions in a defensive or hostile way

Worst of all, presenters can give their audience no strokes by:
- looking bored and indifferent
- looking at the ceiling, the floor or their notes rather than directly at their audience

Preparation

The proper balance between preparation and presentation can be illustrated by the fact that a good presenter is likely to spend several hours on a presentation which may last as little as ten minutes. With this amount of time allocated to planning, the presenter should be able to conquer the *fear* of the unknown by reducing, if not actually eliminating, the *area* of the unknown.

The first stage of the planning process is to decide on one overall aim for the presentation: what, above all else, do you want to achieve as a result of the presentation? This aim should be realistic but it may be something that

Figure 9.2
Overall aim and objectives of a presentation

Aim: To persuade the board of directors of C.G.M. engineering to authorise the purchase of the XYZ desk top publishing system

Objectives: By the end of the presentation, each member of the board of directors will:
  (i) be familiar with two problems related to the present system of producing sales brochures: reliance on one printing company; and lack of flexibility.
  (ii) understand the three basic capabilities of a desk top publishing system: the production of page layouts, graphics and text editing
  (iii) have seen a demonstration of the XYZ system
  (iv) appreciate that the purchase of the XYZ system and appropriate hardware will pay for itself within 2 years by cutting the annual cost of printing brochures and will, thereafter, save the company the sum of £15,000 a year.

you cannot guarantee to achieve. For example, a final decision on the adoption of your proposals may be outside your control.

The next step is to decide on a list of four or five objectives. Objectives should be carefully chosen to match your perception of the audience's needs and, in contrast to the aim, should be ones that you can *guarantee* to deliver. Thus objectives should always begin with the phrase, 'by the end of the presentation, the (audience) will ...' (see *Figure 9.2*). In addition, objectives should always be measurable: those in the Figure could be tested by giving each member of the board a questionnaire to fill in after the presentation. Furthermore, the key to setting objectives is simplicity. If they are too complicated or if you have more than four or five key objectives you may not be able to deliver, as the audience will only be able to retain a limited amount of the information you have given them.

The next stage in the preparation process is to find out about the people to whom you will be giving the presentation. If possible, interview key members of the audience to explore their experience, technical knowledge and interests. This will elicit useful background on the required style for the presentation. For example, what level of technical knowledge you should assume and how much jargon you can use. Interviews will also help to anticipate any possible objections to the arguments you will be putting forward.

Having carried out the initial research, the next step is to decide on the best structure for the presentation. The most widely used structure for presentations is the classic three stages: beginning, middle, end.

The first stage is the introduction - *tell them what you're going to tell them*. In terms of making an impact, the introduction is the most important stage of all. Next comes the middle stage or main body of the presentation - *tell them*. The third, and final, stage is a summary of the main points and recommendations you have already covered in the presentation - *tell them what you've told them*.

A major advantage of this simple structure is that it gives the audience the opportunity to hear your key points three times. Repetition can be a valuable aid to the presenter.

The next stage is to write the presentation. It is a good idea to write the speech out in full at first, so that you are sure that you have thought of the most vivid and concise ways of expressing your ideas. This particularly applies to the all-important introduction (see *Figure 9.3*). However, there are dangers in giving a presentation from a completely prepared script. In particular, you will find yourself reluctant to tear your eyes from the reassuring script and will lose some of that all-important eye contact with the audience (politicians and television presenters solve this problem by using an 'autocue', but, unfortunately, this is not a piece of technology which will be readily available to most readers of this book).

So the next step is to reduce your script into note form: headings and key words which will trigger your memory. Many presenters prefer to write these on 'prompt cards', as these are easier to handle. But if you do this, remember to fasten the cards together so that it is impossible to arrange them in the wrong order inadvertently. Your notes should also highlight points where you intend to use visual aids.

The next stage in the preparation process is perhaps the most important of all, and that is to *rehearse, rehearse and rehearse*. For a first run through you may decide to lock yourself in a room and give a presentation to the mirror. Subsequently you should rehearse in front of real people: a friend or spouse or sympathetic colleagues. Work colleagues, in particular, can help to anticipate the questions you are likely to be asked at the end of your presentation and to prepare some draft answers.

Figure 9.3
Introduction: 'Tell them what you're going to tell them'

'Good afternoon, ladies and gentlemen. My name is John Smith of Effective Business Systems Limited. I am here to talk to you about the XYZ Desk Top Publishing System [Overhead Projector Foil 1 - 'company logo'].

Before I begin, may I thank you for giving up some of your valuable time to listen to my presentation. As a small - but growing - software company we are delighted to be associated with a successful and prestigious organisation like C.M.G. Engineering and we look forward to building a close working relationship with you.

I hope that you will find my presentation both informative and interesting. I intend to talk for about ten minutes and will cover the following areas [OHP Foil 2 - 'plan of talk']

I will begin by reviewing your present procedure for producing sales brochures and highlight two problems which my interviews with members of your staff have highlighted. Firstly, it is unacceptable for a prestigious and successful company like C.M.G. Engineering to be totally reliant on one outside printing company; and secondly, your present procedure for producing manuals seems to be inflexible and slow.

Next, I will show you some actual examples of text, graphics and pages produced on the XYZ Desk Top Publishing System to give you an appreciation of what this new and exciting system can do.

Then, I will explain how I believe the XYZ System can solve the problems with the present system for producing brochures which we have already identified. I will also show you a detailed break-even chart showing how the system will pay for itself within two years by cutting the time taken to design and produce brochures.

Finally, after a brief summary of the main points of my presentation, I will give you an opportunity to ask me any questions about the XYZ system and I will answer them to the best of my ability.

Is this format acceptable? [pause to look around the audience] Fine. Let us look first then at the problems associated with the present system ...'

Many inexperienced presenters worry about being 'floored' by a question they cannot answer. By all means try to minimise the risk of this happening by careful preparation - but do not worry too much. If you get a question you cannot answer, first try 'reflecting' the question back to the questioner: '... that is a very good point - I wonder if you have any ideas for overcoming that problem?' The questioner may be waiting to show off his superior knowledge or experience and it is a good idea to let him have some strokes as you will increase your chances of winning him over to your side. Alternatively, throw the question open to the audience: '... has anyone else any experience that can shed some light on this question?'

If the question remains unanswered, the golden rule is: do not try to bluff your way out. The safest option is to respond to the effect that: 'I'm afraid I don't have enough information to give you an answer now but if you let me have your name and address, I will find out and come back to you by the end of the week' (needless to say you must make a note in your diary to ensure that you keep that promise).

The final stage in your preparation is to check the room where you are going to give your presentation (but note that you should have previously reconnoitered the room to establish its suitability and the availability of audio-visual equipment). On the day in question, arrive early, check that all the equipment such as overhead projectors is working, and, if necessary, move the furniture around to get the seating arrangement that you want.

You should now have 10 or 15 minutes to compose yourself, both physically and mentally, confident that you have done everything in your power to cut down the area of the unknown and ready to make an impact in that first four minutes ...

Delivery

Finally, some thoughts on the delivery of a talk. The two commonest faults of inexperienced presenters are 'gabbling' and 'mumbling'.

Nervous presenters wish to get through their ordeal as quickly as possible and so rush through the talk, with barely a pause for breath (gabbling). The key to solving this problem is, as we have already discussed, preparation and rehearsal to ensure maximum confidence and to make sure that you have not included too much material for the time available. But in addition, make a conscious effort to introduce pauses in the 'natural breaks' of your presentation. For example, when changing a transparency on an overhead projector, take your time over the change:

1. stop talking

2. switch the projector off

3. remove the transparency

4. place the next transparency on the projector

5. switch the projector back on.

Your audience will be patient and welcome the opportunity to shift their sitting position. Furthermore, by taking your time and concentrating on one thing at a time you minimise the danger of putting the new transparency on the wrong way up.

Similarly, good presenters always 'paragraph' their talk. For example, when you get to the end of a section of your talk say '... so that concludes our review of the problems associated with the present system.' Then pause ... take a breath; break eye-contact with your audience for a moment to check your notes and satisfy yourself that the next visual aid is ready for use. Then continue: '... But how can desk-top publishing solve these problems? Well, firstly ...' By this means, you can make your presentation easier to follow and give yourself more time to think and cut down the chance of mistakes.

The problem for 'mumblers' is that they speak too quietly ... and drop their voices at the end of their sentences ... and send their audience to sleep and then WAKE THEM UP AT THE END WHEN THEY'VE FINISHED. The antidote is rehearsing: listen to yourself on audio tape and practice keeping your voice UP AT THE END OF SENTENCES.

Some old actors' tricks to practise diction and breathing can be beneficial here. For example: take a deep breath and see how many times you can say the alphabet out loud; or, repeat over and over again: *the lips, the teeth, the tip of the tongue*. These are excellent 'warm up' exercises and are used by actors and actresses just before they go on stage. They can serve exactly the same purpose for the presenter.

Chairing a meeting

Meetings are notorious consumers of time in many organisations. Common complaints that are heard include 'I seem to spend all my time in meetings ...' or '... oh no, not another meeting - when can I get down to some real work?'.

It can be a salutary experience to add up the real cost of meetings. At the next meeting you have to attend, try to estimate the hourly salary of each person sitting around the table, total them and multiply by the time the meeting takes; then add on some estimated totals for travelling and secretarial support. The final figure may surprise you.

The most important person at any meeting is a chairperson or chairman (for the purpose of this discussion we shall use the latter term to mean a male or female chair). The chairman is at the hub of the communications system within the group. It is up to the chairman, therefore, to ensure the right decisions are taken during the meeting in the most cost effective way. In order to achieve this end, the chairman needs an understanding of two familiar concepts: inter-personal skills and preparation.

Inter-personal skills

The primary purpose of most meetings in organisations is to take decisions. But in order to build good decisions, a chairman needs to develop a sensitivity to the complex personal interactions which will be occurring at the meeting. His or her task can be divided into three stages:

1. unite the meeting
2. focus the meeting on the task in hand
3. mobilise the meeting to take and follow up decisions.

Many meetings consist of a collection of individuals with widely differing attitudes and interests. Take, for example, project team meetings where representatives of diverse departments such as production, design and sales are brought together to improve overall co-ordination. Unfortunately, such meetings are often dominated by inter-departmental politics, with each member defending narrow sectional interests rather than taking an overview of the development of the project. The chairman faces a difficult task in trying to unite the group in these circumstances and there is a danger that aggression within the group can get out of hand; an enormous amount of time and energy can be wasted at such meetings in arguing at cross purposes.

If you find yourself in the position of trying to unite a divided group, you will need to a number of inter-personal skills. Firstly, allow individuals to let off some steam by identifying strong emotions and reflecting them back:

'... clearly, John, you are very angry ... can you tell us why you feel so strongly about this?'

Next bring in other people to the discussion:

'... right, we've heard John's views on the subject. Kathy and Tony, you've been closely involved with this problem from the start ... what do you think?'

Always focus on the facts: '... yes, but the fact is that we are now two weeks behind schedule and we need to establish why this happened.'

Above all, the golden rule for the chairman here is: *stay neutral; do not take sides*.

Having taken the heat out of the situation, you can now focus the group on the task in hand: '... OK, now we've established what went wrong, we need to decide what we must do to get back on target. Has any one got any ideas?'

The main danger now is that the group will start wandering off the point or individuals will begin to talk among themselves. Therefore, you, as chairman, will have to stay alert and keep a firm hand on the wheel: '... we seem to be getting drawn back into a discussion of the problems here ... let's concentrate on solutions' or: '... Kathy and Tony, can we have one meeting at a time please?'

At this point you will want to check understanding by paraphrasing individual contributions:

'... in other words what you are saying is that ... is that right?'

You should now be ready to mobilise the group to build a decision. The overall aim now should be to motivate the group and stimulate individuals to build on each others ideas and to be creative, so make sure that you are giving out plenty of positive strokes. Negative strokes not only destroy ideas and initiatives, they also depress people's energy, drive and enthusiasm. Another point to remember is that the most dominant and assertive members of the group are not necessarily the most able or knowledgeable: the solution you are looking for may come from the quietest person in the room. So, make sure that you are harnessing the collective brain power or 'synergy' of the group by asking them one by one:

'... John, have you anything to add? ... OK, ... Steve?'

Check that the person acting as secretary makes a note of all suggestions that have been made (if necessary, ask the secretary to read them back to remind the group towards the end of the discussion) and protect the weaker members: '... Kathy, will you please let Tony finish - I think he may have an interesting idea there ...'

Finally, making the decision. You will need to give a short summary of the discussion so far and put forward a tentative decision: '... it seems to me that the feeling of the group is that we should ... does anyone dissent from that view?'

If there is still some disagreement, you will need to devote some more time to discussion in the hope of winning the agreement of all the group; but there will be many times when such a consensus is not forthcoming.

What you do next depends on the amount of authority delegated to you. You may have to defer a decision to another occasion and move on to the next item on the agenda. Alternatively, if it is a formal negotiating meeting you may decide to adjourn the meeting and see the main participants individually to seek possible compromises. However, if you are the senior person present, you may be empowered to make the final decision yourself: '... thank you for your comments ... I have listened carefully to both sides of the argument but I have not been convinced that the advantages outweigh the disadvantages, so I think we should stick with the present system.'

In reality, most meetings within organisations employ an autocratic or 'leader decision' style of decision-making (normally it is only at governing body or board of director level that decisions are made by 'majority voting'). The obvious question then is: is it worth spending so much time and effort on building a consensus? The answer is 'yes' for two reasons.

Firstly, the time spent building a consensus, within resource constraints, is time invested in building good communications and team spirit. If a consensus can be achieved, team members will be more committed to implementing the decision than if it is simply announced to them. Secondly, because of power relationships within organisations, certain groups enjoy an effective 'right of veto' anyway. For example a design manager would be unable to gain acceptance for modifications to an existing product without the approval of the production manager. The analogy here is with the Security Council of the United Nations, the Council of Europe or other power-sharing bodies, where no decision can be made unless all participants agree.

The lesson is that the good chairman should aim to be flexible in his approach to decision making and choose an appropriate style to suit the contingencies of each situation (our discussion on leadership styles and decision-making in *Chapter 8* is also pertinent here).

Preparation

The first stage in the preparation for any meeting is to pose two simple and related questions. Is the meeting really necessary? And, what would the consequences be of not holding it? If there are no important decisions to be discussed, or if you can deal with all the items on a one to one basis with the individuals concerned, then you will do everyone a favour if you cancel the meeting. This particularly applies to those regular meetings which are programmed to occur once a week or once a month regardless of whether or not there is anything new or important to discuss.

Having established the need for the meeting, you can begin detailed planning. You should telephone, or speak in person to, some or all of the people who will be attending in order to find out what they want to talk about and to brief them on your own ideas. The next step is to draw up an agenda.

An agenda should be a detailed planning document; not just a list of headings to remind the chairman of the items to be discussed at the meeting itself. Therefore, treat an agenda as a 'mini- report': concentrate on producing a clear structure and style, logical order (e.g. problems before solutions), and presentation. These skills are discussed at length in *Chapter 10*.

The good chairman decides on the order of items on the agenda, and the time allocated to each item, in relation to the *importance* and *urgency* of each item. Thus each agenda item can be placed in one of four categories:

1. urgent and important

2. non-urgent but important

3. urgent but not important

3. non-urgent and not important.

You could place an *unimportant but urgent* item at the beginning of the agenda and allocate it five minutes discussion to get it out of the way quickly. *Urgent and important* items should be placed near the top of the agenda and allocated enough time to reflect their importance: thirty minutes, an hour or more. *Non-urgent but important* items should come next and be similarly allocated a generous amount of time for discussion. *Unimportant and non-urgent* items, if they are to be discussed at all, should be relegated to the end of the agenda and allocated the minimum of time.

It is particularly important to express agenda items as objectives and to start with active verbs: 'to discuss ... to agree on ... to decide whether ...' and include target dates where relevant. And do not forget to include the time, date, and location of the meeting at the top. Finally, it is important to send out copies of the agenda to the relevant people well in advance of the meeting. You will want them to arrive at the meeting fully briefed and ready to make a positive contribution (for an example of an agenda, see *Figure 9.4*).

The last stage of your preparation, as with a formal presentation, is to arrange the furniture in the room where the meeting will take place. Arrange the seating in a circle, or in a square around a table so that you, as chairman, will be able to catch the eye of every person in the room whenever you need to do so.

Figure 9.4
The agenda

PRODUCTION DEPARTMENT MEETING

DATE: 27th November TIME: 9:30 am - 12 noon LOCATION: Committee Room 1

AGENDA

1. PRODUCTION TARGETS
   1.1 To review the production targets for December (15 mins)
   [see Annex 1 attached for details]
   1.2 To decide how many hours of overtime will be required to meet these targets
   (10 mins)
   [NB: this information is required for the Joint Consultative Meeting on 30th November]

2. BREAKDOWN OF CNC LATHE ON 20th November
   2.1 To receive an oral report on the result of the investigations into this breakdown
   from Charles Wright and John Burton (20 mins)
   [see attached paper written by Charles and John - Annex 2]
   2.2 To discuss the causes of the breakdown (30 mins)
   2.3 To agree a plan of action to prevent further breakdowns in the future (40 mins)

3. CD/1 DESIGN PROJECT
   Jill Harding and Bob Ash to report on the progress on this project (20 mins)

4. STATE OF THE TOILETS
   To decide what action to take over the poor state of toilets on floor 1 (5 mins).

If you are expecting a 'difficult' meeting, you may want to go further and decide where each individual will sit. If you expect opposition from an individual who has a reputation for dominating meetings, sit him next to you (where you can place an occasional, friendly and restraining hand on his arm). Never seat him directly opposite you where he is in an ideal position to challenge your authority. Instead, place an ally or an unassertive person in this key position.

After the meeting

The chairman's job is not finished at the end of the meeting. A written summary of all the decisions taken, together with target dates and the names of those responsible for implementing any agreed actions, is absolutely vital given the vagaries of people's memories. It is your responsibility to ensure that minutes which contain this information are produced and circulated to all members by the end of the next working day (although the actual task of producing the minutes may be delegated to someone else). But your responsibility does not stop here. It is good practice to make a note of the decisions and target dates in your diary, so that you can monitor people's progress and issue tactful reminders when, and if, necessary. In this way effective meetings can become part of a continuous co-ordinating and monitoring process; rather than isolated and ineffective events in organisational life.

Selection interviewing

Subordinates are often heard to complain of their managers: 'if only he (or she) would listen ...' Consequently, a manager trained in interviewing skills will always try to create an environment in which the person they are interviewing is encouraged to relax and talk at length. For example, in a discipline interview, the interviewee must be given a fair chance to put their side of the case. There is always the possibility that important extenuating circumstances might be discovered which will remove the need for some form of punishment.

Similarly, experience has shown that appraisal interviews are much more likely to be effective in improving an employee's performance, if the person being appraised is helped to make a realistic self-appraisal of their weaknesses, rather than simply being lectured about their faults.

And a selection interviewer must ensure that the candidate does at least 80 or 90 per cent of the talking during the interview. If interviewers spend most of the time venting their own ideas and answering their own questions rather than listening to the candidate, the opportunity of building a detailed profile of the candidate will be lost.

In this final section we will concentrate on the skills required of the selection interviewer. However, the skills discussed are readily transferable to other situations such as appraisal and discipline interviews.

As with formal presentations and chairmanship, we will look at the skills associated with selection interviewing under two main headings: *inter-personal skills* and *preparation*.

Inter-personal skills

Non-verbal strokes or body language during an interview are very important. During the interview, adopt a relaxed posture with your body positioned towards the other person to show that you are paying attention. If you begin fidgeting or shifting position, the interviewee will sense that you are losing interest and will become inhibited and less willing to talk; so keep your body still (although you may occasionally lean forward to show special interest in specific points).

Similarly, the interviewee will sense your lack of interest and stop talking if you begin to look out of the window or around the room in a distracted fashion. Therefore maintain direct eye contact with the other person for 70 to 80 per cent of the time (any more than this will make the interviewee feel uncomfortable). A good way of breaking eye contact occasionally is to glance down to the notes that you are making of the key points discussed. Finally, smile, grunt and nod at appropriate points in the interview. By these non-verbal communications, you can often keep the interviewee talking without having to ask a follow-up question. Incidentally, never feel nervous about any awkward silences or 'pregnant pauses' which occur during the interview: the interviewee will feel even more nervous and it is precisely at these points that he or she is likely to volunteer some vital piece of supplementary information.

At the same time use verbal strokes to show that you are sensitive to the other person. Two techniques which we have already discussed in relation to chairing a meeting are also useful here: *reflecting* and *paraphrasing*.

Good interviewers always behave in a dispassionate and neutral manner. If they get drawn into showing strong negative feelings the interview is likely to degenerate into an argument. The best way to defuse such strong feelings, if they emanate from the other person, is to reflect them back. Thus if a subordinate rushes into your office and spurts out angrily - 'what right have you to change the system for ordering new supplies behind my back!' - resist the temptation to 'put him in his place'.

Figure 9.5
Asking for information

Start with easy questions - questions that you know the interviewee can answer and that will help to 'break the ice'; build up slowly to the more testing and probing questions

Offer an invitation to talk - open up the dialogue by using encouraging phrases such as: 'tell me about ..., what do you feel about ...? I'd like to hear your views on ...'

Pose fact-seeking questions - these ask for information which the person can provide or which you think they should know; use such questions with care to avoid sounding like an interrogator

Ask open-ended questions - i.e. questions that cannot be answered by a straight yes/no reply; open questions demand that the interviewee expands, thinks and elaborates

Put comprehensive questions - mention a broad topic area and suggest several specific things that the person can comment upon: 'tell me about the problems with the new system, when did they start, have others had the same experience ...?'

Probe - in the later stages of an interview, attempt to make the person more specific and do this in a patient, interested manner that is fairly neutral: 'in what way do you mean that team pressures are increasing ...? can you give me any examples ...?'

Confront - towards the end of the interview, put any doubts you have directly to the interviewee; after all this will be his only chance to answer them: 'your actual experience on the mark III model seems fairly limited. Is this a fair comment or can you convince me I'm wrong?'

Instead, identify that strong feeling and reflect it back to him with a phrase such as: 'obviously, you feel very angry - sit down, and let's talk about it. Now why exactly do you feel so upset by this change?'

Paraphrasing means repeating what the interviewee has said, but using slightly different words. Thus you can demonstrate that you have been listening closely and trying to understand. Additionally, paraphrasing also allows the interviewee to correct any possible misunderstanding. For example: 'Are you really saying that your main reason for applying for this job is to increase your salary? Or have I misunderstood you ...?'

Finally, the type and style of questioning you employ is important in focusing attention on the interviewee rather than yourself (some guidelines on the type of questions which work well are contained in *Figure 9.5*).

Preparation

Painstaking preparation is as vital for interviewing as it is for oral presentations and meetings. A job selection interview is the culmination of a careful decision-making process (but note that discipline or appraisal interviews require similar amounts of preparation).

When recruiting a new employee, the first task is to draw up a job description which defines the duties and responsibilities of the post to be filled. (See *Figure 9.6*)

Next, build a profile of the ideal candidate to fill the post. How much relevant experience would an applicant need in order to cope with the level of responsibility detailed in the job description? Similarly, what qualifications would suggest that the holder had sufficient intelligence and understanding to cope with the job? Are any additional skills required, such as the ability to drive or fluency in a foreign language? A useful framework for relating these questions to the job description is provided by the so called 'seven point plan' (see *Figure 9.7*).

Having gone through this initial planning, the next step is to write a job advertisement for circulation to newspapers, professional journals or employment agencies.

After drawing up a short list, the next job is to plan a selection process lasting for up to a complete day (or longer depending on the number of candidates on the short list). You will want to give the candidates a tour of the premises and a chance to meet the people they might be working with. You will also need to consider whether to set candidates a technical problem or case study to be solved individually or in groups. And are you going to use aptitude or intelligence tests? Note that such tests are not always valid or reliable and should only be used if expert advice on their interpretation is available. You will also need to decide whether to rely solely on your judgement, or to share responsibility for the decision by involving others in the selection process. For example, you could ask a colleague to 'second interview' the candidates and compare notes afterwards or you could decide to invite one or two colleagues to join you on an 'interview panel'. Finally, you should devise

Figure 9.6
The job description

Basic Details
job title and grade; department and section in which the job is located

Objectives
primary objectives of the postholder in relation to the aims of the organisation.

Tasks
what tasks are to be done and how are they to be done? Order of priority

Standards
standards for effective performance of the job; criteria indicating that these have been met

Responsibilities
position of job in organisation structure; superior to whom job holder is accountable; subordinate staff for whom job holder is responsible; responsibility for budget, equipment, etc.

Physical and Social Environment
particular features of work environment (indoor/outdoor, static/mobile etc.); contacts with others (individuals/groups, internal/external, etc.)

Training and Education
training required to bring new jobholders to required level of performance (induction programme, job rotation, internal/external courses)

Career Plan
possible opportunities for promotion and career development

Conditions of Employment
salary and other benefits; probationary period, fixed term/permanent contract; hours of work and leave entitlement; sickness and pension schemes; trade union involvement

a structure for the interview and start thinking about the type of questions to be asked under each heading.

Having sent invitation letters to those on the short list, and taken up references (opinions vary as to whether this is better done by letter or by telephone) all that remains is to prepare the interview room on the day itself.

Figure 9.7
The Job Specification: Seven Point Plan

1. Intelligence

general intelligence and specific abilities

2. Special Aptitudes

mechanical, artistic, manual, verbal, numerical etc.

3. Attainments

academic qualifications; training, experience, skills and knowledge already acquired

4. Physique

health, strength, age, appearance, bearing, speech

5. Disposition

desirable personal qualities (e.g. ability to work in a team or alone, ambitious or
dependable, motivation) but note that these subjective qualities are notorious-
ly hard to measure

6. Circumstances

personal and domestic (e.g. mobility, commitments, family circumstances and oc-
cupations).

7. Interests

personal interests and hobbies (as possible indicators of aptitudes, abilities or personality traits)

The most important point here is to arrange the furniture to create the
right environment for an effective interview. Many managers choose to sit in
an impressive 'executive chair' behind a massive desk, while the applicant co-
wers on the other side. While this arrangement may make the manager feel
important and in command of the situation, it creates a barrier to good communications. Consequently, the candidate is more likely to be on the defensive and to withhold important information.

A much better arrangement is to have two equal size chairs on the same
side of the desk, so that the physical distance between interviewer and interviewee is reduced. This will create a more relaxed and informal atmosphere
which will encourage the candidate to talk freely and at length. On the other
hand, a panel interview is inevitably more formal, and a conventional layout

Figure 9.8
Interview plan

Selection panel: Managing Director (M.D.), Technical Manager (T.M.), Personnel Manager (P.M.)

Introduction (M.D.)
Each member of the panel should be introduced personally to the candidate. This is an ideal opportunity to pose a few easy questions to relax the candidate and establish some degree of 'rapport'

Education and Qualifications (P.M.)
The emphasis here will be on allowing the candidate to expand on his or her particular interests and perceived strengths and weaknesses

Work Experience (T.M.)
Details of previous jobs undertaken by a candidate are very relevant to the final decision on a candidate

Technical Knowledge (T.M.)
This is an opportunity to 'probe' the depth of a candidate's experience and ability by asking detailed technical questions

Motivation (M.D.)
Why does the candidate want to work for this company in particular? What first attracted him or her to engineering as a career?

Personal Circumstances (P.M.)
Care must be taken here not to offend equal opportunities legislation; no questions should be reserved exclusively for female candidates (for example 'when do you plan to start a family?')

Hobbies and Interests (P.M.)
Useful for forming an impression of the candidate's personality e.g. extrovert or introvert?

Conclusion (M.D.)
To include an opportunity for the candidate to ask questions. He or she will be thanked for attending and given a clear indication of how he or she will be informed of the outcome of the interview.

with the interviewers seated behind a desk is probably justified. Finally, you must ensure that the interview will be free from interruptions. Make sure that there is a notice which says something like - 'Interview in Progress, Do not Disturb' - posted on the door and that your secretary or telephonist is briefed to divert callers:

> '... I am sorry, the Manager is interviewing at present, can I take a message?'

Finally, to judge the amount of time needed and the right pace of the interview you will need a plan. This is particularly important if the interview is to be conducted by a selection panel (see *Figure 9.8*).

Delivery

Judging the pace of your delivery is important. Inexperienced interviewers are often more nervous than the person they are interviewing and consequently rush through the interview, failing to give themselves time to think and not allowing the interviewee time to expand. The way to overcome this tendency is 'paragraphing'. Pause occasionally to summarise what has been said, give yourself time to think, and check understanding with the candidate. Then you can introduce the next topic: '... that concludes the questions I want to ask you about your education and qualifications. Is there anything else you want to add? (pause) OK. Now let's turn to your work experience ...'

Suggestions for further study

Clearly, the key to acquiring effective oral communication skills is practise. To this end, student engineers should take every opportunity to attend meetings, give presentations, and practise interviews.

Participation in the local activities of their professional institution or the Engineering Council regional activities is an ideal way of gaining relevant experience.

One useful exercise for students working in small groups is to select a job from a newspaper or journal and use this as a basis for role play. Participants can take it in turn to play members of the selection panel and the interviewee. The educational value of this exercise can be enhanced by recording on video for play-back and analysis.

All presenters can learn a lot from seeing themselves as others see them and video is the ideal medium for recording and playing-back practice presentations. Finally, the giving of careers talks in schools, as suggested at the end of *Chapter 2*, can offer the young engineer valuable experience of oral presentations.

Chapter 10

Written Communications

The Fennell Report into the 1988 King's Cross fire (see *Chapter 5*) criticised the management of the London Underground for adopting a 'management by memo' approach. Officials at various levels in the hierarchy were aware of safety hazards and salved their consciences by writing memos about them; but no one actually took any action to eliminate the hazards. Similarly, memos were written in the Townsend Thoresen organisation about the dangers of ships leaving harbour with the bow loading doors open before the capsize of the *Herald of Free Enterprise* at Zeebrugge; but these memos were not taken seriously by top management.

The disasters at King's Cross and Zeebrugge illustrate in a dramatic way the inherent weakness of the written word as a channel of communication between people in organisations. Henri Fayol, one of the pioneers of classical management, was aware of this weakness as long ago as 1916:

'In dealing with a business matter or giving an order which requires an explanation to complete it, usually it is simpler and quicker to do so orally rather than in writing. Besides, it is well known that differences and misunderstandings which a conversation could clear up, grow more bitter in writing. Thence, it follows that, wherever possible, contacts should be oral; there is a gain in speed, clarity and harmony. Nevertheless, it happens that in some firms, employees who could quite easily meet, only communicate with each other in writing. Hence arise increased work and complications and delays harmful to business. At the same time, there is to be observed a certain animosity prevailing between the employees of different departments. The system of written communication usually brings this result. There is one way of putting an end to this deplorable system and that is to forbid all communications in writing which could easily be replaced by oral ones.'

The continuing validity of Fayol's statement can be proven by a simulation exercise which is sometimes used by communications lecturers and training officers.

Four small groups of people are placed in separate rooms. Each group is then given a simple task to do which they can only achieve successfully by communicating with the other groups. But the rules of the simulation forbid the groups from meeting or talking to each other; instead they have to pass written messages to the other groups via the lecturer or training officer (the groups are also forbidden from speaking to this 'postman'). The rules of the simulation state that each group must answer any written questions sent by another group truthfully.

If the groups were allowed to meet and talk to each other they could complete the task in a few minutes, by simply comparing their information. However, when they are only allowed to communicate with each other in writing, few groups are able to complete the task within the time allowed (normally one hour). Typically when the groups are debriefed, they are fiercely antagonistic towards each other and seek scapegoats for their failure to complete the exercise. They are also amazed to see the amount of paperwork which has been generated.

During the exercise the groups make numerous mistakes which hinder communication and occasionally cause a complete communication breakdown. Written messages are not addressed to anyone in particular and are not delivered by the 'postman'; similarly, groups forget to sign their message and grow increasingly impatient as they wait for a reply (which will never arrive as the other groups do not know to whom to reply). Some show considerable creativity in devising answers which are deliberately misleading, even if they are technically truthful. Others answer messages according to the 'letter' rather than using their initiative to interpret the true intention of the sender.

Above all, most groups tend to see the exercise as a competition, despite the fact that at no time have they been told that they are competing with each other. Consequently the groups seek to acquire information from the other groups without giving anything away themselves. Few realise that the secret to the successful completion of the exercise is the creation of a spirit of trust by first sending a copy of all the information they hold to the other groups; in other words if you want to get something back you first have to give something yourself.

The exercise is, of course, a simulation of what can go wrong in bureaucracies when they are stifled by 'red tape' and unnecessary paperwork. The solution is, as Fayol realised, to keep written communication to a minimum and to rely on direct oral communications (either face to face, or by telephone) wherever possible. To this we can add two other guidelines for the engineer.

Firstly, if a written communication is essential because of the need to put something 'on the record', make sure you also use an oral method of communication as a 'back up': for example, an oral presentation of a written report, or a telephone call to reinforce an instruction contained in a memo.

Secondly, pay careful attention to the *quality* of everything you write. Three factors which contribute to the overall quality of a written communication are:

1. style

2. structure and logical order

3. presentation.

These principles are applied here to report writing; but they are just as relevant to anything else an engineer might have to write, such as the agenda and minutes of meetings, press releases, publicity brochures and instruction manuals. Later, we will consider some additional points which relate specifically to the writing of *memos and letters*.

Style

For many years apostles of 'plain English' have fought a campaign against 'gobbledygook' and sought to promote a writing style which is concise, unambiguous and vivid. The origins of this movement can be traced back to two writers working in the 1940s: Sir Ernest Gowers and George Orwell. Both produced basic rules for writing style which are still valid today.

Gowers' rules are:

1. Write for others rather than yourself.

2. Be short, be simple, be human.

3. Avoid the superfluous word.

4. Choose the familiar word.

5. Choose the precise word (Gowers, 1973).

Orwell's rules are very similar:

1. Never use a metaphor, simile or other figure of speech which you are used to seeing in print.

2. Never use a long word where a short one will do.

3. If it is possible to cut a word out, cut it out.

4. Never use the passive where you can use the active.

5. Never use a foreign phrase, a scientific word or a jargon word if you can think of an everyday English equivalent.

6. Break any of these rules sooner than say anything outright barbarous (Orwell, 1970).

Let us focus here on three of the most widely accepted rules for producing a clear and concise style of writing:

1. prefer familiar and simple words.

2. keep sentences short.

3. prefer the active to the passive voice.

Prefer familiar and simple words

Orwell illustrated this point by quoting a classic verse from Ecclesiastes:

'I returned, and saw under the sun, that the race is not to the swift, nor the battle to the strong, neither yet bread to the wise, nor yet riches to men of understanding, nor yet favour to men of skill; but time and chance happeneth to them all.'

This is a stylish and impressive piece of writing. But it does not contain any impressive-looking words: all the words are everyday words which are simple and familiar (apart from the old-fashioned use of 'happeneth'). Yet many people feel that they have to use long and unfamiliar words, which they would never use in everyday speech, when they are committing pen to paper or sitting at a word processor. The end result is usually a long-winded, verbose and pompous piece of writing which impresses no one. Orwell brilliantly illustrated this point by translating the verse into modern English of the worst kind:

'Objective consideration of contemporary phenomena compels the conclusion that success or failure in competitive activities exhibits a tendency not to be commensurate with innate capacity, but that a considerable element of the unpredictable must invariably be taken into account.'

The original passage is superior in every way yet it contains only a couple of words of three or more syllables; the rewritten version contains fifteen. Orwell also points out that the rewritten version contains eighteen words with Latin (as opposed to old English or Saxon) roots.

Orwell went on to identify a more sinister use of Latin words: their use as euphemisms by politicians to disguise the true meaning of their speeches and ideas. He described how a comfortable English professor who wanted to defend the Stalinist regime in Russia might go about this task. The professor cannot say outright, 'I believe in killing off your opponents when you can get good results by doing so'. Instead, Orwell suggested that the professor would say something like this:

'While freely conceding that the Soviet regime exhibits certain features which the humanitarian may be inclined to deplore, we must I think, agree that a certain curtailment of the right to political opposition is an unavoidable concomitant of transitional periods, and that the rigours which the Russian people have been called upon to undergo have been amply justified in the sphere of concrete achievement.'

Orwell commented that:

'The inflated style is itself a kind of euphemism. A mass of Latin words falls upon the facts like soft snow, blurring the outlines and covering up all the details. The great enemy of clear language is insincerity. When there is a gap between one's real and one's declared aims, one turns ... to long words ... like a cuttlefish squirting out ink' (Orwell, 1970).

Thus there is no reason to feel defensive about favouring simple and familiar words. If you have a choice between a simple Anglo-Saxon word - for example, *start* or *end* - and a more complicated Latin word - *initiate* or *terminate* - use the Anglo-Saxon word. In a technical report the information is already likely to be complex and does not need wrapping up in pretentious language. Well expressed information in a technical report has its own inner dignity and needs no fancy wrapping. Some suggestions of words and phrases to avoid, and their 'antidotes' can be found in *Figure 10.1*.

The same criteria can be applied to the use of 'jargon'. Jargon is acceptable as long as it is used to describe new ideas or objects or can replace a

Figure 10.1
Some examples of over-long words and phrases and their antidotes

DO NOT USE	WHEN YOU COULD SAY
aforementioned	these
in which eventuality	if so
circumstances occasionally arise	sometimes
in the near future	soon
accounted by the fact that	because
after the conclusion of	after
in view of the fact that	because
for the purpose of	for; to
there is reason to believe that	I think, we think
advantageous	useful
alleviate	ease, improve
disseminate	spread
facilitate	ease, help
implement	do
modification	change
necessitate	require
predominant	main
proximity	near
unavailability	lack, absence
utilise	use

string of old words. And there is no alternative to the precise terms needed in a complex technical report - for example, the chemical engineer is saddled with such terms as *trichlorophenol* and *tetrachlorobenzene*. In such cases the writer has to make a judgement on the technical competence of the readership and decide how much help they need. This help could be an explanation in brackets directly after the technical term, a footnote, or a cross reference to a 'glossary of terms' at the end of the report.

However, the widespread use of complicated technical terms in a report makes it all the more important to ensure its overall readability by keeping the rest of the language as clear and simple as possible.

Abbreviations are fine if they are used for proper names such as the names of organisations and their use may help to improve readability by cutting the number of words used. A common practice is to write the name out in full first with the abbreviation in brackets: for example, Manpower Services

Commission (MSC). Thereafter use the abbreviation only. You may also choose to include abbreviations in the glossary.

Keep sentences short

One of the findings of the Fennell Report into the King's Cross fire was that the Underground's rule book on emergency fire procedures was too long and verbose, and did not clearly state what staff had to do in the event of a fire. Subsequently, the Underground employed a firm of communications consultants to rewrite the manual. Their aim has been to jettison clauses and subclauses that have been added over the years and rewrite the manual in positive and easy to understand terms (see *Figure 10.2*).

If you find yourself writing too many long and complex sentences you will have simply to chop them into two or more pieces. Sometimes this is as simple as changing a comma into a full stop and converting the first letter of the next word into a capital; sometimes you will have to change some of the words to cauterise the wound. For example:

> 'The working party recommended the purchase of six new terminals and printers for the purpose of increasing the number of staff able to gain easy access to the mainframe system.'

There are 30 words in this sentence. After the 'chop', and with a few words changed, we have two sentences of 12 and 16 words:

> 'The working party recommended the purchase of six new terminals and printers. This will increase the number of staff able to gain easy access into the mainframe system.'

However, you can go too far in keeping sentences short. Try reading the following extract from a computer manual:

> 'BASIC was invented many years ago. It was originally designed as a programming language that was simple to learn. Its purpose was to aid teaching. There are now many versions of BASIC. These have been developed to run on modern microcomputers.'

Here the sentences are too short and jerky, the writing does not flow, and the whole paragraph is rather patronising. The solution is to downgrade the less important ideas and put them in subordinate clauses:

Figure 10.2
London Underground emergency procedures
(*Daily Telegraph*, 1989)

The inquiry into the King's Cross fire criticised the wording of rules such as rule D2 in the official manual:

D2 If fire or smouldering is small enough to be dealt with by members of staff, speed is of the utmost importance. If a member of staff observes, or is informed of, a small fire or smouldering in or around railway buildings, tracks, cables or other property (including tunnels and the sides of cuttings and embankments) he must take immediate action to extinguish it. Most fires can be extinguished or kept in check by buckets of water and/or hand pumps or beating with lengths of hose.

While these instructions included words like 'must' and 'speed', the approach was long winded and softened its impact by using the words 'if' and 'smouldering'. These and similar instructions have been replaced with instructions in plain English such as:

Fire or smoke in stations - tell the line controller where the fire is and the best way for the fire brigade to reach it.

Station Evacuation - close the station to incoming passengers.

'BASIC was originally designed, many years ago, as a simple to learn programming language which could aid teaching. There are now many versions of BASIC developed to run on modern microcomputers.'

An average of 15 to 20 words per sentence is a reasonable target to aim for. But vary your sentence length to create interest and guide the reader; read your work 'silently aloud' to make sure that you have the right harmony and rhythm; and use short sentences without any subordinate clauses to highlight key points or ideas. For example: 'Always remove the disc before switching off!'

In technical reports and manuals where the information cannot be easily cut, you may be able to alter the layout to create an impression of shorter sentences. For example:

'The current value of a variable can be lost in three ways: firstly when you load a program, secondly when you run a program and thirdly when you leave BASIC'.

This sentence is rather clumsy and could be rewritten as follows:

'The current value of a variable is lost whenever you:
1. load a program
2. run a program
3. leave BASIC'.

This is still one sentence although it may not look like it.

Prefer the active to the passive

'The operator pulled the lever' is an example of the *active* voice - the operator is the *subject* of the sentence and the lever is the *object*. However, it is possible to rephrase the sentence in the *passive* voice: 'the lever was pulled by the operator'. Notice how in the second example, the subject and object of the sentence have changed places: somewhat illogically, the lever is now the subject and the operator the (indirect) object.

Similarly, in describing a simple scientific experiment, it would be logical to use the active voice: 'I then observed that the liquid turned green and started to effervesce ...' However, generations of school children have been taught instead to use the passive voice: 'it was observed that the liquid ...'

The aim here is to switch the subject of the sentence from the person conducting the experiment to the experiment itself and replace the personal pronoun 'I' with the impersonal 'it'. By this linguistic device, the writer hopes to create an impression of impartiality and objectivity. For the same reasons the passive voice has traditionally been used in report writing, for example: 'it is recommended that ...' rather than: 'I recommend that' (the justification is that the recommendation itself is more important than who made it).

But excessive use of the clichéd 'it ... that' construction (see *Figure 10.3*) can lead to an impersonal and sterile style. The danger here is that important and useful information may be lost. For example:

'It has been suggested that a working party should be set up to review current working practices.'

Why not write instead:

'The managing director suggested that the personnel department should set up a working party to review current working practices?'

The passive tense is inadvisable when writing procedures or other instructions. Do not write:

Figure 10.3
The 'it ... that' construction

There are a number of variations on the passive 'it ... that' construction - most of which have a bad effect on style:

- It is assumed that ...

- It is felt that ...

- It might be thought that ...

- It has been brought to my attention that ...

- It has been shown that ...

- It has been previously remarked that ...

- It has been established that ...

- It has been found by experiment that ...

'the level of lubricant in the L17 machine must be topped up every Friday or after 60 hours of continuous use'.

By whom - a robot? Instead write:

'the operator of the L17 machine must top up the level of lubricant every Friday or after 60 hours of continuous use'.

This second version is more direct and the instruction is more likely to be carried out.

Another device for achieving a certain 'pseudo-objectivity' is to use expressions such as 'the writer believes' or 'in the author's opinion'. The overall effect can be very clumsy and heavy. Why not say, instead, 'I believe that the best option is to ...' or 'in my opinion, we should ...'? This more direct style brings the writer and reader into closer contact and the writing becomes more vivid. One advantage of the use of the personal pronoun is that it discourages vagueness and emphasises the author's responsibility for what he or she writes. But overuse of the words 'I' and 'we' can be intrusive and irritating - the key is to achieve balance in your writing.

A note of caution is necessary here. Some long-established companies still insist on an impersonal 'house style' for report writing based on the

Figure 10.4
The Fog Index (Gunning, 1952)

The following passage is an example of deliberate verbosity taken from *The Engineer in Society*' Part 2B Examination 1988 (Engineering Council).

'Given the present state of the art, of the renewable energy sources sun, wind, and biomass are under the most severe competitive pressure from the conventional systems whenever the latter are available even though they may be expensive. This is generally the result of the comparatively low energy densities of the renewable energy sources which necessitate the installation of material-intensive systems for concentrating the energy flows. The example of solar energy demonstrates this aspect when considering the large absorber areas required, even for a relatively low output. Likewise although an energy flow of high density is produced when gasifying forestry waste and converting to electricity, the preceding collection of the biomass from a defined catchment area presents a laborious process of concentration. From this one is easily led to the standard optimised solution i.e. that units of this kind should preferably be operated where there are already concentrations of suitable quantities of biomass e.g. at sawmills. However, a careful optimisation is much more complex if all the technical and economic characteristics of system components are to be considered with reference to a competitive overall system.'

To calculate the fog index of the passage:

1. Count the number of words in the passage	185
2. Count the number of sentences	6
3. Calculate the average number of words per sentence	31
4. Count the number of 'polysyllables'	49
[polysyllables are words with 3 or more syllables, discounting proper names and verbs which become three syllables after the addition of -ed -es -ing etc.]	
5. Calculate the percentage of polysyllables in the passage	38%
6. Add step (5) to (3) and multiply the result by 0.4 to give ... THE FOG INDEX =	27.4

The fog index of a piece of text is said to correspond to the number of years of formal education that a reader of average intelligence would need to read and understand it.

Fog Index	Comments
Under 8	childish
8-14	easy to read
15-17	heavy
18-20	very heavy
over 20	virtually unreadable

passive tense. If such a company is your employer or a client, you will have to adapt your style accordingly. It is a good idea, anyway, to practise writing in both the impersonal, passive and the direct, active styles as this will help develop your writing skill. The disciplined use of both styles can add some variety and elegance to your writing.

Finally, there is a mathematical formula for measuring the readability of a given piece of text: this is the so-called 'fog index' (see *Figure 10.4*). The fog index can give no real indication of style or whether a piece of writing is good or bad but it is a useful indicator of verbosity; try applying it to 200 words of your own writing.

Structure and logical order

Figure 10.5 summarises four alternative structures which can be adapted for use with the majority of topics to be covered by a report. These structures are: *Conventional Report Structure*; *Court Structure*; the *Four P's*; and the *Inverted Pyramid*. Each has its own internal logical order.

Most engineers will be familiar with the five-part conventional report writing structure which has been in use for many years. This structure starts with a clear statement of the *Terms of Reference* of the report. As well as specifying the main aims and objectives of the report, this section could include a description of the background events leading to the request for the report.

Next comes the *Method of Investigation*. This should include an account of the resources available to the author (such as staff-time, authority to collect evidence and so on) and how these influenced the method. The actual methods and techniques used in the study (for example: interviews, postal questionnaires or experiments) should also be described and justified in relation to the objectives already stated in the terms of reference.

These first two sections are introductory in nature and should not take up too much space. The main part or body of the report should be devoted to the *Findings* section. You will need to devise your own detailed structure here, depending on the subject. You will also have to pay attention to logical order.

Wheatley (1988) has analysed the logical order in which the findings of the inquiry into the Flixborough disaster (see *Chapter 5*) were presented in the final report. She summarises this order as:

1. what happened

Figure 10.5
Four alternative structures for report writing

Conventional Report Structure: TERMS OF REFERENCE
METHOD OF INVESTIGATION
FINDINGS
CONCLUSIONS
RECOMMENDATIONS

Court Structure: PROPOSITION, EVIDENCE,   INTERPRETATION
CONCLUSION - based on practice in the courts and
good for scientific and investigative reports (e.g.
accident reports)

The Four Ps: POSITION, PROBLEMS, POSSIBILITIES, PROPOSAL
good for problem solving or sales reports

The Inverted Pyramid   particularly good for punchy short reports (including
letters and memos)

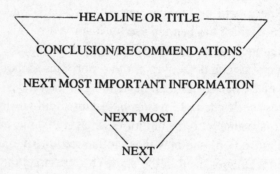

2. the problem stated - the need to discover why

3. the two-stage hypothesis - quickly rejected

4. evidence from eye witnesses

5. the 8-inch hypothesis - examined in detail and rejected

6. the 20-inch hypothesis - compared with the 8-inch and accepted.

The strength of this structure lies in its logic and simplicity. The report proper
(which is written in a style which is clear to any non-scientific reader) is only
37 pages long.

The next two sections in the conventional report structure are the most important: the *Conclusions* and *Recommendations*. Some readers may read these two sections in detail but only skim through the rest of the report.

The conclusions should flow from and be linked to the findings section of the report with appropriate cross references. Some reports have mini-conclusions at the end of each sub-section in the main body of the report. If you decide to adopt this structure, an additional section entitled *Summary of Conclusions* is useful as a means of drawing all the strands of your arguments together in preparation for the recommendations which are to follow.

Recommendations should be presented as a numbered list of action points. These should be written as though they are to be given to a robot who needed to know what to do but not why ('why' is covered in the rest of the report). If appropriate, include the names of the individuals or groups who are to implement your recommendations. Remember, that in the conventional structure, recommendations should always come after conclusions (in a short report it is acceptable to combine the two in a section entitled *Conclusions and Recommendations*).

An alternative to the conventional report structure, is the *Court Structure*, which, as the name implies, is based on practice in a court of law. This structure starts with the *Proposition* ('it is alleged that on the night of the 14th, the defendant did ...'). The court then hears the *Evidence* in strictly logical order. The case for the prosecution comes first, followed by the case for the defence. Next comes the *Interpretation* stage when the counsel for the prosecution and the defence, followed by the judge, sum up the arguments as they see them. Finally, the *Conclusion* is reached when the jury give their verdict: guilty or not guilty. This proven structure and logical order can be adapted to report writing and works particularly well for formal investigative reports.

The *Four P's* provide a simple structure for report writing which is less formal and, perhaps, more stylish than the conventional or court structures. In this structure you first set the scene with a description of background events which have contributed to the current *Position*. Then identify the *Problem* (or problems) to which you are seeking a solution in the report. Next list all the *Possibilities* or alternative courses of action which may solve the problem identified and summarise their respective advantages and disadvantages. Finally, choose the one option from your list of possibilities which seems to offer the best solution and rewrite this in more detail as your *Proposal*. The main strength of this structure is the logical way in which it separates problems from solutions.

Incidentally, the Four P's can make a very effective sales pitch. Show your customer that you understand his position. Show that you understand his problems. Then list the possibilities for solving his problem - including what your competitors would offer. Show him the limitations of these solutions. Then make your proposal - show him how your product or service could solve his problems.

The *Inverted Pyramid* is the least formal structure of the four structures discussed here. Its main advantage is that it wastes no time in getting straight to the point and it is ideal for short reports, memos and letters in which you want to make an immediate or dramatic impact. It is also ideal for press releases. Its main disadvantage is its lack of subtlety. If you are writing on a contentious subject you may want to build your case slowly, taking your reader with you, before revealing your solution; if so, one of the other structures would be more suitable. Similarly, if you use this structure for a complex technical subject you might be criticised for being too simplistic or journalistic. This would not be surprising as the inverted pyramid is a structure which is taught to journalists and is widely used in the tabloid press.

The inverted pyramid is top heavy and tapers into nothing at the bottom. First comes the *Title* or *Headline*. This must be carefully chosen to get to the heart of the main idea of the report. Next - in reversal of the normal order - come the conclusions and recommendations. Journalists are taught to use Rudyard Kiplings' six honest serving men:

'I keep six honest serving men (they taught me all I know)

Their names are What and Why and When

And How and Where and Who.'

In most reports, what action you propose to take is the most important piece of information, and the six serving men can help you write these first. Next write the conclusions using the same methodology. From then on you can add the next most important piece of information and so on.

The choice of an appropriate structure before you start will considerably ease the process of writing. Nevertheless, many engineers dread the moment when they have to sit down with a blank piece of paper and start writing a major report. Inspiration rarely arrives easily. One approach is to apply a technique called 'patterned note-taking' to the all-important preparation and planning stage of writing a report.

First, ask yourself the question: what above all else am I hoping to achieve as a result of writing this report? Take a large piece of blank paper and write this question at the centre of the paper (not at the top as in conventional notes). Next write your main headings - for example the four P's - in a circle around the centre and join them to the centre with lines. Now 'brainstorm' and write key ideas around each of the main headings. Highlight the ideas which seem to be most important and which will warrant the status of subsidiary headings in the final report. Look for additional ideas or connections and add them to your diagram; and use 'graphic design' (geometrical shapes, arrows, colour etc.) to highlight connections.

Buzan (1974) argues that patterned notes have a number of advantages over conventional 'linear' notes (the latter defined as notes written in sentence form, starting in the top left hand corner of the page and writing from left to right). In patterned notes, the central or main idea stands out. The relative importance of each idea is clearly indicated: more important ideas will be near the centre and less important ideas near the edge. Links between key concepts will be immediately recognizable because of their proximity and connection. Finally, the open-ended nature of the pattern produced will enable the brain to make new connections far more readily.

In linear notes, Buzan suggests that time is wasted recording and re-reading words which are not crucial to the main idea of the report. Similarly, time is wasted searching for 'key' words which are hidden among other less important words. Finally, the connections between key words are interrupted by the words and spaces that separate them making it more difficult to make proper connections between ideas.

Let us assume that you have completed a patterned note diagram of the structure of your proposed report. Your next step is to review the integrity and logical order of the whole structure and add a decimal numbering system to all the headings and sub-headings highlighted on the diagram. For example:

1. main heading

1.1 sub-heading

1.1.1 sub, sub-heading.

It is theoretically possible to go on to 1.1.1.1 (sub, sub, sub-heading), but this would almost certainly indicate an over complicated structure. If you find yourself in this position, take another look at your patterned note diagram and see if you can promote some of the sub-headings into main headings.

Having designed a suitable structure and collected any necessary information or data, you are now ready to start writing. If you are using pen and paper, collect some blank pages of A4 and write out your main headings with their numbers - with one heading per page. If you are using a word processor, type in all your headings and sub-headings together with the numbering system.

Now start writing in your text under the appropriate headings. The advantage of having already established a clear structure and logical order is that you can start writing anywhere you like. Start with the bit you think will be easiest to write: if you run out of inspiration, you can always move on to another section and come back to the original one later. Remember that you have already carefully numbered all your headings so that you cannot lose your place in the overall scheme of things. Collation of the report when you have finished writing is simply a matter of sorting your papers, or printing files from a word processor, into the correct order.

Presentation

At every stage in the process of producing a report you should be thinking of your readers. Will they be other engineers, colleagues in other professions, or members of the public? Or a mixture of groups? Clearly you will need to adjust your style of writing accordingly (the appropriate use of technical terminology is an obvious example). An appreciation of the needs of your readers is particularly important in the final stage of the report writing process: the presentation and layout of the report itself.

Let us assume that you have written an important report for your board of directors. Now let us try to visualise how the report will be received and perceived by one member of the board ...

The managing director is going through his in-tray at 8:30 a.m. before his first engagement at 9:30 a.m. He works his way methodically through the pile of paper, taking action on each item. He scribbles a note on one piece of paper and files it in his action tray for his secretary; another piece of paper is read and then immediately crumpled up and 'filed' in the bin. The M.D. picks up your report. You now have his attention for five minutes at most.

Figure 10.6
Title page and summary

C.G.M. ENGINEERING plc

A PROPOSAL FOR THE INSTALLATION OF A FIRE DETECTION SYSTEM
AT HEAD OFFICE

By Janet Smith, Trainee Engineer

1st September 1990

Summary
This report compares three types of fire detector (flame detectors, heat detectors and
smoke detectors). The author recommends the installation of a smoke detector system
for the management offices and conference rooms as this system responds quickest to
the outbreak of a fire. However customers are allowed to smoke in the display showrooms - in this area a heat detector system is recommended. Finally, the report recommends that both systems be linked to a master control panel designed to show quickly
where an alarm has been set off.

Distribution: *Board of Directors, Safety Officer*

His first impressions are good. The report looks professional and well laid
out. The title page tells him the topic, the name of the author, who else has
got copies of the report and its date of publication (he is pleased to see that
the report is 'hot off the press'). He opens the report and is delighted to find,
on the first page, a summary of the whole report including the main conclusions and recommendations. Having read every word of the summary with
interest, he then turns the page to find a page entitled 'Table of Contents'.
He reads this and notices that the 'conclusions' and 'recommendations' sections are on pages 15 and 16 respectively. He turns to these pages and reads
them in detail (remember that he has already seen a summary of them).

He then leans back in his chair and flicks through the pages of the report
in a distracted way. You can tell he is thinking. An interesting-looking graph
takes his attention and is studied carefully. Then his body stiffens - clearly he
has come to a decision. He throws the report on the table and picks up the
telephone: 'John, I'd like you to make an appointment for me to see that
young engineer - what's her name?' He pauses to look at the title page of the

report - 'Ah yes, Janet Smith. Tell her that I want to discuss the report she's just written.' The managing director puts the report into his briefcase - he will read it at his leisure that evening - and goes back to the contents of his in-tray.

This scenario illustrates the importance of providing an 'overview' of your report for your readership and the way in which a 'title page', 'summary' and 'table of contents' can help you to achieve this (see *Figure 10.6*). Whether a summary is included on the title page or whether it merits a page of its own depends on your judgement and the length of the report. An important point to remember here is that the order should always be:

1. title page

2. summary

3. table of contents

4. text (your page numbering system starts here)

5. appendices (if any).

Another good reason for providing a clear overview of your report is that research has shown that it helps readers to master difficult subjects. If the brain is made aware of the conclusion first, it can more easily make the connections between the findings leading up to that conclusion. An overview then is equally important if you are writing for top executives or shop floor workers.

You can also make your report easier to read by relegating detailed technical information to 'appendices' at the back of the report. If left in the main text, this information could interrupt the 'flow' of your writing and alienate non-technical readers. Appendices should be numbered differently from the headings in the main body of the report to avoid confusion (e.g. Appendix A, Appendix B etc.). A full list of the appendices should be included in the table of contents and individual appendices cross-referenced in the text (e.g. 'see Appendix B').

The actual layout or design of the printed page can also have an important impact on the psychology of the reader. It can be an enervating experience to open a report and see page after page of closely packed text unfolding before you. The generous use of white space to break up blocks of continuous prose and to create a feeling of lightness will make the report more readable. The use of double line spacing (i.e. one empty line between two lines of text) rather than single line spacing is one way of achieving this effect.

Finally, use indenting, capital and lower case letters, and underlining to clarify the relative importance of headings and paragraphs, for example:

1. <u>CAPITALS UNDERLINED</u>
  1.1 CAPITALS NOT UNDERLINED
    1.1.1 <u>Lower Case Underlined</u>
    1.1.2 Lower case not underlined (paragraphs without
        headings).

A report which contains a mixture of numbering systems - for example, arabic (1,2,3), roman (I,II,III or i,ii,ii,) and letters (A,B,C, or a,b,c) - can be very confusing. Therefore, stick to one numbering system: preferably arabic (with decimals).

Memos and letters

The efficiency of face-to-face communication is undermined by the notorious unreliability of the human memory: for example, it is common for people to have substantially different recollections of the same conversation. Hence the need for written minutes of meetings and the need for the 'memo' - the most commonly used channel of internal written communications (see *Figure 10.7*).

The key to the proper use of the memo is contained in the original Latin meaning of the word in its full version - *memorandum* literally means 'something to be remembered.' In the course of a day, an individual may take part in many face-to-face communications - in corridors, at meetings and interviews and so on. Inevitably, there is a risk that important information and agreements may be forgotten. Therefore, it is usually a good idea to follow up such contacts with a memo to ensure that the important parts of the communication will be remembered. By sending copies to other people in the organisation who may have a legitimate interest, proper use of the memo can help to spread accurate information and prevent misunderstanding and duplication of effort.

The fundamental difference between a memo and a letter is that while a memo is normally reserved for internal communication, a letter is used for external communication and, as such, acts as a form of ambassador from one organisation to another. When writing a letter you should always be aware of this fact and pay particular attention to presentation and proof reading.

Figure 10.7
The successful completion of memos

A memo is designed for simple, efficient communication between people who are working together. Although courtesy is essential, over-elaborate language and platitudes are out of place

The full addresses are unnecessary as employees should be familiar with these (moreover an internal delivery system will probably deliver the memo anyway)

Salutation (Dear Sir) and *subscription* (Yours faithfully etc.) are not needed

Layout is strictly functional. Usually headed pro-formas are provided within the organisation.The heading should include:
1. 'MEMORANDUM' (or 'MEMO)
2. 'TO', 'FROM', and 'COPY TO' indicating the spaces where the names and/of titles of the sender, recipient/s and those who are to receive the information are to be typed or written. N.B. if there are too many names to be fitted in the spaces following 'TO' and 'COPY TO', write 'See below' and list the names at the end of the memo
3. 'DATE' followed by a space in which the date is written (normally in abbreviated form)

Often included in headings are:
1. the name of the organisation - this is not strictly necessary as everybody should know who they are working for.
2. 'REF' - the reference may be the initials of the sender and the typist, or, preferably, a filing code (efficient filing is essential if the memo is to act as a memory aid).
3. 'SUBJECT' - this means that a heading or title for the memo must be given. This is a desirable practice in correspondence, for a heading immediately identifies the subject matter

It is useful to include a list of possible responses in the standard heading so that you can tick an appropriate box for each memo you send out:
[ ] FOR INFORMATION [note this and remember it, but you are not required to do anything about it]
[ ] FOR ACTION [the text of this memo will tell you what to do]
[ ] FOR FILE [keep this as you may need it in the future]
[ ] FOR COMMENT [the sender wishes you to reply]

If you require the recipient to take some action, always put in a target date; never use the meaningless term 'as soon as possible' (or 'A.S.A.P.'). Make a note of the target date in your diary in case the recipient loses your memo and you have to give him or her a gentle reminder on the day in question

At the end of the memo come the initials of the sender (signed personally). A full signature is not required

Figure 10.8
Some letter writing clichés and their alternatives

Thanking you in anticipation (thank you).

With reference to your letter of the 20th Ult ... (put the subject title of the letter and date in full in your own heading).

It has been brought to my attention that ... (leave it out altogether - you would hardly be writing about it if it had not been drawn to your attention).

I remain your obedient servant ... I beg to inform you that ... (better to omit antiquated phrases like these altogether)

Your early attention to this matter would be appreciated ... (please reply by the 25th because we make up our monthly orders then ...)

However, because of a desire to impress the reader, many people employ a pompous and long-winded style of expression in a letter which they would never use in ordinary conversation. Phrases such as 'thanking you in antici-pation', 'with reference to your letter of the 14th inst.', 'it has been brought to my attention that ...', 'I remain your obedient servant' appear only in let-ters.

However, far from impressing the reader, the net effect of the use of such phrases and words is to make the letter longer and harder to understand and consequently to irritate the reader. Worse still, important target dates and deadlines can be lost behind such woolly phrases as 'your early attention to this matter would be appreciated'.

It is much better to use a more direct, plain English style (see *Figure 10.8*). The secret, if you find it difficult to express yourself in a clear way while writ-ing a letter, is to stop and ask yourself the question - 'how would I phrase this if the person I am writing to is standing in front of me'? Then write this down and polish it.

Finally, wherever possible, make an effort to find out the name and job title of the person you are writing to. If in doubt, telephone them; you may find anyway that you can achieve your purpose more effectively over the tele-phone. If not, at least you should be able to clarify to whom you are writing and avoid the use of the impersonal 'Dear Sir' (or, worse, 'Dear Sir or

Madam') in your letter. Unfortunately, some companies and most government departments state that all letters must be addressed impersonally to the company. Although this is old fashioned, it would be impolite to ignore this instruction. Therefore, show that you are replying to the person who wrote to you by putting an additional heading in ('for the attention of: ...'); then open with 'Dear Sir' or 'Dear Madam'.

Suggestions for further study

The Engineering Council is one of the bodies that has been campaigning for a plain English style in technical writing. Over the years, one question in their *Engineer in Society* examination has been reserved for an example of verbosity which the candidate has to translate into a piece of simple, concise and clear English. These exercises are ideal for engineers who wish to practise their writing skills and we have included a selection of them in the *Study Questions and Assignments* for *Chapter 10*.

The *Complete Plain Words* by Sir Ernest Gowers remains a classic and has not dated in any significant way. George Orwell's essay *Politics and the English Language* contains his rules for plain English and is a passionate defence of the English language. The essay also anticipates many of the issues which Orwell develops in his powerful novel *1984*, where a totalitarian state invents a new language - 'Newspeak' - to mislead and help subdue the masses.

Finally Tony Buzan, in his book *Use Your Head*, gives many practical tips on creative thinking and time planning which are very useful to anyone who has to write reports.

Study Questions and Assignments

Chapter 1

Why did the Finniston Report conclude that engineering could not be regarded as a profession in the strict sense of the term? Give your views on how this situation might be changed.

Suggest points that you would like to see included in a contemporary Code of Professional Practise for Engineers. Justify your suggestions and discuss uses for such a Code.

Do you agree that Britain is an industrial country with an anti-industrial culture?

'The iron law of international comparison requires that you improve your efficiency, cut your costs, by something like three per cent every year *just to stand still*.' (Handy, 1984). What are the lessons here for industry?

Give your views on the reasons why Britain has found herself with a worsening balance of payments deficit in finished manufactured goods from 1983 onwards.

'English schoolboys have learnt that they can earn much more by buying and selling houses and antiques than they can by becoming engineers.' (Lord Bowden). Discuss this statement and give your views on how degree-level recruitment might be improved.

Chapter 2

Why was 1986 designated British Industry Year?

Give your views on how the recruitment of high calibre men and women into the British engineering industry might be increased.

The Engineering Council hopes that an increasingly large number of British women will enter degree courses to study engineering. Discuss the prospects for a continued increase in numbers of women entrants and examine potential benefits to the British engineering industry.

Critically examine the proposals for an improved system of higher education and training to produce top quality engineers, made in the Finniston Report, *Engineering Our Future*.

What are non-price factors? Show why these are so important for the survival of British manufacturing industry.

Explain the term 'post-industrial society'. What are the implications for the engineering profession?

Chapter 3

What do you consider to be the likely impact on the British economy of the increased use of robotics and computer-integrated manufacture (CIM) in engineering?

What were the main criteria that the Government took into account when deciding to order the building of a pressurised water reactor at Sizewell in Suffolk?

Examine the likely impact of cable television and direct broadcasting by satellite on British society.

Describe what you consider the main features of present-day 'post-industrial society' in Britain.

Describe the main features of the British Industrial Revolution, paying special attention to those features which you feel were essential to its rapid development.

What factors do you feel that the current British Government should be taking into account when planning energy supplies for the first decade of the next century.

If you were asked to investigate the impact of a major new piece of technology on society, what criteria would you use? Give examples to support your choices.

Discuss the contention that the study of the social history of engineering is a vital part of any professional engineer's education. Use examples to support your views.

Discuss the major problems that the developing nations are meeting in their efforts to industrialise. Use examples to explain these problems and their possible solutions.

Why might computers be a success in London and a disaster in the developing world?

What do you consider to be the engineering achievement of this century from a social point of view? Explain the criteria you use to make your choice.

Technology is sometimes uncritically regarded as a curse and at other times as an unalloyed blessing. Give your ideas, with examples, on what constitutes 'good' technology.

It has been said that the Apollo project to put a man on the Moon can now only be regarded as a waste of money. Give your views.

Chapter 4

Do you agree that 'acid rain' from coal-fired power stations has made nuclear power an attractive option for Britain's future energy provision?

The problem of waste disposal has been called the 'Achilles' heel' of the nuclear industry. Describe and discuss the problems of nuclear waste disposal in Britain.

Comment on the engineering problems associated with the decommissioning of nuclear reactors. Discuss the possible methods available for the disposal of such radioactive waste.

Discuss the 'greenhouse effect'. In your answer describe how the use of chlorofluorocarbons (CFCs) affects the Earth's ozone layer and outline the problems that this could pose for future generations.

Examine the view that the accident at Chernobyl has marked the end of nuclear power as a solution to world energy needs.

Chapter 5

Discuss the view that major accidents are an inevitable feature of technological progress. Support your argument with examples.

Examine the radical view, that if engineers are to perform the extraordinary feats that society expects of them, accidents are bound to occur.

What lessons can be learnt from major industrial accidents and technological failures? Give examples to illustrate your views.

'Safety should be considered at the drawing board stage of a project rather than after its completion.' Discuss this statement and describe some of the loss-prevention techniques used by engineers to minimise the chance of failure.

Discuss some of the management failures that culminated in:
1. the capsize of the *Herald of Free Enterprise*.
2. the King's Cross Underground fire.
    What organisational changes are required to prevent such accidents from happening in the future?

Chapter 6

What is Taylorism? Describe Taylor's contribution to the development of organisation and management theory.

Describe the work of Henri Fayol with particular reference to the five functions that he saw for management.

Describe and discuss the management principles that underlay Alfred P. Sloan's salvation of General Motors in the 1920s.

Show why Classical Management Theory became discredited and discuss the main criticisms of it.

Chapter 7

Describe and discuss the management theory underpinning the success of Japanese manufacturing industry in the 1970s and 1980s.

Discuss the significance of the 'Volvo experiment' in Sweden for the organisation of factory work.

Describe and discuss the different forms of authority relationship that you would expect to find in an engineering works.

Chapter 8

Contrast McGregor's Theory X with his Theory Y and explain the relevance of Theory Y to team leadership.

Explain the significance of the Hawthorne experiments in the USA (1924 to 1936) and illustrate the 'Hawthorne effect'.

Explain the relevance of Maslow's 'hierarchy of human needs' and the concept of 'self-actualisation' to team leadership.

Give your views on what constitutes effective leadership and support your ideas with examples.

Imagine that you are a management consultant hired to investigate the organisational structure of a SECTION of the company you currently work for or that you know well.

Carry out your own investigation into company organisation, applying the techniques and concepts contained in this book. Then write a report of your findings. A possible structure for your report is set out below.

TITLE: 'A Report on the Organisation and Management of the ... (section) of the ... (company).'

1. POSITION: background information on the company, number of employees, brief history, official organisation chart.

2. ANALYSIS: apply the different concepts covered in the book. Subheadings might be:

    2.1 Classical Management: do 'classical' principles such as specialisation, individual wage incentives, unity of command, small spans of control, etc., apply? Are 'work study' and 'O and M' techniques applied? If so, how effective are they? Does the company's management style correspond to Theory X?

    2.2 Human Relations: are 'human relations' techniques such as quality circles, job enrichment and job rotation used? Does the company's management style correspond to Theory Y?

    2.3 Organisational Structure: using the definitions of work levels and authority relationships discussed in Chapter 8, draw a diagram (or diagrams) to illustrate the 'social reality' of the company (i.e. 'what really happens'). How does this compare with the official organisation chart in section 1 - is there a mismatch between the official and informal organisation structures?

3. PROBLEMS: identify any organisational problems which your analysis has uncovered. However, if you feel that the company is functioning smoothly without significant problems, then you may omit this section.

4. SUMMARY OF CONCLUSIONS: draw together any conclusions made in sections 2 and 3.

5. RECOMMENDATIONS: these should flow naturally from the conclusions and should attempt to solve any problems identified in section 3 (if you did not identify any problems, your recommendations will probably be to leave things as they are). If relevant, include a diagram to illustrate any proposed changes in the organisational structure.

The completed report should be presented with a title page, summary, acknowledgements and table of contents. Sections and sub-sections should be numbered using a decimal system; pages should also be numbered.

Describe the eight roles that Belbin thought were necessary to form an effective team. Do you agree or disagree with his analysis? Give your reasons.

Chapter 9

Examine ways in which oral communication can be made more effective. Consider examples from both a discussion between individuals and the presentation of a paper at a large conference.

Panther Marine is a successful boat-building company on the South Coast specialising in high-performance racing craft - power and sail. The design department consists of a Chief Designer and a team of four experienced designers. Over the past year, two designers have left the company to work abroad. The company has experienced great difficulty in recruiting experienced designers with sufficient adaptability and creativity, so they have decided to give a chance to a college leaver and train him or her up to their own exacting standards.

The Managing Director has called the Chief Designer and some of his staff, together with the Production Manager and Personnel Manager, to a meeting to plan the overall strategy for recruitment of a suitable college leaver.

The purpose of this meeting is to discuss:
  the job description and job specification for the new post
  the design of a suitable application form
  the design of a job advertisement for circulation to colleges and
      newspapers
  a plan for a selection process lasting for up to a day (including details of interview/s, any other selection techniques, introduction to the company, etc.).

The actual production of these documents will be delegated to smaller working parties drawn from those attending the meeting.

Your task, in small groups, is to:

1. Allocate a suitable role to every member of your group, and role-play the meeting described above
2. Form sub-groups to produce the documents described
3. Report back to a meeting of the full group to approve the final documents
4. Distribute application forms and job advertisements to members of another group and role-play the interviews.

Chapter 10

Describe the different circumstances in which information on a technical investigation would best be transmitted by:

1. a written report
2. a memorandum
3. a letter
4. an oral presentation

What principal differences in strategy are involved in each type of communication?

[*The Engineer in Society*, Engineering Council Examination, Q12, 1982]

What are the main considerations that must be taken into account in the preparation of a technical report? Outline the errors that are frequently made in English grammar, style and presentation.

What are the considerations that must be taken into account in the preparation of a machinery maintenance manual.

Discuss the criteria for the successful writing of technical reports.

What are the main considerations that must be taken into account in the preparation a memorandum, particularly with regard to style and presentation.

The following passage is the rough draft of a part of a technical report entitled *Measuring Strain in Multiwall Paper Sacks*. The report is intended for the research manager who commissioned the investigation. The draft is verbose and woolly. For example, the opening sentences could read: 'The first two experiments were exploratory: our aim was to find out why multiwall sacks break. During these experiments we realised that ...'

Rewrite the whole passage in a similarly direct and active style. Include all the information. You are *not* asked to write a summary of the passage.

Preliminary observations

The initial two experiments were exploratory in nature, undertaken with the aim of establishing details of the mechanics of breakage of multiwall paper sacks and in the course of these preliminary experiments it became apparent to the authors that the distribution of strain in the paper of which the sack is fabricated is a factor whose influence must obviously be determined. Due to the heavy work-load in the Bagging and Despatch Department in the pre-Christmas period it was not found practicable to obtain maximum information regarding the strain factor by means of measurements carried out during the course of the routine day-to-day handling as a result of which breakage usually occurs. Hence the restriction of the investigation to tests conducted in the laboratory. In laboratory experimentation, being limited by present knowledge and currently available test methods, the closest simulation that can be achieved is in drop testing. Mechanical and optical methods of strain distribution determination being almost impossible during drop testing, due to the surface of the sack being curved and the shape of the sack changing with each drop, it is necessary to apply methods of converting mechanical strain into an electrical signal which has great advantages, particularly for measurement of transient strain during rapid shock loading. It was thus necessary to investigate the feasibility of the utilisation of electrical methods of strain determination during sack dropping.

Strain gauges

In strain gauges of the conventional type, the degree of increase in electrical resistance of a metal strip on extension is measured, this being related directly to the strain. An initial attempt at the sack problem was made with conventional strain gauges, but it was found that even when foil strain gauges, the most delicate available, were utilised, the gauges and its adhesive exhibited a strength so much in excess of that of the paper that no measurement of the stretch of the paper was being achieved. It was therefore felt that any further work employing conventional strain gauges was unlikely to be of any profit. The desirability of evolving a method of printing a conducting layer directly onto the paper became evident. In discussion with John Brown of the Printing Department the suggestion was made to the authors that a strip of colloidal graphite might provide a suitable conducting coating. This method was adopted and the results are described in the sections below.

[*The Engineer in Society*, The Council of Engineering Institutions, Q1, 1971]

Rewrite the following passage in report form - to include title page, table of contents, numbered sections and paragraphs, appendices (if necessary) - so that it communicates more clearly and effectively. You are *not* asked to write a summary, but you may omit any information that you judge to be superfluous. You will be marked both on content and standard or presentation.

Photography for drawings

As you know, the basic procedure for the preparation of drawings for our hardware manuals is to first take photographs of the equipment, and then to draw from these. Since the closure, in March last year, of the company photographic department, we have had to use local professional photographers. Last year (12 months) we had 500 photographs taken, which were of a very high quality (actually, the quality was *too* high for our needs) and, on average, the photographer took 10 photographs on each visit to us. There are certain disadvantages to this system - notably that we have to fit in with the photographer's schedules, and it takes nearly a week to get the finished photographs. On top of that, there are transport costs which are estimated as an average of £5 per visit - either we have to take our equipment to him, or he has to come to us. Either way, personnel time in travel to the studio or supervising the photographer on our own premises costs an additional £10 for each visit. The photographer has offered to give us a contract which will cost £35 for each set of 10 photographs (not including travel). Finally, I was surprised to find that 'administration' - that is, the paperwork, VAT, secretarial time and telephones - cost us £200 last year, just for the photographs. If you consider that it is not very sensible for a company of our status to rely totally on one supplier, then you will see that we need another answer. I would strongly recommend that, instead, we buy an 'instant' camera, which would mean that we can take photographs of the quality we need ourselves; these could then be enlarged on our own photocopier to the required size for drawings. I have checked with ten suppliers and find that a professional quality camera, with all the necessary lenses and lights, would cost us £700, and would last at least 10 years. Each set of 10 photographs would cost us only £5 for materials, plus 10p a copy for enlarging. As you can see, this would very quickly pay for itself, even allowing for £5 for personnel time for each set of photographs (there would be no other costs).

[Adapted from *The Engineer in Society*, Engineering Council Examination, 1985]

How are considerations of layout likely to influence the effectiveness of an engineering report or paper? In your answer, discuss among other considerations, the front page, table of contents, headings and numbering system.

[Adapted from *The Engineer in Society*, Engineering Council Examination, 1983]

The following material is part of a handbook issued to plant managers. It describes the servicing of chemical filtering equipment. In its present form, the text is a mixture of description, explanation and instruction. It is verbose and poorly organised.

Rewrite the material as INSTRUCTIONS for use by personnel responsible for servicing. Pay particular attention to organisation and layout.

Due to lack of headroom, it is suggested that two properly attested reinforced lifting brackets complete with lifting eyes, be provided and left bolted to the filter cover flanges as part of the unit. By utilising two Type-22 chain blocks from the swinging lifting beam located permanently above, the filter cover can be lifted high enough to expose the filters (having first removed the 8 retaining bolts). There is a distribution tray between the top nine filter elements and the bottom nine, halfway down the column.

Care must be taken to ensure that the flange seats are not damaged (they should normally be replaced at every fifth re-packing operation). If they are damaged either by deterioration or by the re-packing, they must be renewed before the cover is replaced.

The cover is then swung clear and securely supported.

Remove the first three elements singly. Fit a lifting eye to each one in turn and use Type-22 lifting block from lifting beam in order to lift them and swing them clear. The next 6 elements can now be lifted to the top of the column as one lift, and one element removed at a time. This is done by exposing two elements and resting the load on angle irons placed across the top flange of the column between the *second* and *third* element, so that the top element can be removed. There is insufficient headroom for removal of more than one element at a time to be effected.

The distribution tray can now be removed (see section SW1).

Bottom section filter removal is identical to top section filter removal.

To re-pack the column, reverse the procedure, noting that the top element of the bottom section is a 'special' and can only be used in this position. Make sure that all tongue-and-groove joints are really home before final hardening of filter cover bolts.

This operation must be carried out at maximum intervals of 3 months, or earlier if flow rates in the by-pass valve system exceed values expressed in Table 1.

[Adapted from *The Engineer in Society*, Engineering Council Examination, 1984]

The manager of your Head Office has asked your advice on the installation of a fire detection system in the main office building, which houses management offices, display showrooms and conference rooms. He has heard that three types of detector are available: flame detectors, heat detectors and smoke detectors. He has asked you to recommend which type he should evaluate in detail and to mention any specific points he should look out for.

Base your reply on the information below, omitting anything you feel is redundant. Write a memorandum of about 150-200 words, making a clear recommendation.

All modern systems connected to a control board through a cable network.

Fire starts - triggers detector - alarm indicated at control board and (if desired) automatically relayed to local fire service.

Smoke detector: reacts to combustible particles formed as fire starts, often before flames can be seen.

Heat detector: reacts to rise in temperature; sets off alarm when temperature near detector reaches predetermined level, commonly 70 degrees C.

Flame detector: reacts to varying infra-red light from an open flame; sets off alarm when hit by infra-red light.

At control board: both optical and acoustic signals can be given.

Layout of board can show quickly where alarm has been set off separate fault signal can be set off if fault occurs in cable network mechanism to monitor mains power supply continuously can be installed.

Smoke detectors may be triggered by activities that produce much smoke, for example, laboratory work, operation of motor trucks in enclosed space or welding. Other detectors desirable in such areas.

Desirable to install a system that operates even in event of mains supply failure; requires mains supply *and* battery supply connected in parallel so that system will operate even if mains power supply fails.

Development of a fire: early stages - incomplete combustion releases certain particles and gases before open flame and heavy smoke develop and before temperature rises significantly. Smoke detectors triggered by these particles and gases.

Production of flames visible to an infra-red detector or of temperature rise detectable by ceiling-mounted heat detector set at 70 degrees C requires substantial progress of fire.

Smoke, heat and flame detectors can all be linked into same fire protection system. Together they can cover varying demands in any building. Installation of any one type does not preclude subsequent installation of other type.

[Adapted from *The Engineer in Society*, The Council of Engineering Institutions, 1973]

Bibliography

Adair, J., (1986), *Effective Teambuilding*, Pan, London.

Adair, J., (1988), *Effective Teambuilding*, 2nd ed., Pan, London.

Allison, L., (1983), 'Is Britain's Industrial Decline a Myth?', *New Society*, 17th November, 274-5.

Atom, (1988), 'Nuclear Generates over 16% of World Electricity', *Atom*, 378, April, 2.

Bailey, M., (1988), 'Tunnel Vision', *Sunday Observer*, 28th August, 13.

Baker, D., (1986), 'Why *Challenger* Failed', *New Scientist*, 11th September, 52.

Barlow, Sir W., (1988), 'Professional engineers - A Special Report', *The Times*, 14th October, 31-8.

BBC, (1988), *Journey to Excellence*, TV series, 'Business Matters', BBC, London.

Belbin, R. M., (1981), *Management Teams*, Heinemann, London.

Berne, E., (1964), *Games People Play*, Penguin, London.

BNFL, (1983), *The Windscale Vitrification Plant*, British Nuclear Fuels, Risley.

BNFL, (1987), *Annual Report and Accounts*, British Nuclear Fuels, Risley.

Bonnavia, M. R., (1987), *The Channel Tunnel Story*, David & Charles, Newton Abbot.

Bryant, S., and Kearns, J., (1982), 'Workers' Brains as Well as Their Bodies', *Public Administration Review*, 42, 2, 140-50.

Buchanan, D. A., and Huczynski, A. A., (1985), *Organisational Behaviour'*, Prentice-Hall International, London.

Buchanan, R. A., (1989), *The Engineers: A History of the Engineering Profession 1750-1914*, Jessica Kingsley, London.

Burns, T., and Stalker, G. M., (1968), *The Management of Innovation*, 2nd ed., Tavistock Publications, London.

Buzan, T., (1974), *Use Your Head*, BBC Publications, London.

CEGB, (1987), *Supplement to the CEGB and Nuclear Power - Questions and Answers*, CEGB, London.

CEGB, (1988), *Flue Gas Desulphurisation. What it is and why we will be using it*, CEGB, London.

CEGB Research, (1987), *Acid Rain - A Special Issue*, 20, CEGB, London.

Chandler, G., (1985), 'Special Report on Industry Year 1986', *The Times*, 16th December, 27-34.

CIMAH, (1985), *A Guide to the Control of the Industrial Major Accident Hazards Regulations - 1984*, HMSO, London.

Cmnd. 9735, (1986), *Channel Tunnel Fixed Link*, HMSO, London.

Cmnd. 9745, (1986), *Channel Tunnel Treaty*, HMSO, London.

Cmnd. 114, (1987), *Higher Education - Meeting the Challenge*, HMSO, London.

Coch, L., and French, J. R. P., (1948), 'Overcoming Resistance to Change', *Human Relations*, 1, 512-32.

Collier, J. G., and Davies, L. M., (1980), 'The Accident at Three Mile Island', *Heat Transfer Engineering*, 1, January-March, 56.

CSO (Central Statistical Office), (1987), *Annual Abstract of Statistics 1987*, HMSO, London.

CSO, (1988), *Annual Abstract of Statistics 1988*, HMSO, London.

CSO, (1989), *Monthly Digest of Statistics*, HMSO, London.

Daily Telegraph, (1989), 'Underground Gets Fire Message in Plain English', 20th February.

Dainton, F. S., (Chairman), (1968), *Enquiry into Flow of Candidates in Science and Technology*, Cmnd. 3541, HMSO, London.

Davies, J., (1988), 'Greenhouse effect - implications for industry', *Professional Engineering*, 1, December, 34-7.

De Board, R., (1978), *The Psychoanalysis of Organizations*, Tavistock Publications, London.

DoT, (1987), *Kent Impact Study - Channel Tunnel a Strategy for Kent*, Channel Tunnel Joint Consultative Committee, DoT, London.

Draper, R., (1985), 'Robots in the Workplace', *New York Review of Books*, reprinted in *Dialogue Magazine*, 3, 1986, Washington, USA.

DTI, (1983), *Remote Sensing*, DTI, London.

DTI, (1986), *Quality Counts*, DTI, London.

DTI, (1987), *Channel Fixed Link Newsletters*, MMT Division, London.

The Economist, (1987), 'All Aboard for Lots More Chunnels', 10th October.

Hakim, C., (1987a), 'Trends in the Flexible Work Force', *Employment Gazette*, November, 549-60.

Hakim, C., (1987b), 'Higher Education Output in Engineering - International Comparisons', *Employment Gazette*, December, 603-10.

Employment Gazette, (1988), Labour Market Data, HMSO, London.

Engineering Council Documents: see end of bibliography.

European Document, (1987), *European Community and the Environment*, CB-NC-87-003-EN-C, February, Commission of the European Communities, London.

Eurotunnel (1987a), *Eurotunnel*, Share Information Office.

Eurotunnel (1987b), *Environmental and Visual Impact of the Channel Tunnel*, Channel Tunnel Group Information Service, London.

Eurotunnel (1987c), *Disposal of the Soil from the Channel Tunnel*, Channel Tunnel Group Information Service, London.

Eurotunnel (1987d), *Noise, Vibration and Air Pollution from Construction and Operation of the Channel Tunnel*, Channel Tunnel Group Information Service, London.

Eurotunnel (1987e), *Rabies and the Channel Tunnel*, Channel Tunnel Group Information Service, London.

Eyeions, D., (1988), 'The big jobs revolution of today has switched to the information workers', *The Times*, 28th April, 32.

Fayol, H., (1916), *General and Industrial Management*, (translated by Constance Storrar, 1949), Pitman, London.

Feilden, G. B. R., (Chairman), (1963), *Engineering Design: Report of a Committee appointed by the Council for Scientific and Industrial Research to consider the present standing of mechanical engineering design*, HMSO, London.

Fennell, D., (Chairman), (1988), *Investigation into the King's Cross Underground Fire*, HMSO, London.

Ferry, G., (1984), 'Wise Campaign for Women Engineers', *New Scientist*, 12th January, 10-11.

Financial Times, (1987), 'Computers in Manufacturing, 2nd June.

Finniston, Sir M., (Chairman), (1980), *Engineering our Future - Report of the Committee of Inquiry into the Engineering Profession*, Cmnd. 7794, HMSO, London.

Flixborough (1975), *The Flixborough Disaster - Report of the Court of Inquiry*, HMSO, London.

Freeman, C., (1987), in Finnegan, R., Salaman, G., and Thompson, K., (eds), *The Case for Technological Determinism in Information Technology: Social Issues*, OU Reader, Hodder and Stoughton, London.

Gittus, J. H., et al., (1987), *The Chernobyl Accident and its Consequences*, HMSO, London.

Goldsmith, D., and Clutterbuck, W., (1985), *The Winning Streak*, Penguin, London.

Gowers, Sir E., (1973), *The Complete Plain Words*, Penguin, London.

Guardian, (1988), 'Managers Guilty on Tube Fire, 11th November, 4.

Gunning, R., (1952), *The Technique of Clear Writing*, McGraw-Hill, New York.

Hammer, M., (1987), 'Overloaded lorries may have weighed down stricken ferry', *New Scientist*, 11th June, 21.

Hammer, M., (1988), 'The Night that Luck Ran Out', *New Scientist*, 7th July, 29.

Handy, C., (1984), *The Future of Work*, Blackwell, Oxford.

Handy, C., (1985), *Understanding Organisations*, Penguin, London.

Hill, G., (1989), 'Iron horses let loose in the garden', *The Times*, 30th January, 10.

Hooper, E. G., (1988), 'Engineering Health and Safety', *Professional Engineering*, October, 12.

House of Lords, (1987), *House of Lords Select Committee Report 138 on the Channel Tunnel*, HMSO, London.

HSE, (1987), *BNFL Sellafield Post Audit Progress*, Health and Safety Executive, London.

I.CHEM.E., (1981), *A First Guide to Loss Prevention*, I.Chem.E., Rugby.

I.CHEM.E., (1988a), 'News Review', *Chemical Engineer*, June, 6.

I.CHEM.E., (1988b), 'Bhopal 1, 2 and 3', *Chemical Engineer*, August, 4.

Illich, I., (1977), *Disabling Professions*, Marion Boyars, London.

Independent, (1988), 'King's Cross: How the Tube's luck ran out', 25th June, 2.

Independent, (1989), 'Obituary - Professor Kaoru Ishikawa', 26th April, 18.

Industrial Society, (1988), Video, *Quality Circles: Employee Involvement at the Point of Work*, London.

Institution of Production Engineers, (1987), *Rules for Professional Review*.

Janis, I., and Mann, L., (1977), *Decision Making*, Free Press.

Jaques, E., (1976), *A General Theory of Bureaucracy*, Heinemann, London.

JET, (1987), *JET and Industry*, Jet Joint Undertaking, Culham.

JET, (1988), *JET Joint Undertaking Annual Report 1987*, Culham.

Johnson, D., and Johnson, F., (1982), *Joining Together: Group Theory and Group Skills*, 2nd ed., Prentice-Hall, Hemel Hempstead.

Johnson, S., (1988), 'Environmental problems facing the electricity industry', *Atom*, 380, 8-12.

Johnstone, B., (1987), 'Japan's rising man made sun', *New Scientist*, 26th February, 53-7.

Jones, B., (1987), 'Thinking the unthinkable - Fire in the Chunnel', *Chartered Mechanical Engineer*, November, 8-9.

Jones, P. M. S., (1988), 'The benefits of nuclear power', *Atom*, 379, 12-17.

Jordan, A. G., and Richardson, J. J., (1984), 'Engineering a Consensus: From the Finniston Report to the Engineering Council', *Public Administration*, 62, 383-400.

Joyce, C., (1986), 'Space Shuttle: a blueprint for disaster', *New Scientist*, 12th June, 17.

Kharabanda, O. P., and Stallworthy, E. A., (1988), *Safety in the chemical industry - lessons from major disasters*, Heinemann, London.

Kirkman, J., (1971), 'What is good style for engineering writing?', *Chemical Engineer*, 285-92, 343-5.

Kletz, T. A., (1984), *Hazop and Hazan - notes on the identification and assessment of hazards*, I.Chem.E., Rugby.

Kletz, T. A., (1988), *Learning from Accidents in Industry*, Butterworths, London.

Koestler, A., (1978), *Janus - A Summing Up*, Hutchinson, London.

Kolcum, E. H., (1986), 'Morton Thiokol engineers testify NASA rejected warnings on launch', *Aviation Weekly and Space Technology*, March, 18.

Levy, J. C., (1987), 'The Engineering Council - five years of progress', *Naval Architect*, April, E160.

Lewin, K., Lippet, R., and White, R. K., (1939), 'Patterns of aggressive behaviour in experimentally created "social climates"', *International Journal of Social Psychology*, 10, 271-99.

Lihou, D., (1985), 'Why did Bhopal ever happen?', *Chemical Engineer*, April, 18.

Long, A., (1989), 'Activity over inert gases', *Sunday Times*, 19th February, 19.

McClelland, D. C., (1961), *The Achieving Society*, Van Nostrand, New York.

McCormick, J., (1985), *The User's Guide to the Environment*, Kogan Page, London.

McGregor, D., (1960), *The Human Side of Enterprise*, McGraw-Hill, Maidenhead.

MacKenzie, D., (1985), 'Safety under pressure', *New Scientist*, 27th June, 22.

MacKenzie, D., (1986), 'Chemical disasters need not happen', *New Scientist*, 5th June, 42.

McMahon, D., (1987), 'Industry itself must be the first to combat the prejudices against industry', *The Times*, 26th February.

Marshall, V., (1987), *Major Chemical Hazards*, Ellis Horwood, Chichester.

Maslow, A., (1970), *Motivation and Personality*, 2nd ed., Harper and Row, New York.

Mayo, E., (1949), *The Social Problems of an Industrial Civilization*, reprinted in Pugh, D. S. (ed.), (1984), *op. cit.*

Milne, R., (1986), 'Breaking up is hard to do', *New Scientist*, 11th December, 34.

Mitchell, E., (1977), *The Employer's Guide to the Law on Health, Safety amd Welfare at Work*, Business Books, London.

Morgan, G., (1986), *Images of Organisation*, Sage Publications, London.

MV *Herald of Free Enterprise*, (1987), *Report of the Court No. 8074 - Formal Investigation*, HMSO, London.

Naisbitt, J., (1984), *Megatrends*, Macdonald, London.

New Scientist, (1987), *Special Chernobyl Issue*, 23rd April.

Nicholson, Lord, D., (1989), 'Halt: major inconvenience ahead', *The Times*, 27th March, 11.

NIREX, (1987), *The Way Forward - A Discussion Document*, UK Nirex, Didcot.

Open University, (1988a), *Course DT 200, an Introduction to Information Technology: Social and Technological Issues, Block 5 Part A Mainstream: II in Manufacturing*, OUP, Milton Keynes.

Open University, (1988b), *Course DT 200 - Computer Integrated Manufacture*, TV programme.

Orwell, G., (1949), *1984*, Penguin, London.

Orwell, G., (1970), *The Collected Essays, Volume IV - In Front of Your Nose 1945-1950*, Penguin, London.

Overy, R., and Pagnamenta, P., (1984), *All Our Working Lives*, BBC Publications, London.

Parkinson, C. N., (1965), *Parkinson's Law and Other Studies in Administration*, Penguin, London.

Pascale, R. T., and Athos, A. G., (1986), *The Art of Japanese Management*, with Introduction by Sir Peter Parker, Penguin, London.

Peters, T., (1988), *Structures for the Year 2000*, Palo Alto.

Peters, T. J., and Waterman, R. H., (1982), *In Search of Excellence: Lessons from America's Best Run Companies*, Harper and Row, New York.

Petroski, H., (1985), *To Engineer is Human*, Macmillan, London.

Price, R., (1986), *Labour in British Society*, Croom Helm, Beckenham

Pugh, D. S., (ed.), (1984), *Organization Theory: Selected Readings*, 2nd ed., Penguin, London.

Pugh, D. S., Hickson, D. J., and Hinings, C. R., (1983), *Writers on Organizations*, 3rd ed., Penguin, London.

Reason, J., and Mycielska, K., (1982), *Absent Minded? The Psychology of Mental and Everyday Errors*, Prentice-Hall, Hemel Hempstead.

Rostow, W. W., (1960), *The Stages of Economic Growth*, OUP, Oxford.

Roszak, T., (1986), *The Cult of Information*, Paladin, London.

Rowbottom, R. W., (1987), 'Authority relationships', unpublished lecture given at Brunel University.

RSA, (1986), *Action by Industry*, 27th January, RSA, London.

Saunders, P. A. H., (1987), *The Management of Radioactive Wastes*, UKAEA, London.

Sayle, M., (1982), 'The Yellow Peril and the Red Haired Devils', *Harpers*, November, 23-35.

Scala Magazine, (1982), 'The robots are coming!', 3, Frankfurt-am-Main.

Schumacher, E. F., (1973), *Small is Beautiful*, Blond and Briggs, London.

Sloan, A. P., (1965), *My Years at General Motors*, Sidgwick and Jackson, London.

Stanstell, J., and Valery, N., (1977), 'The Great Engineering Debate', *New Scientist*, 28th April, 184-8 and 5th May, 271-3.

Stonier, T., (1982), *The Wealth of Information: A Profile of the Post Industrial Society*, Methuen, London.

Swann, M., (Chairman), (1968), *The Flow into Employment of Scientists, Engineers and Technologists: Report of the Working Group on Manpower for Scientific Growth*, Cmnd. 3760, HMSO, London.

Taylor, F. W., (1912), *Testimony to the House of Representatives Committee*, reprinted in Pugh, D. S., *op. cit.*

The Times, (1984), 'Why isn't there an Engineers' Corner in Westminster Abbey?', 28th November, 9.

The Times, (1987), 'When the chips are down: research and prosperity' - part I, 16th February, 10.

TMI, (1979), *Report of the President's Commission on the Accident at Three Mile Island*, Pergamon Press, Oxford.

Toffler, A., (1971), *Future Shock*, Pan, London.

Toffler, A., (1981), *The Third Wave*, Pan, London.

Tring, M., (1988), 'Oath for engineers', *Chemical Engineer*, August, 12.

Vaidyanathan, A., (1985), 'A sorry technological tale from India', *New Scientist*, 21st February, 36.

Von Bertalanffy, L., (1969), 'The theory of open systems in physics and biology', in Emery, F. E., (ed.), *Systems Thinking*, Penguin, London.

Vroom, V. H., (1974), 'A new look at managerial decision making', *Organisational Dynamics*, 5, reprinted in Pugh, D. S., (1984), *op. cit.*

Watt Committee, (1984), *Acid Rain - Report no. 14*, Watt Committee on Energy, London.

West, R., (1984), *What IS Engineering?*, The Women's Engineering Society, London.

Wheatley, D., (1988), *Report Writing*, Penguin, London.

Wiener, M. J., (1981), *English Culture and the Decline of the Industrial Spirit 1850-1980*, Cambridge University Press, Cambridge.

Wright, P. J., (1980), (for DeLorean, J.,), *On A Clear Day You Can See General Motors*, Sidgwick and Jackson, London.

Engineering Council Documents, 10 Maltravers Street, London

(1983a), *Appraising the Technical; and Commercial Aspects of a Manufacturing Company.*

(1983b), *Technical Reviews for Manufacturing, Process and Construction Companies.*

(1984a), *Policy Statement on Standards and Routes to Registration.*

(1985a), *Raising the Standard - Nominated and Authorised Bodies.*

(1985b), *Discussion Document: Continuing Education and Training.*

(1985c), *Newsletter No. 1.*

(1985d), *Problem Solving: Science and Technology in Primary Schools.*

(1985e), *Career Breaks for Women Chartered and Technician Engineers.*

(1986a), *Opening Windows on Engineering.*

(1986b), *A Call to Action - Continuing Education and Training for Engineers and Technicians (and two Annexes B1 and B2).*

(1986c), *A Special Report on the Young Engineers for Britain Competition.*

(1986d), *Managing Design for Competitive Advantage.*

(1986e), *Take Action for Engineering - Industry Year 1986.*

(1986f), *On Being A School Governor - Opportunities for Engineers and Technicians.*

(1987), *The Board for Engineers' Registration.*

(1988a), *A Comparison of Statistics of Engineering Education.*

(1988b), *A Guide to the Engineering Institutions.*

(1988c), *Continuing Education and Training.*

(1988d), *Management and Business Skills for Engineers.*

(1988e), *Achievements - Six Years On.*

Appendix I

The Major Engineering Institutions - A Chronology

Institution	Established	Royal Charter
Institution of Civil Engineers	1818	1828
Institution of Mechanical Engineers	1847	1930
Royal Institution of Naval Architects	1860	1910
Institution of Gas Engineers	1863	1929
Royal Aeronautical Society	1866	1949
Institution of Electrical Engineers	1871	1921
Institute of Marine Engineers	1889	1933
Institution of Mining Engineers	1889	1915
Institution of Mining and Metallurgy	1892	1915
Chartered Institution of Building Services Engineers	1897	1976
Institution of Structural Engineers	1908	1934
Institution of Production Engineers	1921	1964
Institution of Chemical Engineers	1922	1957
Institute of Energy	1927	1946
Institute of Measurement and Control	1944	1975
Institute of Metals	1945	1975
British Computer Society*	1957	1984

* subject to fulfillment of conditions during a transition period.

Note - these are 'Major Institutions' in the sense that they are nominated Chartered Engineering Institutions. Each professional engineer on the Council's Register who is a corporate member of a nominated Chartered Engineering Institution may use the title Chartered Engineer and the designatory letters CEng.

(*A Guide to the Engineering Institutions*, May 1988, Engineering Council)

Some key dates in the development of the British Engineering Profession

1660 The Royal Society [of London for Improving Natural Knowledge] (Royal Charter 1662)
1754 The Royal Society for the Encouragement of Arts, Manufactures and Commerce (RSA)
1771 The Society of Civil Engineers
1799 The Royal Institution
1818 The Institution of Civil Engineers - Britain's first engineering Institution
1847 Institution of Mechanical Engineers
1851 The Great Exhibition - Hyde Park
1860 The Royal Institution of Naval Architects
1863 The Institution of Gas Engineers
1878 The City and Guilds of London Institute
1888 Institution of Electrical Engineers (from Society of Telegraph Engineers 1871)
1920 The Women's Engineering Society
1921 The Institution of Production Engineers
1965 The Council of Engineering Institutions
1965 The Science Research Council by Royal Charter (became Science and Engineering Research Council in 1981)
1974 The Health and Safety at Work Act
1975 The Sex Discrimination Act and the Equal Opportunities Commission
1976 The Fellowship of Engineering (Royal Charter 1983)
1980 The Finniston Report, *Engineering Our Future*
1981 The Engineering Council (by Royal Charter)
1982 Government White Paper 'Standards, Quality and International Competitiveness' (Cmnd. 8621), July
1984 Women Into Science and Engineering Year (WISE '84)
1984 Standards and Routes to Registration (SARTOR) - Engineering Council
1985 First Engineering Assembly - Birmingham (September)
1986 Industry Year
1987 Government White Paper on Higher Education, 'Meeting the Challenge'
1988 The Education Reform Act
1992 Single European Market Completion
1993 Channel Tunnel scheduled to open

Appendix III

Useful Addresses

Engineering Council nominated bodies

(For London numbers, from 6th May 1990, replace 01 with the code shown in [ ].)

Association of Supervisory and Executive Engineers
Wix Hill House
West Horsley
Surrey
KT24 6DZ
Tel: (0483) 222383

Association of Water Officers
15 Market Place
South Shields
Tyne and Wear
NE33 1JQ
Tel: (0914) 563882

Biological Engineering Society
Royal College of Surgeons
35-43 Lincoln's Inn Fields
London
WC2A 3PN
Tel: (01) [071] 242 7750

British Computer Society
13 Mansfield Street
London
W1M 0BP
Tel: (01) [071] 637 0471

British Institute of Non-Destructive Testing
1 Spencer Parade
Northampton
NN1 5AA
Tel: (0604) 30124

Chartered Institution of Building Services Engineers
Delta House
222 Balham High Road
London SW12 9BS
Tel: (01) [081] 675 5211

Highway and Traffic Technicians Association
3 Lygon Place
Ebury Street
London SW1W 0JR
Tel: (01) [071] 730 5245

Institute of Acoustics
25 Chambers Street
Edinburgh EH1 1HU
Tel: (031) 225 2143

Institution of British Foundrymen
3rd Floor, Bridge House
121 Smallbrook Queensway
Birmingham B5 4JP
Tel: (021) 643 4523

Institute of Ceramics
Shelton House
Stoke Road
Shelton
Stoke-on-Trent ST4 2DR
Tel: (0782) 202116

Institute of Energy
18 Devonshire Street
London W1N 2AU
Tel: (01) [071] 580 7124

Institute of Engineers and Technicians
100 Grove Road
East Dulwich
London SE22 8DR
Tel: (01) [081] 693 1255

Institute of Hospital Engineering
20 Landport Terrace
Portsmouth
Hampshire PO1 2RG
Tel: (0705) 823186

Institute of Marine Engineers
76 Mark Lane
London EC3R 7JN
Tel: (01) [071] 481 8493

Institute of Measurement and Control
87 Gower Street
London WC1E 6AA
Tel: (01) [071] 387 4949

Appendices 279

Institute of Metals
  1 Carlton House Terrace
  London SW1Y 5DB
  Tel: (01) [071] 839 4071

Institute of Physics
  47 Belgrave Square
  London SW1Y 5DB
  Tel: (01) [071] 235 6111

Institute of Plumbing
  64 Station Lane
  Hornchurch
  Essex RM12 6NB
  Tel: (04024) 72791

Institute of Quality Assurance
  8-10 Grosvenor Gardens
  London SW1W 0DQ
  Tel: (01) [071] 730 6154

Institute of Road Transport Engineers
  1 Cromwell Place
  London SW7 2JF
  Tel: (01) [071] 589 3744

Institution of Agricultural Engineers
  West End Road
  Silsoe
  Bedford MK45 4DU
  Tel: (0525) 61096

Institution of Chemical Engineers
  George E. Davis Building
  165-171 Railway Terrace
  Rugby CV21 3HQ
  Tel: (0788) 78214

Institution of Civil Engineers
  1-7 Great George Street
  London SW1P 3AA
  Tel: (01) [071] 222 7722

Institution of Electrical and Electronics Incorporated Engineers
  Savoy Hill House
  Savoy Hill
  London WC2R 0BS
  Tel: (01) [071] 836 3357

Institution of Electrical Engineers
  Savoy Place
  London WC2R 0BL
  Tel: (01) [071] 240 1871

Institution of Engineers Designers
  Courtleigh

  West Leigh
  Westbury
  Wiltshire BA13 3TA
  Tel: (0307) 822801

Institution of Gas Engineers
  17 Grosvenor Crescent
  London SW1X 7ES
  Tel: (01) [071] 245 9811

Institution of Lighting Engineers
  Lennox House
  9 Lawford Road
  Rugby CV21 2DZ
  Tel: (0788) 76492

Institution of Mechanical Engineers
  1 Birdcage Walk
  London SW1H 9JJ
  Tel: (01) [071] 222 7899

Institution of Mechanical Incorporated Engineers
  3 Birdcage Walk
  London SW1H 9JN
  Tel: (01) [071] 799 1808

Institution of Mining Electrical and Mining Mechanical Engineers
  60 Silver Street
  Doncaster DN1 1HT
  Tel: (0302) 310604

Institution of Mining Engineers
  Danum House
  South Parade
  Doncaster DN1 1HT
  Tel: (0302) 20486

Institution of Mining and Metallurgy
  44 Portland Place
  London W1N 4BR
  Tel: (01) [071] 580 3802

Institution of Nuclear Engineers
  Allan House
  1 Penerley Road
  London SE6 2LQ
  Tel: (01) [081] 698 1500

Institution of Plant Engineers
  138 Buckingham Palace Road
  London SW1W 9SG
  Tel: (01) [071] 730 0469

Institution of Production Engineers
  Rochester House
  66 Little Ealing Lane

London W5 4XX
Tel: (01) [081] 579 9411

Institution of Structural Engineers
11 Upper Belgrave Street
London SW1X 8BH
Tel: (01) [071] 235 4535

Institution of Water and Environment Management
15 John Street
London WC1N 2EB
Tel: (01) [071] 430 0899

Institution of Works and Highways Management
Suite 209, Oxford House
2 Cheapside
Reading RG1 7AA
Tel: (0734) 508432

Minerals Engineering Society
32 Field Rise Littleover
Derby DE3 7DE
Tel: (0332) 766812

North East Coast Institution of Engineers and Shipbuilders
12 Windsor Terrace
Newcastle-upon-Tyne NE2 4EH
Tel: (091) 281 3272

Plastics and Rubber Institute
11 Hobart Place
London SW1W 0HL
Tel: (01) [071] 245 9555

Royal Aeronautical Society
4 Hamilton Place
London W1V 0BQ
Tel: (01) [071] 499 3515

Royal Institution of Naval Architects
10 Upper Belgrave Street
London SW1X 0BQ
Tel: (01) [071] 235 4622

Society of Civil Engineering Technicians
1-7 Great George Street
London SW1P 3AA
Tel: (01) [071] 630 0726

Society of Electronic and Radio Technicians
57-61 Newington Causeway
London SE1 6BL
Tel: (01) [071] 403 2351

Welding Institute
11-12 Pall Mall

London SW1Y 5LU
Tel: (01) [071] 925 0082

Other useful addresses

British Nuclear Fuels PLC
Information Services Directorate
Risley
Warrington
Cheshire WA3 6AS
Tel: (0925) 832128

British Safety Council
62/64 Chancellors Square
London W6 9RS
Tel: (01) [081] 741 1231

Business and Technician Education Council
Central House
Upper Woburn Place
London WC1H 0HH
Tel: (01) [071] 388 3288

Central Electricity Generating Board
Press and Publicity Office
Sudbury House
15 Newgate Street
London EC1A 7AU
Tel: (01) [071] 248 1202

Chemical Industry Safety and Health Council of the Chemical Industries Association (CISHEC)
Kings Buildings
Smith Square
London SW1P 3JJ
Tel: (01) [071] 834 4469

City and Guilds of London Institute
76 Portland Place
London W1N 4AA
Tel: (01) [071] 580 3050

Department of Energy
Thames House
South Millbank
London SW1P 4QJ
Tel: (01) [071] 211 3000

Department of the Environment
2 Marsham Street
London SW1P 3EB
Tel: (01) [071] 212 3434

Design Council
28 Haymarket

London SW1Y 4SU
Tel: (01) [071] 839 8000

Engineering Council
10 Maltravers Street
London WC2R 3ER
Tel: (01) [071] 240 7891

Engineering Industry Training Board
54 Clarendon Road
Watford
Herts WD1 1LB
Tel: (0923) 38441

European Communities Information Services
8 Storey's Gate
London SW1P 3AT
Tel: (01) [071] 222 8122

Eurotunnel Information Centre
Tontine House
Tontine Street
Folkestone
Kent CT20 1JR
Tel: (0303) 57466

Fellowship of Engineering
2 Little Smith Street
Westminster
London SW1P 3DL
Tel: (01) [071] 222 2688

Health and Safety Commission
Baynards House
1 Chepstow Place
London WC2 4TF
Tel: (01) [071] 229 3456

Industrial Society
Robert Hyde House
48 Bryanston Square
London W1H 7LN
Tel: (01) [071] 262 2401

Nuclear Electricity Information Centre
22 Buckingham Gate
London SW1E 6LB
Tel: (01) [071] 828 8248

PICKUP
The Adult Training Promotions Unit
Department of Education and Science
Elizabeth House, York Road
London SE1 7PH
Tel: (01) [071] 934 0859

Royal Society of Arts
8 John Adam Street
London WC2N 6EZ
Tel: (01) [071] 930 5115

Royal Society of Chemistry
30 Russell Square
London WC1B 5DT
Tel: (01) [071] 580 3482

Science and Engineering Research Council (SERC)
Polaris House
Swindon
Wilts
Tel: (0793) 26222

Standards and Quality Policy Unit
Department of Trade and Industry
88-89 Eccleston Square, Room 113
Bridge Place
London SW1V 1PT
Tel: (01) [071] 212 6918

United Kingdom Atomic Energy Authority
Information Services Branch
11 Charles II Street
London SW17 4QP
Tel: (01) [071] 930 5454

UK Nirex Ltd
Curie Avenue
Didcot
Oxfordshire OX11 ORH
Tel: (0235) 835153

Watt Committee on Energy Ltd
Savoy Hill House
Savoy Hill
London WC2R 0BU
Tel: (01) [071] 379 6875

Women's Engineering Society
Department of Civil Engineering
Imperial College of Science and Technology
London SW7 2BU
Tel: (01) [071] 589 5111 ext 4731

Index